agency
under
stress

agency under stress

THE SOCIAL SECURITY ADMINISTRATION IN AMERICAN GOVERNMENT

MARTHA DERTHICK

THE BROOKINGS INSTITUTION
WASHINGTON, D.C.

Library of Congress Cataloging-in-Publication data

Derthick, Martha.
  Agency under stress : the Social Security Administration in American
government / Martha Derthick.
    p.   cm.
  Includes index.
  ISBN 0-8157-1824-1 (cloth).—ISBN 0-8157-1823-3
(paperback).
    1. United States.   Social Security Administration.   2. Insurance,
Disability—United States.   3. Supplemental security income pro-
gram—United States.   I. Title.
HD7125.D475   1990
353.0082'56—dc20   90-2123
                                                              CIP

9 8 7 6 5 4 3 2 1

The paper used in this publication meets the minimum requirements
of the American National Standard for Information Sciences—Permanence of Paper for Printed Library Materials, ANSI Z39.48-1984.

Set in Linotronic Janson
Composition by Monotype Composition Co.
  Baltimore, Maryland
Printing by R.R. Donnelley and Sons, Co.
  Harrisonburg, Virginia
Book design by Ken Sabol

℔ THE BROOKINGS INSTITUTION

The Brookings Institution is an independent organization devoted to nonpartisan research, education, and publication in economics, government, foreign policy, and the social sciences generally. Its principal purposes are to aid in the development of sound public policies and to promote public understanding of issues of national importance.

The Institution was founded on December 8, 1927, to merge the activities of the Institute for Government Research, founded in 1916, the Institute of Economics, founded in 1922, and the Robert Brookings Graduate School of Economics and Government, founded in 1924.

The Board of Trustees is responsible for the general administration of the Institution, while the immediate direction of the policies, program, and staff is vested in the President, assisted by an advisory committee of the officers and staff. The by-laws of the Institution state: "It is the function of the Trustees to make possible the conduct of scientific research, and publication, under the most favorable conditions, and to safeguard the independence of the research staff in the pursuit of their studies and in the publication of the results of such studies. It is not a part of their function to determine, control, or influence the conduct of particular investigations or the conclusions reached."

The President bears final responsibility for the decision to publish a manuscript as a Brookings book. In reaching his judgment on the competence, accuracy, and objectivity of each study, the President is advised by the director of the appropriate research program and weighs the views of a panel of expert outside readers who report to him in confidence on the quality of the work. Publication of a work signifies that it is deemed a competent treatment worthy of public consideration but does not imply endorsement of conclusions or recommendations.

The Institution maintains its position of neutrality on issues of public policy in order to safeguard the intellectual freedom of the staff. Hence interpretations or conclusions in Brookings publications should be understood to be solely those of the authors and should not be attributed to the Institution, to its trustees, officers, or other staff members, or to the organizations that support its research.

Foreword

IN 1979 BROOKINGS published *Policymaking for Social Security* by Martha Derthick, in which she sought to explain how so large and costly a program had been established with so little controversy. Viewed historically, social security had been an immense political success, even a "sacred cow," in the words of economist Milton Friedman. Nevertheless, it seemed possible that sharply rising costs would threaten the program's popularity. In 1977 Congress had been forced to rescue the finances of social security with a large tax increase.

Today, social security is no less sacred politically, despite having gone through still another fiscal crisis in the 1980s, but its administering agency has become much more vulnerable to criticism. The present book explores how and why that happened. It focuses on two traumatic events: the initiation of the supplemental security income program in the mid-1970s and a review of the eligibility of disability insurance cases in the early 1980s. On both occasions, beneficiaries and staff suffered and Congress and other overseers judged the Social Security Administration to have performed poorly.

Derthick argues that the quality of public bureaucracies' performance depends heavily on the quality of policymaking institutions' guidance—and she shows that in many ways the guidance is not conducive to good administration. Some of the problems lie in the most basic features of American government: the changes in policy and leadership that accompany frequent elections, the fragmentation associated with federalism, and the interbranch tensions of separation of powers. Others lie in the low priority that policymakers attach to administration and in their inability to anticipate the administrative consequences of particular policy choices. Although Derthick's evidence is drawn from the recent experience of the Social Security Administration, her analysis applies generally to the major administrative agencies of the federal government.

Formerly director of the Brookings Governmental Studies program, Martha Derthick is currently the Julia Allen Cooper Professor of Government and Foreign Affairs at the University of Virginia. For their support of this project, she wishes to thank Thomas E. Mann, current director of Governmental Studies, and his predecessor, Paul E. Peterson. She also wishes to thank Diane Hodges, Sandra Z. Riegler, and Eloise C. Stinger for administrative support and Renuka D. Deonarain, Vida R. Megahed, and Teresita V. Vitug for secretarial assistance. Nancy D. Davidson edited the manuscript, Linda Keefer verified its factual content, and Susan L. Woollen prepared it for typesetting. Diana Regenthal prepared the index.

The views expressed here are solely those of the author and should not be ascribed to the persons whose assistance is acknowledged above, to the organizations that supported the project, or to the trustees, officers, or other staff members of the Brookings Institution.

BRUCE K. MAC LAURY
President

May 1990
Washington, D.C.

Acknowledgments

I BEGAN TO THINK about this book early in 1984, when I was named to a panel created by Congress to consider how the Social Security Administration should be organized if it were severed from the Department of Health and Human Services. In the course of the meetings, I learned a great deal about the agency's problems and acquired an abundance of source material, thanks to P. Royal Shipp, executive director of the panel, and the staff and witnesses he assembled.

Originally, I sought to explain why the performance of the SSA had deteriorated. Why had an agency that had once performed so well suffered a decline? Thanks to Edward D. Berkowitz, I had a chance to sketch out the inquiry in a conference at George Washington University in 1986 and in a collection of the conference papers that he edited (*Social Security after Fifty*, Greenwood Press, 1987). However, I began to make good progress only when I realized that my original question was misconceived. It was wrong to suppose that the agency's performance had worsened. Because its tasks had expanded enormously, it was impossible to compare the quality of current and past performance. Among those who helped me to see this and to frame a better inquiry were R. Shep Melnick and Stanford G. Ross, who commented on a presentation I made at the Gordon Public Policy Center at Brandeis University.

The study would have been all but impossible without the help of insiders in recapturing source material on the supplemental security income program. I am deeply indebted to Arthur E. Hess, retired deputy commissioner of social security, who both drew on his own memory and opened doors for me at SSA headquarters in Baltimore. John H. Trout, who had been deeply engaged in planning for SSI, searched his personal files for me. Renato A. DiPentima sent me a copy of his doctoral dissertation. Jack S. Futterman, retired assistant commissioner for administration, gave me access to his reports on the agency. Beryl Radin, a fellow academic, loaned me the material she had saved after serving on the SSI study group in 1975. I also drew on the resources of the historian's office at SSA and the library at the Department of Health and Human Services.

Had I not been teaching at the University of Virginia, the book would have been done more quickly but less well. Teaching and research do complement each other, especially when the students are good and faculty colleagues and university administrators are supportive. All of this is true at the University of Virginia. In addition, the university's Alderman Library contains a complete and superbly administered collection of U.S. government documents. Walter Newsome and his staff were unfailingly helpful. Jim Yoho, a University of Virginia graduate student, provided skillful and efficient research assistance in the summer of 1989.

Had I been obliged to teach full time, the book would have taken still longer. A Ford Foundation grant financed a semester off in the fall of 1986 as well as summer research. Support from the Center for Advanced Studies at the University of Virginia reduced my teaching load in 1984–85 and 1985–86.

Had I not learned before starting the book to use a personal computer for word processing, it might not be done yet. For benign encouragement to a beginner, I thank Paul J. Quirk. For frequent technical assistance, I thank my former colleague Donald F. Kettl.

By January 1989 a draft manuscript was ready to circulate to critics. Thanks to them, the published version is much better than the draft. Robert M. Ball, Louis D. Enoff, Erwin C. Hargrove, Jr., Arthur E. Hess, Jean H. Hinckley, Thomas E. Mann, Richard P. Nathan, Paul J. Quirk, Stanford G. Ross, Deborah A. Stone, John H. Trout, and James Q. Wilson read the entire manuscript and made many corrections and useful suggestions. Quirk called attention to some serious conceptual weaknesses and proposed solutions. Like *The Politics of Deregulation* (Brookings, 1985), this is a far better book because of his contribution, even if he is not this time a coauthor. For less extensive but nonetheless helpful criticism, I am grateful to Robert A. Katzmann, Donald F. Kettl, Jerry L. Mashaw, and R. Kent Weaver.

None of these institutions or persons should be blamed for surviving defects.

MARTHA DERTHICK

Contents

agency
under
stress

Part I
Introduction

CHAPTER 1

The Governmental Setting

THE PERFORMANCE of large public agencies in the United States has become a source of disappointment, dissatisfaction, and even shock and grief—as in the extreme case of the explosion of NASA's space shuttle *Challenger*, which killed seven astronauts in 1986.

The explanations offered for error or dysfunction typically rest on properties internal to the organization, such as quality of leadership; motivation, morale, and training of staff; the incentives leaders have devised to motivate members; the locus of responsibility; conceptions of mission and other ideological influences; procedures for decision-making; the flow of operational cues down and responses up the organizational hierarchy; the organization's capacity to gather, store, and analyze information; and its ability to learn from experience. The pathologies of bureaucracy itself are found to be at fault.[1]

Granting the importance of such factors, this book nevertheless rests on the premise that agency performance cannot be understood apart from its institutional context. The tasks of public agencies are defined by policymaking institutions. If the agencies repeatedly fall short, the flaw may be in the source of instruction rather than in the objects of it—or, more precisely, in the relation between the two. The

1. *Report of the Presidential Commission on the Space Shuttle Challenger Accident* (Washington, 1986), esp. chaps. 5, 6, and 7; and, also on NASA in the aftermath of that accident, Stuart Diamond, "NASA Wasted Billions, Federal Audits Disclose," *New York Times*, April 23, 1986, p. 1; Diamond, "NASA Cut or Delayed Safety Spending," *New York Times*, April 24, 1986, p. 1; Douglas B. Feaver, "Building the Shuttle," *Washington Post*, April 6, 1986, p. 1; and Feaver, "Success Relaxed NASA's Vigilance," *Washington Post*, May 26, 1986, p. 1. There is a very large, mostly sociological, literature on bureaucratic dysfunction. Among the places to begin are: Michel Crozier, *The Bureaucratic Phenomenon* (University of Chicago Press, 1964); Charles Perrow, *Complex Organizations: A Critical Essay* (Scott, Foresman, 1972); and Victor Alexander Thompson, *Modern Organization*, 2d ed. (University of Alabama Press, 1977).

3

quality of public bureaucracies' performance depends heavily on the quality of the policymaking institutions' guidance.

I argue that the institutions of American government function in ways that are not conducive to good administration. Policymaking neglects administration. Policymakers, who define administrative tasks with their choices, act with limited understanding of administrative organizations and without attaching high priority to anticipating the consequences of their choices for the agencies' performance.

More fundamentally, the most cherished structural features of American government pose obstacles to good administration. Democracy, which entails regular and frequent elections, fosters instability in policy guidance. The laws that agencies administer are subject to constant revision as officeholders change and incumbents seek to serve and satisfy a heterogeneous and ever-changing society. The pace and timing of policy decisions are likely to be determined by electoral events, both recent and anticipated. The separation of powers, with its calculated division among chief executive, legislature, and courts, fosters inconsistency in policy guidance. Each institution, wanting the bureaucracy to behave in its own image, frames policy instruction in a distinctive way, expecting conformance. Federalism, likewise embedded in the constitutional scheme, fragments administrative structures, necessitating the construction of elaborate arrangements for intergovernmental cooperation.[2]

To support and illustrate this argument, I will analyze two much-publicized cases of poor performance by one of the biggest and best-established American bureaucracies, the Social Security Administration (SSA). Created in 1935 by the Social Security Act, the SSA is responsible for administering the federal government's principal programs of support for individual incomes. As of 1987 it employed 70,176 persons, down from a peak of 82,034 reached in 1980. In size and impact on the average citizen, it is roughly comparable to the Internal

2. While I know of no other book that takes the same approach, my purpose bears a general similarity to that of James Q. Wilson in *The Investigators: Managing FBI and Narcotics Agents* (Basic Books, 1978). In his study of the Federal Bureau of Investigation and the Drug Enforcement Administration, Wilson sought to demonstrate that rational management—adapting an organization to its critical tasks—is hindered in public agencies by their subservience to political institutions, which stipulate their goals and supply their resources. Support from these institutions, Wilson argued, was contingent (it could be withdrawn, altered, or reduced at any time) and conditional (to secure it required public executives to accept many and severe constraints on their authority). Wilson's account focused on official roles internal to the agency; mine concentrates on the external sources of guidance and constraint.

Revenue Service (IRS). Whereas the IRS is the government's big collector of revenue from individuals, the SSA is the big dispenser of benefits. The two events I have chosen for study are the initiation of the supplemental security income program (SSI) in 1974 and a review of the eligibility of recipients of disability insurance in the early 1980s.

SSI is the federal program for supporting the income of needy blind, aged, and disabled persons; in the mid-1970s it replaced the federally aided state programs that had prevailed for several decades. The SSA, which was made responsible for administering the new program, was not ready for the task. Many payments were made in error, and many eligible persons failed to receive payments. Because computer systems were insufficiently developed, it was impossible to trace the sources of error or make corrections. Mobs jammed big-city social security offices, and federal marshals and private security forces under contract had to maintain order in some places. Field employees worked millions of hours of overtime. Other agency programs suffered. A decade and a half later, SSI is still remembered inside the agency as a disaster.

The disability review conducted in the early 1980s was also traumatic. Concerned that the disability insurance program was being abused, Congress in 1980 ordered the SSA to undertake periodic reviews of the eligibility of recipients. Those who were not classified as permanently disabled would have to be reviewed every three years. A massive initial review was begun in the first months of the Reagan administration. The administration's budget projected that billions of dollars would be saved by removing hundreds of thousands of ineligible recipients from the rolls. The SSA and the state agencies with which it collaborates in the administration of disability insurance reviewed over 1,203,000 cases in three years and benefits were terminated for 495,000. Opposition grew intense as it became clear that obviously disabled persons were being summarily deprived of benefits. Flooded with appeals, the courts ruled against the SSA in more than 200,000 cases (many of which were encompassed in class actions), and many state governments ceased to cooperate with the agency in carrying out the review. In the spring of 1984 the secretary of the Department of Health and Human Services, in which the SSA is located, suspended the review pending development of fresh legislation.

Presumably, administrative organizations are most vulnerable and error-prone when tackling unfamiliar tasks, as was the case with SSI, or otherwise departing from their routines. The review of the eligibility of disability recipients, while not different in kind from what the SSA had done in the past, was attempted on a far greater scale. One might expect policymakers to be most vigilant in their concern for administration at such moments. If policymakers do not carefully inquire into organizational capacities when imposing new burdens, presumably they never do so. Thus these cases should be well suited to provide some insight into the weight given to administrative questions in the course of policymaking. That is a prime purpose of part II of the book, which describes how the presidency, Congress, and the SSA leadership itself went about deciding to impose these added tasks on the SSA.

Because they were "bad" cases, much deplored as examples of incompetence and injustice, these two are richly documented by the government itself. Whatever the explanation may be for poor performance by U.S. government agencies, when it occurs it is abundantly confirmed by critical self-examination. That is one reason for choosing to study these cases. But it is not just the documentation of administrative dysfunction that makes them suitable for study. Institutional guidance for administration develops in the course of oversight as well as in policymaking; much of it comes directly in response to administrative actions. When things go wrong, oversight flourishes, yielding rich data on both the overseers and the object of oversight. Part III of the book analyzes the presidency, courts, and Congress as sources of oversight.

The relations here portrayed between the SSA and the primary governing institutions are intense. When departures in policy are being attempted or when administrative trouble develops, an agency and its political and judicial supervisors perforce become deeply engaged with each other. An examination of the SSA's routines would show much less institutional supervision. In 1986 the SSA issued 5.7 million new social security cards, received and posted 230 million earnings reports for 124 million workers (virtually everyone in the country who was employed), processed 6 million applications for benefits, and made benefit payments to 41.8 million persons. At the core of its functions is retirement and survivors' insurance. Under this program employed workers are taxed on their earnings and employers on their payrolls; the employees qualify for benefits when they retire, and their survivors receive benefits when they die. This program was the SSA's initial responsibility and remains its largest single one, consuming 44 percent of the effort of its work force.[3] Both of the events described here

3. Disability insurance consumes 27 percent; SSI, 25 percent; and medicare, 5 percent. Social Security Administration, *Executive Handbook of Selected Data*, SSA Pub. 47-085 (May 1988), p. 10.

occurred outside this core, relatively routinized, function. As sources of information on relations between the SSA and its institutional supervisors—and on the character of the institutions' supervision—they are the more revealing precisely because they entailed policy innovations.

If, as I argue, administrative agencies are ill served by the working of American government, that may not seem a very serious matter. Government does not exist to serve bureaucracy. Administrative agencies are means to the ends of government, not ends in themselves. It is far more important that American governing institutions work well at defining and redefining consensus—that they be vigorously representative and responsive—than that they work well as sources of guidance to the administrative apparatus of government.

And yet bureaucracies are indispensable means to virtually all of government's desirable ends, and they have become the principal medium of the relation between government and the public. Increasingly, Americans are acted upon by government—they are bureaucracy's clients—as well as being citizen actors who seek to influence government by voting or otherwise participating in politics.[4] When agencies perform poorly, all citizens are victims, and particular citizens may be victimized in cruel and very damaging ways. The clients of the Social Security Administration, which is to say its current beneficiaries, include between 15 and 20 percent of the population, and most of the other 80 percent will be beneficiaries eventually. All have a stake in being well served by the agency, and a stake therefore in its being well served by its overseers in the government.

ADMINISTRATION IN CONSTITUTIONAL THEORY

Because this is a book about relations between an administrative agency and its institutional supervisors, it will be useful at the outset to review how American constitutional theory has treated administration. In the U.S. system of government, where do administrative agencies fit? How are they supposed to relate to the three primary branches of the government? What follows is a thumbnail guide to some very complicated constitutional issues.

4. Michael Nelson develops this point in "Bureaucracy: The Biggest Crisis of All," *Washington Monthly*, vol. 9 (January 1978), pp. 51–59.

An Elliptical Inheritance

The Framers of the Constitution and the authors of the *Federalist* papers—to whom Americans turn first for guidance in constitutional theory—were not indifferent to administration. The *Federalist* more than once asserts the importance of good administration. Nonetheless, Hamilton and Madison had relatively little to say there about how administration was to fit into the constitutional scheme, and the scheme that had been devised in Philadelphia guaranteed that a fit would be problematic.

The bedrock principle of the Constitution is republicanism. Executive power and legislative power were lodged in officeholders who were to be picked directly or indirectly by the people and were to serve fixed terms. To remain in office, they would have to be reelected. The lower house of the legislature was to be directly accountable to the people. The upper house and the chief executive were only indirectly accountable to a popular electorate at first, but eventually became more directly so.[5]

Other principles of the regime, less fundamental than republicanism but nonetheless deeply embedded, have been constitutionalism, federalism, and the separation of powers. The newly created government had only those few powers granted to it in a written constitution. All others remained with the state governments and the people. Although the principle of states' sovereignty had in general been repudiated in favor of popular sovereignty, the repudiation was not complete, and the result was not pure. In Madison's phrase, the republic was "compound"; it mixed the features of a unitary government with those of a federal government. The states were represented equally in the upper house of the legislature—a surviving vestige of the old, purely federal form. Elected by the state legislatures, the upper house was to serve as a check on the lower, popularly elected one. The powers of government were divided among three branches—executive, legislative, and judicial—an arrangement pronounced by the Framers to be the very definition of free government. They were deeply committed to that principle.

Under this scheme of government, there were major obstacles to

5. On the Senate, see William H. Riker, *The Development of American Federalism* (Boston and Lancaster: Kluwer Academic Publishers, 1987), chap. 7; and on the presidency see, for example, W. E. Binkley, *The Powers of the President: Problems of American Democracy* (Doubleday, Doran, 1937), later rev. as *President and Congress* (Vintage, 1962), chap. 4.

creation of administrative agencies at the national level. Historically, the presumption has been that domestic functions of government rested with the states. Advocates of national action of any kind—and specifically of the creation of national administrative agencies—have faced a heavy burden of proof. They had to establish that the function was one that the national government constitutionally could, and otherwise should, undertake. And if this threshold were successfully crossed and national administrative agencies were created, it was then necessary to confront the deeper constitutional question of how they were to be held accountable. All uses of governmental power must ultimately, even if indirectly, be subject to popular control. In a system of separated powers, how was this to be achieved? To which of the branches should administrative agencies report? Or could accountability somehow be made direct?

Insofar as the Framers supplied an answer to such questions, it favored the president. In *Federalist* number 72, Hamilton wrote that "The administration of government . . . in its most usual . . . [and] precise signification . . . is limited to executive details, and falls peculiarly within the province of the executive department." He continued:

> The actual conduct of foreign negotiations, the preparatory plans of finance, the application and disbursement of the public moneys in conformity to the general appropriations of the legislature, the arrangement of the army and navy, the direction of the operations of war . . . constitute what seems to be most properly understood by the administration of government. The persons, therefore, to whose immediate management these different matters are committed, ought to be considered as the assistants or deputies of the chief magistrate, and on this account, they ought to derive their offices from his appointment, at least from his nomination, and ought to be subject to his superintendence.[6]

Moreover, the first Congress, which may reasonably be viewed as a continuation of the Constitutional Convention, in framing statutes for creation of the first executive departments decided that the president alone should have the power to remove his department heads. Even when the Senate had the right to advise and consent to their nomination, as provided for in the Constitution, it should not similarly participate

6. Edward Mead Earle, ed., *The Federalist* (Modern Library, n.d.), pp. 468–69.

in their removal. This was a constitutional decision of utmost importance.[7]

However, what the Framers supplied was a mere fragment of guidance to future generations. Hamilton's essays on the chief executive offer no comment, for example, on the "take care" clause of the Constitution, that part of Article II, section 3, which provides that the president shall "take care that the laws be faithfully executed." Does this mean that the president and his assistants and deputies are confined strictly to what the legislature has authorized, or do they have discretion in interpreting the law? How much discretion, if so? If the chief executive and members of the legislature disagree over what the law requires, from which source do administrators take orders? Nor does Hamilton comment on a further provision of Article II, which says, after defining the president's appointment power: "But the Congress may by law vest the appointment of such inferior officers, as they think proper, in the President alone, in the courts of law, or in the heads of departments." If Congress can create departments and vest the power of appointment directly in department heads, it has an important source of control over administration. In short, the Constitution lays the basis for a contest between the executive and the legislature for the control of administrative agents.

The Framers could be elliptical on the subject of the supervision of administration perhaps because there was so little administrative organization at the time, and also perhaps because they did not expect that very much of it would ever develop at the national level. In *Federalist* numbers 45 and 46, in which Madison argued that the federal government would not have an undue advantage in the new system, he said that the number of persons employed by the federal government would be much smaller than the number employed by the states. In a rather different spirit, Hamilton too anticipated a bottom-heavy administration. He predicted a "regular and peaceable" execution of the laws because the federal government would depend so heavily for

7. Though taken very early, this decision did not settle the question. The scope of the president's power of appointment and removal has been the subject of Supreme Court decisions in this century, and to this day, the president does not have complete freedom to remove his appointees to the independent regulatory commissions, such as the Federal Trade Commission and Federal Communications Commission. (That is what makes them "independent.") Yet on the whole, the power of appointment and removal has developed to the president's advantage, sustained in large part by the legislative decision of 1789. For a succinct account of that decision, see Leonard D. White, *The Federalists: A Study in Administrative History* (Macmillan, 1948), pp. 20–25.

that purpose on state governments, to which the populace would be attached. He wrote:

> The plan reported by the convention, by extending the authority of the federal head to the individual citizens of the several States, will enable the government to employ the ordinary magistracy of each, in the execution of its laws. . . . Thus the legislatures, courts, and magistrates, of the respective [states], will be incorporated into the operations of the national government *as far as its just and constitutional authority extends*; and will be rendered auxiliary to the enforcement of its laws.[8]

From the perspective of the late twentieth century, one can see that Hamilton was at least half right. The administrative apparatus of state and local governments, with over 10 million employees in 1985, *has* been harnessed very much to the federal government's purposes. Yet it is also true, to a degree that he and Madison probably did not anticipate, that the federal government has developed an administrative apparatus of its own. As of 1985 the federal government had 3 million civilian employees, who were distributed among a wide variety of agencies.[9] Subsequent generations have had to figure out how to reconcile this development with the constitutional scheme without much help from the scheme's designers.

The Doctrine of Presidential Responsibility

The need for a theory covering the place of administration in the American regime became more urgent as government developed and became more national. As government acquired more functions and the functions became more complex, legislatures began routinely to give administrative bodies broad grants of discretion. Decisions formerly made by legislatures themselves or by courts began to be made by administrative agencies. In the period of rapid industrialization

8. Earle, ed., *Federalist* no. 27, pp. 169–70 (emphasis in original).

9. For an overview of their development, see *The Federal Executive Establishment: Evolution and Trends*, Committee Print, Senate Committee on Governmental Affairs, 96 Cong. 2 sess. (Government Printing Office, 1980). For a scholarly analysis of the foundations of national administration, see Stephen Skowronek, *Building a New American State: The Expansion of National Administrative Capacities, 1877–1920* (Cambridge University Press, 1982).

immediately following the Civil War, this occurred at both the state and national levels. Federal government employment doubled (from 53,900 to 107,000) between 1871 and 1881. In the following decade, Congress passed the Pendleton Act, creating a federal civil service, and the Interstate Commerce Act, creating the first of the national government's independent regulatory commissions. Events compelled attention to the place of administration.

One response, highly ambivalent, came from the courts. They said that Congress could not delegate legislative power to the executive branch because that would violate the separation of powers. However, until the New Deal the courts never actually invalidated any congressional acts on the ground that they contained unconstitutional delegations. The leading case was *Field* v. *Clark*, decided by the Supreme Court in 1892. Justice John Marshall Harlan wrote: "That Congress cannot delegate legislative power to the President is a principle universally recognized as vital to the integrity and maintenance of the system of government ordained by the constitution."[10] Yet in that case the Court upheld a provision of the Tariff Act of 1890 that authorized the president to suspend favorable tariff treatment for nations that imposed on American products duties deemed to be reciprocally unequal and unreasonable. In decisions both before and after that one, the Supreme Court upheld statutes that gave the president or other executive officers a large role in formulating as well as executing national policy. Not until Congress passed the National Industrial Recovery Act, a Depression measure that gave the president sweeping power to impose anticompetitive regulation on the economy, did the Court find a congressional delegation to be excessive.[11] Thereafter it reverted to its customary permissiveness. The result of this line of doctrinal development was to permit all but unlimited scope for rulemaking by executive agencies in practice, yet to leave it clouded with the suggestion of constitutional impropriety. By the 1930s everyone was prepared to concede that broad delegations to the executive were necessary, but neither Congress, which made them,

10. 143 U.S. 649 at 692.

11. The New Deal decisions were *Panama Refining Co.* v. *Ryan*, 293 U.S. 388 (1935) and *Schechter Poultry Corp.* v. *United States*, 295 U.S. 495 (1935). For good brief summaries of the history of the nondelegation doctrine, see Jerry L. Mashaw and Richard A. Merrill, eds., *Administrative Law: The American Public Law System: Cases and Materials*, 2d ed. (West Publishing Co., 1985); and Edward S. Corwin's *The Constitution and What It Means Today*, 14th ed., rev. by Harold W. Chase and Craig R. Ducat (Princeton University Press, 1978), pp. 7–8.

nor the courts, which generally approved them, pretended to like that fact or to find it consistent with the spirit of the Constitution.[12]

A second and equally influential set of reactions to the growth of administration came from the nascent Progressive Era profession of political science, within which Woodrow Wilson and Frank J. Goodnow were crucially concerned with the ordering of relations between administration and politics. On this subject, Wilson offered simple precepts, and Goodnow, a complex, extended discussion.

As an instructor in government at Bryn Mawr College in 1887, Wilson wrote an essay, "Study of Administration." Its publication has come to be viewed by scholars as a seminal event, marking the emergence of the self-conscious study of public administration.[13] "It is getting to be harder to 'run' a constitution than to frame one," Wilson wrote, in what has become probably the article's most-quoted passage. Until then, he said, America had been preoccupied with the framing of constitutions; it was now time to turn to the organization and methods of government offices and to the quality of governmental personnel. He argued for a "science of administration."

Wilson's was of course a professorial view: there was a right way to run a government, which could be discovered through inquiry and research. But, perhaps because he was weary of all the constitution making, perhaps because he was fundamentally out of sympathy with the separation of powers (as his book *Congressional Government* had already shown), Wilson did not come to grips with the crucial constitutional dilemma: to whom should public administrators be

12. For extended discussions of the historical development of rulemaking by the executive, see James Hart, *The Ordinance Making Powers of the President of the United States* (Johns Hopkins Press, 1925; AMS Press, 1971); John Preston Comer, *Legislative Functions of National Administrative Authorities* (Columbia University Press, 1927; AMS Press, 1968); and James Hart, "The Exercise of Rule-Making Power," in The President's Committee on Administrative Management, *Report of the Committee with Studies of Administrative Management in the Federal Government*, 74 Cong. 2 sess. (GPO, 1937). Delegation doctrine continues to receive attention from constitutional scholars. For example, see Sotirios A. Barber, *The Constitution and the Delegation of Congressional Power* (University of Chicago Press, 1975); and Edward L. Rubin, "Law and Legislation in the Administrative State," *Columbia Law Review*, vol. 89 (April 1989), pp. 369–426, and a response by Peter L. Strauss, "Legislative Theory and the Rule of Law: Some Comments on Rubin," pp. 427–51.

13. Paul P. Van Riper has debunked this view, however, pointing out that the essay did not attain prominence until the 1950s. "The American Administrative State: Wilson and the Founders," in Ralph Clark Chandler, ed., *A Centennial History of the American Administrative State* (Free Press, 1987), p. 9.

responsible? His prescription was characteristically Wilsonian—and unhelpful. He said they should be responsible to public opinion, which should "play the part of authoritative critic." The corps of civil servants ought to carry out the policy of the government they served, and the people would be the source of that policy. He favored "large powers and unhampered discretion" so that responsibility could be fixed. "Public attention must be easily directed, in each case of good or bad administration, to just the man deserving of praise or blame. . . . If [power is] centered in heads of the service and in heads of the branches of the service, it is easily watched and brought to book." Wilson wrote as if chief executives, legislatures, and courts did not exist as intermediaries between the public and public administrators. He said that public office must be nonpartisan and businesslike. Crucially, "administrative questions are not political questions. Although politics sets the tasks for administration, it should not be suffered to manipulate its offices."[14]

Wilson and Goodnow are both recalled today for the argument that politics and administration ought to be separated, but Goodnow's book-length formulation was far more complex. Politics had to do with policies or expressions of the state will, and administration had to do with the execution of those policies, he stipulated. He said they had to be separated in some respects and connected in others, and he tried to define which was which. A large part of administration is unconnected with politics "because it embraces fields of semi-scientific, quasi-judicial and quasi-business or commercial activity." In other words, it entails "the exercise of foresight and discretion, the pursuit of truth, the gathering of information, the maintenance of a strictly impartial attitude towards . . . individuals . . . and the provision of the most efficient possible administrative organization."[15] Such activities should be carried out by government agents having considerable permanence of tenure. Also, clerical and ministerial officers who simply carry out orders of their superiors should have tenure. Because these two groups of officials were engaged in work that was unconnected with expression of the "true state will," they should be insulated from politics.

14. Woodrow Wilson, "Study of Administration," *Political Science Quarterly*, vol. 2 (June 1887), pp. 197–222.

15. Frank J. Goodnow, *Politics and Administration: A Study in Government* (Macmillan, 1900), p. 85. Van Riper credits Goodnow with having founded the academic study of public administration in this country. "The American Administrative State," p. 21. See also Nicholas Henry, "The Emergence of Public Administration as a Field of Study," in Chandler, *Centennial History*, pp. 37–85.

However, insofar as administration entailed execution of the state will, it should be coordinated with politics, not separated. Goodnow therefore supposed that the highest executive officers—those to whom was entrusted the general execution of the law and who had a determining influence on policy—should not enjoy tenure of office. On the contrary, he wrote:

> Permanence of tenure in the case of the highest executive officers entrusted with large discretionary powers is incompatible with popular government, since it tends to further the formation of an immense governmental machine whose very efficiency may make it dangerous to the existence of popular government. . . . Too great strength in the administrative organization tends to make popular government impossible.[16]

The necessity for the separation of politics from administration was greatest in municipal government, where most administration is of the narrowest kind. At higher levels of government, executive officers would necessarily bear more responsibility for policy choice.[17]

Goodnow stipulated that the political body should have control over the administrative body.[18] But what of a system in which the function of expressing the state will was divided between two political bodies? He did not claim to have a solution, for he well recognized how deeply embedded the separation of powers was in American theory and practice, but he knew the direction in which he wished the governmental system to move. He wanted strong, responsible chief executives and strong, responsible political parties. On the whole, his book was an argument for the reform of parties, which at the time seemed strong but irresponsible. Parties, he believed, were the indispensable mechanism for coordinating the divided parts of the government. Indeed, they had come to be so strong in the United States because the system of separated powers especially required them. Being necessarily strong, they must also be made responsive if government were to be responsive. Party bosses must be made to answer to party members at large and be readily removable by them, just as chief executives should be answerable to, and removable by, electorates at large.

16. Goodnow, *Politics and Administration*, p. 90.
17. Goodnow, *Politics and Administration*, p. 84.
18. Goodnow, *Politics and Administration*, p. 92.

The president, Goodnow believed, already exemplified what a chief executive should be. He was the sole elected executive (in contrast to the numerous executive officers in state governments). He had power to remove as well as appoint other executive officers. Opinions of attorneys general and decisions of the Supreme Court had held that subordinate executive officials of the national government should defer to superior officials and thus ultimately to the president. Goodnow cited specifically the following language from an opinion of the attorney general: "I hold that no head of a department can lawfully perform an official act against the will of the President; and that will is by the Constitution to govern the performance of all such acts." The president stood at the head of an "official hierarchy" with "large if not complete powers of appointment, removal, direction, and supervision." He was linked to the electorate by party, and party also bound the members of his administration to him.[19]

This Progressive Era prescription, expounded preeminently although not exclusively by Goodnow, had an enduring influence.[20] Students of American public administration ever since have tended to favor concentration of authority and responsibility in the president as elected chief executive. With the coming of the New Deal, the prescriptions of the Progressive Era were reaffirmed and converted into institutional practice. The national administration grew explosively. New agencies proliferated; they received encompassing grants of discretion; and federal government employment nearly doubled (from 580,494 in 1930 to 1,014,117 in 1940). As before, the legitimacy of administrative power was called into question. The answer of the Roosevelt administration, embodied in the report of the President's Committee on Administrative Management (the Brownlow committee), was that administrative power was legitimate as long as it was responsible to the president. The committee sought to make sure that the executive branch was so organized and the president so staffed that he could play his part as manager and supervisor. In pursuance of its recommendations, the Executive Office of the President was created, with the Bureau of the Budget at its core. The report rested squarely on the theory that Goodnow had propounded.

19. Goodnow, *Politics and Administration*, pp. 114–19.

20. See Dwight Waldo, *The Administrative State: A Study of the Political Theory of American Public Administration* (New York: Ronald Press, 1948), chap. 7. Waldo treats W. F. Willoughby along with Goodnow as a "classic" source and discusses numerous other treatments of the separation of powers as well.

Congress and the Courts

Congress, however, has never subscribed to the theory of presidential responsibility. It has sought to supervise administration closely. Among the practices it has relied on have been investigations of administrative conduct; appropriations made annually for narrowly specified purposes; laws that prescribe in detail the structure and functions of administrative agencies and even of particular offices within them; and the legislative veto, a procedure whereby it has sought to reserve the right to review and disapprove action contemplated by the executive.

Using such instruments, Congress has often contested the president very forcefully for control of administration, even to the point of attaining dominance during parts of the nineteenth century. At other times, it has acknowledged the necessity of vesting powers of supervision in him, as when it passed the Budget and Accounting Act of 1921, giving him responsibility for preparing a budget for the government. Nonetheless, even when it initiated or assented to the expansion of presidential powers of administrative supervision, it made no constitutional concessions. Taking care not to endorse any notions of executive prerogative, it made clear that it was making delegations that it retained the right to withdraw or overrule. "Presidents may see themselves . . . as general managers by constitutional intent," James L. Sundquist has written. "But the Congress sees them as agents of the Congress."[21] Congress also sees administrative agencies as its own. In making delegations to them or calling them to account, it does not feel bound by any obligation to defer to the president. As a matter of constitutional principle, it feels entirely justified in combating him. The laws that agencies carry out are laws that Congress has enacted; the money they spend is money that it has appropriated. The will of the legislature, in the legislature's view, should control administrative acts.

The judiciary—third in the American triumvirate of governing branches—has been variously an arbiter between the other two in their struggle for control of administration; a direct rival to administrative

21. James L. Sundquist, "Congress as Public Administrator," in Chandler, *Centennial History*, p. 267. This article condenses themes developed in Sundquist, *The Decline and Resurgence of Congress* (Brookings, 1981). Other accounts of contests between the president and Congress for control of administration may be found in Binkley, *The Powers of the President* ; and Leonard D. White's administrative history of the United States, contained in four volumes: *The Federalists* (Macmillan, 1948); *The Jeffersonians* (Macmillan, 1951); *The Jacksonians* (Macmillan, 1954); and *The Republican Era: 1869–1901* (Macmillan, 1958).

agencies for the function of interpreting and applying the law; and an independent source of supervision of administrative agencies. The first of these functions, though not unimportant in American constitutional history, is not crucial to understanding the place of administrative agencies in the constitutional system, and hence need not be described here. The other two roles are crucial and interrelated.

The British tradition brought to this country made courts the only legitimate interpreters of the law as applied to individual citizens. Shaped over centuries, this tradition was authoritatively expounded by Albert V. Dicey late in the nineteenth century. The essential characteristic of the English constitution, he argued, was the supremacy of law. What that meant in practice was "in the first place, that no man is punishable or can be lawfully made to suffer in body or goods except for a distinct breach of law established in the ordinary legal manner before the ordinary Courts of the land."[22] Government could not act against individuals as it pleased. It could act only according to preexisting general laws passed by a representative legislative body, and no one could be punished for violating such laws except through judicial proceedings. Moreover, in such proceedings the government would have no special standing. It would be treated as simply one of the parties.[23] This tradition formed one of the several bases for distrust of administrative power. The view that Americans inherited from England was that a government "of laws" was superior to a government "of men," and for a government to be "of laws" the courts must interpret and enforce laws passed by the legislature. There was no place in this tradition for administrative discretion.

Courts and their partisans, like Congress and its partisans, over time bowed to necessity and accepted the growth of administrative agencies that were given powers to make rules and enforce them upon private parties. But the courts and their partisans—principally the elite of the legal profession—resisted strenuously. Their efforts, the lingering effects of the Diceyan tradition, and the specific American practice of judicial review, whereby courts decide whether even legislative acts conform to a "higher law," combined to secure a very large role for courts in supervising administrative action. At the turn of the century, in a masterful book on the principles of administrative law in the

22. A. V. Dicey, *Introduction to the Study of the Law of the Constitution*, 8th ed. (Macmillan, 1915), pp. 183–84.

23. I here borrow the paraphrase of Dicey that appears in Martin Shapiro, *Who Guards the Guardians? Judicial Control of Administration* (University of Georgia Press, 1988), p. 36.

United States, Goodnow noted that the courts had the same power over legislative acts of the executive—what today are commonly called regulations—as they had over the statutes of the legislature: "That is, they may interpret them, and in most cases declare them void or refuse to enforce them in case they are contrary to the law." In regard to individual acts—what today is called adjudication—Goodnow wrote:

> When an individual act of the administration is not of a political . . . character [such as carrying on diplomatic relations, making treaties, commanding military forces, or conducting relations with the legislature, all of which were governed by the principle of popular responsibility], the courts have a very large control over it. In many cases they may annul it, amend it, interpret it, and prevent the administration from proceeding to execute it.[24]

An enormous amount of debate has ensued since then, reaching peaks during the New Deal and during the expansion of agency regulatory power that took place in the 1970s. Much more might be said on this subject, but in essence Goodnow's turn-of-the-century observations remain sound. Whether it be rulemaking or adjudication, virtually everything that agencies do that has an effect on citizens is subject to judicial review. The courts are a full-fledged competitor of the president and Congress for the control of administrative acts.

The summary answer, then, to how national administrative agencies fit into the American system is that they fit uneasily, under stress. Modern government dictates that they bear very large responsibilities. Yet much in the U.S. constitutional tradition casts doubt on the legitimacy of whatever power they possess. In a system that values constitutional status, they are the creatures of statutes. In a system that rests on the bedrock of popular sovereignty, they are unelected. In a federal system that honors a tradition of decentralization, they are creatures of the center. Finally, by combining executive, legislative, and adjudicative functions, they flout the separation of powers. Yet they are also conspicuous victims of that separation, for they are often the focus of conflicting interaction among the three primary branches, each of which has a solid claim to a right to supervise them.

24. Frank J. Goodnow, *The Principles of the Administrative Law of the United States* (G.P. Putnam's Sons, 1905), p. 51.

THE PLACE OF THE SSA

If only in form, the SSA illustrates the constitutional tensions to which federal administrative agencies are subject. Its form has been unstable and even after more than fifty years remains open to dispute.

To administer the Social Security Act, in 1935 Congress created a bipartisan Social Security Board of three members to be appointed by the president for staggered six-year terms. This was roughly consistent with the recommendation of the President's Committee on Economic Security, whose report laid the foundation of the Social Security Act. The committee had recommended the creation of a presidentially appointed social insurance board within the Department of Labor, whereas Congress chose to make the board independent of any executive department.

This form of organization lasted only a decade. The Brownlow committee, reporting less than two years after the act was passed, firmly condemned boards as a form of management. "The conspicuously well-managed administrative units in the Government are almost without exception headed by single administrators," it said.[25] It also condemned the proliferation of agencies outside the regular executive departments. It recommended the consolidation and grouping of the various units into twelve departments specialized by function, among which would have been a new Department of Social Welfare. The functions of the Social Security Board would have been divided between it and the Department of Labor, with administration of benefits to the needy in the Department of Social Welfare and that of benefits by right in the Department of Labor.[26] Reorganization plans effectuated in 1939, 1946, and 1953 conformed only in part to the Brownlow committee's recommendations.

In 1939 the Federal Security Agency was created, with a single head reporting to the president, and the Social Security Board was subsumed under it, along with the Public Health Service, the Employment Service, and other agencies. In 1946 the Social Security Board was abolished and its functions were transferred to the federal security administrator, who delegated them to a commissioner of social security. In 1953 the Department of Health, Education, and Welfare was created, superseding the Federal Security Agency, and the commissioner of social security was made a presidential appointee.

25. President's Committee on Administrative Management, *Report*, p. 32.
26. President's Committee on Administrative Management, *Report*, pp. 31–36.

(The Department of Health, Education, and Welfare metamorphosed into the Department of Health and Human Services during the Carter administration when education was given its own department.)

In summary, the structure and location of the SSA within the executive branch have more often than not reflected the view that responsibility for executive functions ought to be fixed in single administrators rather than boards or committees and that such administrators ought to be responsible to the elected chief executive. Yet this view has been subject to challenge. Since the mid-1970s partisans of the SSA have argued for removing it from the Department of Health and Human Services and reestablishing it as an independent agency under a bipartisan board appointed by the president. A social security commissioner or executive director, the agency's chief operating officer, would be appointed by the board. Advocated as a way of taking social security "out of politics"—the standard argument for multimember, bipartisan boards—the independent-agency proposal responds to presidential attempts in recent years to achieve greater control over the SSA. The change would reduce the president's present share of control, to the relative benefit of Congress. Therefore presidential appointees have opposed this proposal.

In contrast with the SSA's shifting formal relation to the presidency, the statutory language governing its relation to the courts has been quite stable. Social Security Act amendments in 1939 enlarged the original program, accelerated the initiation of it from 1942 to 1940, and spelled out the agency's rulemaking powers and citizens' rights to an agency hearing and thereafter to judicial review. The law provided that any citizen who had been a party to a hearing could appeal the result to a U.S. district court by filing a petition within sixty days. The agency's findings of fact, if supported by substantial evidence, were to be conclusive. But while the language of this law governing judicial review of the SSA has persisted, the actual relation of the agency with the courts has been transformed, as later chapters will show. Whereas courts once treated the agency with deference, they have turned into active overseers. That development is an important part of the story that follows.

CHAPTER 2

What Went Wrong

WHEN THE Social Security Administration undertook to administer the supplemental security income program, it fell heir to several programs of income support that had previously been administered by state governments. When it undertook to review the eligibility of disability insurance recipients, it was in effect rendering judgment on its own prior performance. Thus neither effort represented a fresh beginning. In both cases, policymakers were seeking to "fix" something they judged to be "broken." The fixing then created problems of its own. This chapter will describe what went wrong. It is background for the analysis of institutional roles that constitutes the core of the book.

SUPPLEMENTAL SECURITY INCOME

The Social Security Act Amendments of 1972 made the federal government primarily responsible for supporting the incomes of the aged, blind, and disabled, and thus represented a major change in policy and administrative practices. Correspondingly, the legislation imposed a major new burden on the Social Security Administration.

Historically, aid to the poor had been a function of state and local governments. However, beginning with the Social Security Act of 1935 the federal government gave grants-in-aid to the states to assist them with that function. The grants were confined to certain categories of needy persons—the aged, the blind, children in a home where the wage earner was absent or incapacitated, and, after 1951, the disabled. The grants-in-aid were accompanied by conditions, yet the state governments retained essential responsibility. They set the standards of eligibility (how poor a person need be to qualify for aid) and the standards of payment (how much a person would get). The states' decisions determined how much the federal government spent in grants-in-aid. The federal law promised to pay to the states a certain proportion of their payment to an individual, up to a specified maximum, but put no limit on the number of individuals aided.

The Social Security Act Amendments of 1972 provided that for those categories subject to reform (after intense debate, aid to families with dependent children, or AFDC, was excluded), the federal government would now set standards of need and eligibility and make and finance the basic payment to the individual. In short, the adult categories were federalized.

Although the federal role had now become predominant, it was still not to be exclusive. The new law provided that states might supplement the federal payment. Nonetheless, the centralizing purport of the policy change was evident here as well. States were given the option of having the federal government administer supplemental payments on their behalf at no cost. The law offered a number of inducements to choose this option, but states doing so would have to abide by whatever rules the secretary of Health, Education, and Welfare judged necessary to achieve "efficient and effective administration" and they would have to make any supplements available uniformly to all SSI beneficiaries. Assuming that states chose federal administration, the result would be a program nationally uniform except for variations in the amount of state supplements to the federal minimum payment. If the design of the program was not purely national, it came close. The change was indubitably fundamental.

Why SSI Was Difficult

For the SSA, the new law meant taking on a new task, more difficult and burdensome by far than its basic responsibility of administering retirement and survivors' insurance. The differences between the two programs derived from the way in which beneficiaries qualified for payments: in one by demonstrating financial need, in the other by establishing that they had earned the right to benefits through paying taxes.

Need-based income support programs are hard to administer because need is hard to determine. At a minimum, it requires determining how much income, earned and unearned, individuals have, and what financial assets they possess. There is no quick, reliable, and easy way to do that. The federal government, from the reports of organized employers (the W-2 form well known to the American taxpayer), gets a good deal of information about income earned through conventional employment, but it knows much less about other forms of income and depends heavily on the recipients to tell it. If, for example, the government wishes to treat as income the value of room and board for people who live in the household of a friend or relative, it must gather the information. By contrast, recipients of retirement insurance have only to establish that they have qualified for benefits through the necessary length of time in taxable employment, have retired from work (a limited amount of postretirement earnings is permitted), and have reached the minimum age for eligibility.

From this basic difference, others follow. The decision to award retirement insurance benefits can be anticipated by both the agency and the beneficiary and therefore can often be made at a deliberate pace. Beneficiaries are likely to apply in anticipation of their retirement, perhaps as much as three months before actually retiring. Needy people, by contrast, are presumably in need at the moment they apply, and the agency correspondingly is under pressure to act promptly on their applications. In the case of retirees, the agency already possesses the information that is needed to act, for it has kept track of the applicants' taxable earnings; in the case of the needy, the agency must obtain the information. Once people qualify for retirement insurance benefits, they will ordinarily remain qualified until death. "Postentitlement changes," as they are called, are relatively simple, involving changes of address or changes in postretirement earnings; by contrast, the income and living arrangements of the poor may change in ways that affect eligibility for payment. Clients embrace virtually the whole population in the former case, including the most competent, socially adjusted part of it; the financially dependent population is more troubled, and hence more trouble to serve.

In sum, the SSA's new job was intrinsically hard. And there was not much time to prepare for it. Action on the law was completed in late October 1972, and the new program would go into effect on January 1, 1974. Strictly speaking, the lead time was longer than fourteen months, inasmuch as it was clear by the spring of 1971 that the adult categories might be federalized. Leading policymakers from the executive and legislative branches made the crucial decisions to approve the new program and assign it to the SSA in executive sessions of the House Ways and Means Committee at that time. The SSA's internal planning for the change began in March 1971, even before the committee reported a bill. However, it was not clear for some months thereafter whether the Senate would agree to the House's decision.

Not until the fall of 1972, shortly before the legislation passed, did the Senate Finance Committee declare support for federal administration. Realistically, the SSA's planning effort could not gain much momentum until the outcome had been settled. When that happened, the pressure to perform suddenly became intense.

There was much to plan for. On one hand, the SSA had to start from scratch, inasmuch as no applicable body of administrative rules existed. As a federal program, SSI was brand new. On the other hand, the SSA had to assume responsibility for programs that had long been operating at the state level. Specifically, this meant that it had to do the following in order to be ready.

—Develop formal rules and other guidance, consistent with the law, to govern the administration of individual cases and relations with the states in regard to federal administration of supplemental payments.

—Secure critical information about 3 million aged, blind, or disabled recipients from 1,350 state and local administrative units, and either verify this information independently or run the risk that it would be inaccurate.

—Publicize the new program and receive and process applications from individuals made freshly eligible by it. The SSA's original estimates were that SSI would add 4 million to 6 million people to the rolls.

—Open new field offices and expand and relocate others. Hire and train 15,000 new field employees, the number at first estimated to be needed, and train veteran employees in the new program.

—Negotiate agreements with the states covering their supplemental programs and other aspects of SSI implementation.

—Develop the systems—the information processing and decision procedures and associated computer software and equipment—by which the SSA would make determinations of eligibility and render payments in individual cases.

Even before January 1, 1974, it was painfully evident to some persons—namely, the SSA field employees on whom the main burden would fall—that the organization was not ready to do all this. Excerpts from the monthly trend reports sent from district offices to SSA headquarters in the last three months of 1973 reveal their plight:

> A new dimension to SSI not encountered with previous amendments is the slowness of getting decisions made and information about them. We are continually embarrassed by questions we are unable to respond to. (Dayton, Ohio)

SSI could well be the program that ruins the reputation of the Social Security Administration. (Lima, Ohio)

We anticipate that the situation from a standpoint of backlog and waiting time will rapidly worsen. The instructions for this new program are conveyed in too many forms. (Berkeley, California)

Even with the mandatory overtime of four hours per interviewer per week, our SSI leads accumulate faster than we are able to process them. Training is next to impossible on our current work schedule of only 30 minutes per day. (Walnut Creek, California)

We see the next few months as the most demanding and challenging times that we have ever known. And while we readily and willingly accept our responsibilities, we have serious doubt that we'll have the time with which to do justice to the public we serve. (McAllen, Texas)

It is almost inconceivable that the *policies* are still not set re such important items as food stamps and medicaid when we've known for four years that we would someday have this program to administer. Operational technicalities that change frequently are understood, but not policy. Both trainers and trainees are asea. (Cincinnati, Ohio)

When January arrived and operations began, the tone grew more desperate. The district office in Lancaster, California, resorted to black humor in its March report: "By mid-February we tried 'Dial a Prayer,' and by mid-March were negotiating for an exorcist."[1]

Where Errors Came From

In the first week of 1974, the federal government sent checks to more than 3 million recipients of SSI who had formerly been on the welfare rolls of the state governments. Thus the ultimate disaster did not occur; the conversion was accomplished. Data were assembled from states and localities despite the large number of data sources and the wide variety of forms in which the data had been stored. (A few jurisdictions had used modern disk storage systems, others had used magnetic tape, and many others had used paper files and ledgers.)

The converted cases contained many errors, however. The first

1. *Administration of the Supplemental Security Income Program*, Hearings before the Subcommittee on Oversight of the House Committee on Ways and Means, 94 Cong. 1 sess. (Government Printing Office, 1975), vol. 2, pp. 1–2.

systematic efforts at quality assurance, put in place six months after the program began, showed that between July and December 1974 payments in virtually one-fourth (24.8 percent) of all cases contained errors. There were overpayments in 13.3 percent of the cases, underpayments in 5.4 percent, and payments to ineligible people in 6.1 percent (not counting disability cases, for which quality reviews were separately conducted).[2] Roughly $400 million—just under 7 percent of total expenditures—was spent in error in the first year of the program.[3] In retrospect, this does not seem like a very high proportion under the circumstances, but because it exceeded the standard of performance that the federal government was seeking to impose on the states in the AFDC program, the SSA took a great deal of criticism for it.

There were many reasons for the volume of errors, including, of course, flaws in the data transferred from the states. The Social and Rehabilitation Service, the federal agency responsible for administering federal welfare grants to the states, in 1973 permitted the states to transfer the cases to be converted to SSI without redetermining their eligibility. This was done after consultation with the SSA, and for the apparent purpose of easing the conversion, but it surely did not improve the quality of the converted data.[4] When the conversion occurred there were still 100,000 to 200,000 cases for which data were missing. In these cases, the SSA made whatever assumption was most advantageous for the beneficiary.[5]

Other explanations for error derived more directly from the SSA's own difficulties in implementing the new program. Because the SSA was unable to develop policy guidance expeditiously, for a long time it was unclear just what data would be needed to carry out the program, and instructions to SSA field offices and the states changed constantly. Moreover, until the late fall of 1973, the SSA did not have an automated system for keeping records up to date as changes occurred. Data

2. *The Supplemental Security Income Program*, Committee Print, Senate Committee on Finance, 95 Cong. 1 sess. (GPO, 1977), pp. 49–50.

3. Renato Anthony DiPentima, "The Supplemental Security Income Program: A Study of Implementation," Ph.D. dissertation, University of Maryland, 1984, pp. 193, 208. This scholarly account by a participant is invaluable and is richer in detail than the several analyses produced by official evaluations such as the Senate Finance Committee staff report cited above.

4. *Report of the Supplemental Security Income Study Group*, Department of Health, Education, and Welfare Pub. (SSA) 76-10609 (January 1976), p. 17.

5. Jack S. Futterman, "A Two-Level Review: SSA Organization for Administering SSI; SSA's Organization as a Whole," March 1, 1974, pp. 35–36, copy in author's files.

spontaneously reported by the states about changes in recipient status or newly requested because of changes in SSA's policies were chronologically queued so that they could be properly entered whenever the capability to do so was developed. In the process, mistakes mounted. Correspondingly, once operations began, there was no way to issue corrected checks promptly in cases where errors were discovered. The payment system had been designed so that all payments had to be issued by the computer system rather than allowing for a manual substitute in exceptional cases. But when the program began, the computer system was not running daily, as had been assumed, but only about once a week. In combination with Treasury Department regulations for reissuance of government checks, which required that the first check be canceled before a new one was issued, this meant that the issuance of new checks could take weeks. A procedure for emergency issuance of corrected checks had to be improvised, inasmuch as welfare recipients could not wait for weeks.[6]

Another source of error was the SSA's inability to integrate the new SSI information system with its data for retirement and survivors' insurance. Many errors in SSI payments occurred because of mistaken information about social security benefits. Others occurred because of the SSA's failure to verify the social security numbers of SSI recipients expeditiously and assign new numbers to people who did not already have one. Dummy numbers were freely assigned in converted cases to facilitate computer operations; as of early February 1974 there were more than 475,000 dummy numbers in the SSI master record, constituting an important source of error. Recipients who received more than one check were likely to have a regular social security number and one or more dummy numbers.[7]

Given the many opportunities for error inherent in the conversion, one might expect that new claims—those from people made freshly eligible by the law of 1972 and therefore subject simply to the SSA's own processing—would have fared much better. In fact, they fared far worse. In those cases, the ultimate disaster *did* occur: most of the checks did not go out on time. SSA headquarters could not tell why. Under the pressure to get the program running, systems planners had given a lower priority to collecting information for management. Thus no one at headquarters knew initially how many applications had been

6. DiPentima, "Supplemental Security Income Program," pp. 192–93, 206–07.
7. Futterman, "Two-Level Review," pp. 33–34.

received, were pending, or had been approved. By May 1974 head-quarters officials had ascertained through field investigation that approximately 1 million new claims had been received since July 1973 but only 300,000 had been processed. In all the field offices they visited, they found hundreds of claims filed away because field office workers had been unable to put data into the computer system. The system had been programmed so intricately that many cases were rejected, but it had not yet been reprogrammed to accept corrected input. These cases, in limbo, piled up in all available storage spaces, while the field office staff struggled with the day-to-day interviewing work load, much of which stemmed from these unprocessed and unprocessible claims. By the late summer of 1974 the SSA was making progress with this backlog, but the new claims continued to have a higher error rate than the converted cases.[8]

It is clear that the SSI program depended crucially on computer operations and that these operations had not been adequately developed and tested when the program began. To administer SSI, with its unique properties, the SSA had decided to build a completely new computer system. This entailed at least three major design and development projects: an automated system to process information, maintain recipients' records, and calculate monthly benefits; a telecommunications system through which the 1,400 field offices could quickly communicate with the data processing system; and a system (the State Data Exchange) for communicating to the states the information they needed for making supplemental payments and also for determining eligibility for medicaid. (The program through which medical care for the dependent poor is financed, medicaid remained a state program with federal grants-in-aid.) Developing any of these three elements would have been a major undertaking in the time available. None of the three was operating reliably when the program began.

The first SSI payment tapes were created in late December 1973 and were sent to the Treasury Department containing largely untested and unvalidated computer programs. The telecommunications system on which the field offices would rely for inputting data to the system and securing access to recipient records was still being installed and had not been tested or debugged. Computer programs for processing changes in recipient records had not been completed. The State Data

8. DiPentima, "Supplemental Security Income Program," pp. 208–09, 214–16; and John Fialka, "Welfare Payments Wrong 23% of the Time," *Washington Star*, August 16, 1975.

Exchange had yet to be tried. In short, the statutory program, begun in January 1974, was the trial run for a brand-new computer system, and it was a trial for which the SSA was not ready.

Within days of the start of the program, field offices were inundated with questions from people who had not received checks or had received an unusual amount. To answer such questions, field employees had to query a central data base to see if a recipient's record existed and if so what the payment was based on. This was to be done through a system called SSADARS (SSA Direct Access and Response System), which was the SSA's first on-line, disk data base system providing field offices access to an up-to-date file of recipients' records. For the first time, field offices would use interactive terminals rather than teletype machines to communicate with headquarters. SSADARS had been designed to handle about 10,000 inquiries a day. Within the first week of the program, field offices were generating about 50,000 to 60,000 inquiries a day, and by week's end SSADARS stopped working. Each time it was restored, the flood of backlogged inquiries introduced by the field offices would cause it to collapse again. Field offices were cut off from the information they needed to do their work and were incapable of doing anything to initiate or correct a payment.[9]

Massive crowds developed at district offices in some of the cities having the greatest concentration of dependent persons. Lines formed in early morning hours. Because the weather was cold in the Northeast, the SSA rented hundreds of buses and parked them outside local offices to provide shelter. In New York, where the crowds were worst (or most publicized), some SSA employees were physically threatened by younger SSI recipients who were disabled because of drug addiction, alcoholism, or mental disorders. Federal marshals were called to provide crowd control; when they proved insufficient, private security guards were hired.[10]

Even though most field offices did not experience such extreme disorder and crowding, all were overwhelmed by the burden of SSI and continued to suffer the manifest effects of the initial unreadiness for at least a year. Overtime was far above the normal level. The Bureau of District Office Operations reported that 1.86 million overtime hours were used in the fall quarter of 1974, compared with 24,000 hours for the same quarter in 1972.[11] Morale suffered. Employees

9. DiPentima, "Supplemental Security Income Program," pp. 197–202, 209–10.
10. DiPentima, "Supplemental Security Income Program," pp. 211–12.
11. From material supplied to the SSI Study Group by the SSA in 1975 and

reported that even with heavy overtime it was not possible to complete work satisfactorily.[12] Administrative performance with respect to other programs deteriorated. By 1975, SSI consumed 23 percent of the total work-years expended by the SSA's work force, mainly at the expense of the basic retirement and survivors' insurance program, whose share of work-years fell from 63 percent in 1970 to 47 percent in 1975.[13] Backlogs rose sharply. At the end of 1973 the district offices had 249,000 claims pending in the insurance programs (those in which payments were not subject to a need test); by the end of February 1974 that figure had risen to 383,000.[14] The incidence of errors in payment also rose in the other programs. The struggle to administer SSI reduced the length of training for new employees, doubled the number of inexperienced workers in technical jobs, and almost eliminated on-the-job training for incumbent employees.[15]

This lengthy account should serve to establish that the SSA was unready for SSI, but it does not exhaust the agency's trouble with that program. It also was forced to compromise its own commitment to nationwide uniformity of administration and thus to sacrifice something of its essential character.

Effects on the Agency

The SSA decided that the characteristics of SSI, especially the need for promptness in processing applications, required placing a high degree of responsibility at the lowest professional level of the organization, the claims representatives in the field offices. In the insurance programs, by contrast, control was highly centralized. Authority to approve payments was located in six large payment centers around the country, and a large proportion of the field offices' initial decisions were reviewed there. Thus it was a radical departure from the traditional practice for the final decision on all SSI claims to be made in the district office by a claims representative. No provision was made for

preserved in the files of Professor Beryl Radin of the University of Southern California's Washington branch.

12. *Supplemental Security Income Program*, Committee Print, p. 43.

13. Social Security Administration, *Executive Handbook of Selected Data: Administrative Data, Program Data*, SSA Pub. 24-085 (1983), p. 10.

14. Futterman, "Two-Level Review," p. 119.

15. John Fialka, "Social Security Scandal: Other Programs Infected," *Washington Star*, August 21, 1975, citing an internal SSA memo.

further professional review, either of authorizations for payment or of denials. This made the job of the claims representatives far more difficult in every respect. They not only had to receive claims, their traditional function, but also had to abstract, manipulate, and compute data and bear responsibility for evaluating and acting upon the results, even in the numerous complicated, problematic cases. This radical decentralization increased the risk of error, disparities in judgment, and fraud.[16]

If decentralization characterized SSI operations within the SSA, it also characterized the SSA's arrangements with the states. Consistent with the intent of the law, the SSA sought to induce states to turn over administration of their supplements. But the states, as governments in the federal system, turned out to be hard and powerful bargainers, whereas the SSA, anxious to win their assent to federal administration before the program became operational, proved to be a very weak one. The outcome embraced so many variations in state supplements that the new program looked very much like the old ones.

The states sought to reduce their financial obligations by negotiating with the SSA for intrastate variations in supplements based upon such factors as geographic location, living arrangements, and program category (aged, blind, or disabled). California, for example, wanted a variation based on whether recipients had a cooking facility—a stove or hot plate—in their residence. In state after state, the SSA yielded, until it had approved dozens of actual variations and more than 2,000 potential ones (if all states chose federal administration, with all possible intrastate variations). The pressure to do so mounted as January 1974 approached and the states gambled that the SSA would not wish to bear the onus of having failed to get the checks out, complete with supplementary amounts. On December 18, 1973, only two weeks before the checks were to be mailed, the last of the federal-state agreements—that with California—was concluded. The variations that the SSA had agreed to administer added heavily to the operations burden in local offices and the complexities of computer programming. The SSA was obliged to gather and process, at no cost to the states, a large amount of information that was not essential to the basic federal program, but only to the states' supplementation. Thus an SSA claims representative in California was supposed to ascertain whether applicants did or did not have a stove or a hot plate.[17]

16. *Supplemental Security Income Program*, Committee Print, pp. 47–49; and Futterman, "Two-Level Review," p. 53.

17. *Supplemental Security Income Program*, Committee Print, pp. 68–71; DiPentima,

In sum, the program that was to remove discretion at the lowest levels of administration instead increased it. A high-ranking SSA official distilled the experience of SSI as follows:

> People came in, sat down, and negotiated how much they were going to get. And that really wasn't what we were about. Our motto had been . . . "you get every penny that's coming to you, not one cent more, not one cent less." But the clients—they were coming out of an environment . . . where they had a negotiated benefit. And in January 1974 they would come into an office that has a supposedly fixed benefit structure . . . but it could vary on forty-five different variables, plus mandatory State supplement.[18]

Thus the program that was to become efficient and uniform when the SSA took charge was neither. It was wasteful and riddled with variations from state to state and possibly even from one claims representative to another. The reform that was to nationalize welfare instead radically decentralized the SSA.

THE DISABILITY REVIEW

Congress authorized the extension of social insurance to cover disabled people in 1956. Until then coverage had been limited to retired workers and the survivors of deceased workers. By the mid-1970s the disability program had grown very large. Beneficiaries, including dependents as well as disabled workers, numbered 3.5 million in 1974. In 1975 there was a record number of new awards, 592,000. Along with 663,957 dependents, this enlarged the rolls by 1.2 million persons. Expenditures rose from $2.5 billion in 1969 to $13.7 billion in 1979. This was a leading cause of the fiscal crisis that engulfed social insurance in the mid-1970s.

The drastic enlargement of the disability rolls had numerous causes. One was statutory liberalization of the program. In 1965 the law was changed to permit benefits for people whose impairments were expected to last for at least twelve months. (Previous language had stipulated "long continued and indefinite duration.") In 1967 Congress made it

---

"Supplemental Security Income Program," pp. 168–73; and *Report of the SSI Study Group*, p. 111.

18. Office of Technology Assessment, *The Social Security Administration and Information Technology*, OTA-CIT-311 (October, 1986), p. 106.

easier for workers under age thirty-one to qualify by reducing the amount of time they were required to have spent in covered employment. As of 1973, beneficiaries who had been on the rolls for at least two years became eligible for medicare benefits, and cash benefits also increased sharply in the early 1970s, so that their value in relation to previous earnings rose. All of this increased the proportion of potentially eligible recipients and increased the incentives to apply.

More people did apply: applications jumped by 77 percent between 1969 and 1974. The higher rate of applications also may have been fueled by rises in unemployment, increased awareness of the program, and a weakening of the work ethic in the population, particularly in the younger "counterculture." While the proportion of applications initially approved did not increase, more applicants began at this time to pursue appeals—and to win them. And, once on the rolls, few people left. Even as the number of beneficiaries rose, the number of persons leaving the rolls as a result of recovery from their disability declined (it was 38,000 in 1969 and 36,000 in 1974). The principal reasons for leaving were reaching age sixty-five (and thus qualifying for retirement insurance) or death. Only 11 percent of those who quit the rolls in 1974 reported recovery.[19]

Controlling Growth

Viewing this experience with the program, policymakers of the mid- and late 1970s in both the executive and legislative branches became determined to contain its growth. The Social Security Disability Amendments of 1980, which required the SSA to regularly review the eligibility of all recipients who were not permanently disabled, were a result.

In principle, the SSA had always conducted reviews of the eligibility of disability insurance recipients—but selectively. Its policy had been to review those cases in which the health of the recipient was expected to improve, the recipient's earnings record indicated work activity, or the recipient voluntarily reported work activity or medical improvement. Relatively few cases were ever scheduled for reexamination, and even those that were scheduled often did not receive it. One might have expected that as the law changed to make it easier for young adults to qualify for disability benefits, administrative practice would

19. Mordechai E. Lando and Aaron Krute, "Disability Insurance: Program Issues and Research," *Social Security Bulletin*, vol. 39 (October 1976), pp. 3–17.

have responded with expanded reviews so as to verify that recipients continued to be disabled. That would have been logical, but the agency was accustomed to thinking of initial adjudications as the crucial task in disability insurance, and, with work loads generally rising, it was not likely to conceive of expanding any particular activity. The proportion of cases reviewed in the 1970s was small (fewer than 4 percent a year) and stable, except for a sharp drop in the year SSI was initiated.[20] Under these circumstances, beneficiaries could be confident of receiving disability payments until they reached retirement age, whereupon they qualified for retirement insurance.

By requiring in 1980 that the SSA review all recipients except the permanently disabled at least once every three years (and even the permanently disabled at intervals found by the secretary of Health and Human Services to be "appropriate"), Congress sought to make routine and comprehensive what had earlier been episodic and partial. This was not a fundamental redefinition of tasks, such as SSI entailed, but an increase in the scope and frequency of a procedure that had already been established. Yet it signified an important policy change, for it challenged the implicit operating premise that most people, once on the rolls, would stay on.

Just how fundamental this challenge might be was not clear in 1980. While the impression was widespread that many people getting disability benefits were not entitled to them, at the time no one professed to know what the rate of ineligibility was. Furthermore, because the agency did not routinely classify recipients as permanently disabled or not, no one knew just what proportion of the caseload would be reviewed under the new law. The congressional conference report on the bill estimated very modest savings from the review—a net of $10 million in the first four years. For the first two years, savings on benefit payments were projected to be more than offset by increased administrative costs.[21]

Nonetheless, it was not long before it became evident that the challenge would be fundamental indeed. Two events in 1981 conjoined to make it so: the appearance of official evaluations, originating in the SSA and amplified by the General Accounting Office, suggesting that as many as 584,000 out of the program's 2.9 million primary beneficiaries

20. General Accounting Office, *More Diligent Followup Needed to Weed Out Ineligible SSA Disability Beneficiaries*, HRD-81-48 (March 3, 1981), p. 6.

21. *Status of the Disability Insurance Program*, Committee Print, Subcommittee on Social Security of the House Committee on Ways and Means, 97 Cong. 1 sess. (GPO, 1981), p. 4.

(not including dependents) might be ineligible and were costing the government $2 billion a year,[22] and the arrival in office of a newly elected Republican president whose domestic program consisted of reducing expenditure.

The GAO report, an early version of which was presented to members of the Reagan transition team in December 1980, recommended that the secretary of HHS direct the commissioner of social security to expedite efforts to remove ineligible recipients from the disability rolls. Incoming officials, caught up in preparing the new president's first budget, heartily concurred. Vowing that "a new management team" would "weed out" all of the ineligible recipients cited by the GAO, the Reagan administration—with support from the new findings and in its zeal to maximize budget savings—projected savings from the disability review totaling $3.45 billion in six years (1981–86). This was a complete departure from the earlier estimate of a mere $10 million net in four years (1982–85). Furthermore, the SSA elected to begin the review right away, in the spring of 1981, rather than on January 1, 1982, as the law contemplated.[23] The effect of these changes was to alter the spirit of the undertaking. What had been conceived by Congress in 1980 was deliberate invigoration of a review procedure that had been too feeble to have much effect. What was set in motion in 1981 was more like a purge.

The review lasted until the spring of 1984. By then opposition was so powerful and the chaos was so complete that the administration was compelled to suspend the review and wait for Congress to try to restore order with new legislation. Congressional hearings (more than twenty of them in two years) and the media were filled with "horror stories," as they were commonly called—accounts of cases in which obviously disabled persons had been summarily deprived of benefits. In its effort to remove ineligible persons from the rolls, the SSA was causing hardship among the genuinely qualified, whom it was apparently unable to distinguish. The state governments, which function as administrative agents for the SSA in determining disability, refused to continue cooperating with it. In the year beginning in March 1983,

22. GAO, *More Diligent Followup Needed.*

23. *Program for Economic Recovery, Message from the President of the United States,* H. Doc. 97-21, 97 Cong. 1 sess. (GPO, 1981), pp. 95–96; Executive Office of the President, Office of Management and Budget, *Additional Details on Budget Savings,* April 1981, pp. 174–75; and *Social Security Financing Issues,* Hearings before the Subcommittee on Social Security of the House Committee on Ways and Means, 97 Cong. 1 sess. (GPO, 1981), pp. 227–29.

eighteen states, including New York, Pennsylvania, Virginia, Michigan, Illinois, and Texas, announced suspension of disability reviews. The federal district courts were flooded with appeals. By 1984 the SSA was regularly being defeated in both individual and class action cases.[24]

Why did the SSA prove so inept and vulnerable to judicial defeat? In contrast to its experience with SSI, the agency was not instituting a new program. It was only performing on a much larger scale and at a faster pace procedures that were well established. But therein lies much of the explanation: under extraordinary circumstances, the pitfalls of ordinary procedures were magnified and dramatized. More fundamentally, the agency fell victim, along with many of its clients, to the inherent difficulty of determining disability under any circumstances.

The Determination Process

Determinations of disability are inescapably subjective. The law defines disability as the "inability to engage in any substantial gainful activity by reason of any medically determinable physical or mental impairment which can be expected to result in death or which has lasted or can be expected to last for a continuous period of not less than 12 months." The impairment is supposed to result from "anatomical, physiological, or psychological abnormalities which are demonstrable by medically acceptable clinical and laboratory diagnostic techniques." And it is supposed to be so severe that, considering his age, education, and work experience, the individual cannot engage in any kind of work that exists in the national economy, "regardless of whether such work exists in the immediate area in which he lives, or whether a specific job vacancy exists for him."[25] Evidence on each of the crucial criteria—the severity of the impairment, its likely duration, its effect on the ability to perform gainful work, the availability of work somewhere in the national economy—is often inconclusive. Administrators must exercise their judgment.

Perhaps because administration of disability benefits is known to be subjective, its organization and procedures are complex and redundant

24. The data on congressional hearings, state government actions, and court cases are from Katharine P. Collins and Anne Erfle, "Social Security Disability Benefits Reform Act of 1984: Legislative History and Summary of Provisions," *Social Security Bulletin*, vol. 48 (April 1985), pp. 30–32.

25. Sec. 223(d) of the Social Security Act, in *Compilation of the Social Security Laws*, H. Doc. 93-117, 93 Cong. 1 sess. (GPO, 1973), vol. 1, pp. 170–71.

in the extreme. Authority to make determinations of disability is divided between the federal government and the states, and then, within the federal government, is further divided among administrators, judges, and a sizable class of officials who, having some of the attributes of each, are called administrative law judges.

As of the early 1980s, the formal procedure for determining disability, stated simply, was as follows: SSA district offices received applications for disability insurance and established that the applicants had worked and paid taxes long enough to be covered by social insurance, but, beyond gathering the names of treating physicians and hospitals, they played no part in judging the claim of disability.[26] They referred applications to state agencies, which were usually located in departments of vocational rehabilitation. Guided by policies issued by the SSA, these agencies gathered detailed medical data and rendered a decision on disability, using a two-person team consisting of a physician and a lay disability examiner. This team made its decision on the basis of the paper record only. It did not interview the applicant. A rejected applicant then could request reconsideration by the state agency, which repeated the original procedure but with a different team. An applicant rejected at this stage could request a hearing before an administrative law judge (ALJ) in the SSA's Office of Hearings and Appeals, who was responsible for perfecting the record of evidence. Here claimants appeared in person and could produce witnesses, submit additional evidence, and be represented by counsel. The ALJ might require medical examinations and otherwise solicit expert testimony. The ALJ hearing, then, was no mere review of the state agency decision, but a *de novo* determination of disability. An applicant denied by an administrative law judge might request a review by the Appeals Council, a fifteen-member body in SSA's Office of Hearings and Appeals, which could uphold, deny, or remand the ALJ's decision. From there the case might, and very often did, enter the federal courts.

The process for redetermining eligibility, as in the review of 1981–84, was the same as that for initially determining it, except that the SSA's district offices did not need to review the recipient's insured status. Redetermination began in the state agency, with receipt of the SSA's instructions. If the state agency decided in favor of termination,

26. For a brief description, see *Staff Data and Materials Related to the Social Security Disability Insurance Program*, Committee Print, Senate Committee on Finance, 97 Cong. 2 sess. (GPO, 1982), pp. 75–100. For an extremely subtle and sophisticated book-length analysis of the process, see Jerry L. Mashaw, *Bureaucratic Justice: Managing Social Security Disability Claims* (Yale University Press, 1983).

benefits ended after two months, rather than continuing through the appeals process, but were restored retroactively if the beneficiary was ultimately found eligible.

The involvement of state governments was one of many legislative concessions made to conservative opponents of disability insurance in order to create the program in the mid-1950s. To conservatives, the state governments were more acceptable than the SSA as field administrators because they were presumed to have no stake in expanding the federal government's social insurance program, they were thought to pose no political threat to the private practice of medicine, and they had experience in running vocational rehabilitation programs. The legislation gave the SSA authority to reverse the states' positive findings but not their negative ones.[27] The appeals procedure, involving first an ALJ and then the Appeals Council, was not peculiar to the disability program, but paralleled that which the Social Security Board, predecessor of the SSA, instituted in 1940 for the old-age and survivors' insurance program.[28] Judicial review is provided for by statute, under amendments to the Social Security Act enacted in 1939.

By the mid-1970s, the disability determination process was under enormous strain. It had always been subject to criticism for its duration and complexity. Now congressional documents invariably referred to a "crisis." Caseloads at all stages were very large, delays were very lengthy, and both were growing.[29] Requests for ALJ hearings were never fewer than 100,000 a year after 1973, and were often twice that. The ALJs' backlog of pending cases averaged around 90,000 between 1972 and 1980, and appellants had to wait months for a hearing.

As caseloads and complexity grew, the SSA's control of field operations eroded. An internal SSA task force constituted in 1974 to study the disability claims process found that most field units, federal and state, "had locally written and issued internal operating guides and handbooks because of difficulty in locating instructions issued centrally." In nearly every state agency visited, the task force was told that the disability insurance state manual, headquarters' basic source of guidance for state agencies, was out of date and "virtually unuse-

27. Martha Derthick, *Policymaking for Social Security* (Brookings, 1979), p. 308.

28. Edwin Yourman, "Report on a Study of Social Security Beneficiary Hearings, Appeals, and Judicial Review," in *Recent Studies Relevant to the Disability Hearings and Appeals Crisis*, Committee Print, Subcommittee on Social Security of the House Committee on Ways and Means, 94 Cong. 1 sess. (GPO, 1975), p. 132.

29. *Committee Staff Report on the Disability Insurance Program*, Committee Print, House Committee on Ways and Means, 93 Cong. 2 sess. (GPO, 1974), pp. 5–6, 31–44.

able."[30] As field units resorted to independent improvisations, so increasingly did the administrative law judges. In 1965, 97 percent of all allowances—242,000 of 249,000—had been made at the state agency level. However, as claimants showed an increasing tendency to pursue appeals, the ALJs responded with a rising tendency to rule in their favor. They were overturning 40 to 50 percent of agency findings under review in the early and mid-1970s and close to 60 percent by 1980.[31] By 1982, allowances by ALJs, the Appeals Council, and courts together constituted roughly 30 percent of the total.[32]

There were several explanations, each compelling, for the great discrepancy between state agency and ALJ decisions. These two decisionmakers used neither the same evidence nor the same decision criteria. The ALJs came face-to-face with the claimants, in contrast to the state agency adjudicators' reliance on only the paper record (typically a thinner one than was presented to the ALJs). Often, they also faced appellants' lawyers. In a random sample of ALJ cases studied by SSA's task force, 40 percent of the appellants were represented by attorneys.[33] State agencies attempted to be faithful to policy guidance from SSA headquarters, which was relatively explicit and detailed, though hardly rigid or confining.[34] Also, they were under pressure to meet production goals and deadlines. ALJs, by contrast, purported to follow law and formal regulations, which were less detailed, thus permitting more scope for discretion. Also, they often took cues from the federal courts in their circuits. In keeping with the norms of judicial decisionmakers (for they thought of themselves as such), they sought to dispense individualized justice and to avoid being overruled by judicial supe-

30. "Report of the Disability Claims Process Task Force" (the Boyd Report), in *Recent Studies*, Committee Print, pp. 41–42. For a sympathetic analysis of the SSA's approach to maintaining central control of field disability units, see Mashaw, *Bureaucratic Justice*, chap. 7.

31. *Staff Data and Materials Related to the Social Security Disability Insurance Program*, Committee Print, pp. 146–47.

32. "Two Year Report of the Social Security Disability Foundation Recommending Changes in the Social Security Disability Adjudicatory System Prepared Pursuant to Grant No. 85-10-3 of the Alfred P. Sloan Foundation," n.d., pp. I-15, I-16.

33. *Recent Studies*, Committee Print, p. 101. The 40 percent who were represented by attorneys had a success rate of 78.4 percent; those who had other representation had a success rate of 51.5 percent; those who were unrepresented had a rate of 28.3 percent.

34. Mashaw, *Bureaucratic Justice*, summarizes the SSA's stance in the Disability Insurance State Manual as saying: "Give each case the development it needs, remembering the general requirements of timeliness and fiscal responsibility." Mashaw writes: "The norms of this system do not say to adjudicators, 'Be generous!' or 'Be stingy!' They say instead, 'Be right!' " (pp. 158, 159).

riors.[35] Finally, it was easier for them to grant appeals than not to; an ALJ who granted a claim did not need to write an extensive opinion justifying that result, whereas a denial required an opinion good enough to withstand scrutiny at the next level of appeal.[36]

Thus two systems of adjudication had developed, and they were in increasing tension with each other. In the late 1970s SSA headquarters sought to resolve this tension by asserting control over the ALJs, treating them like administrators integral to the agency rather than judges appended to the judicial system. They too were given production goals and subjected to "peer review." This of course only created a new dimension of conflict. The ALJs responded by suing the government on the ground that management actions of this sort violated both constitutional due process guarantees afforded to disability claimants and statutory guarantees of the ALJs' own independence embedded in the Social Security Act and Administrative Procedure Act.[37]

One other characteristic of the disability determination process needs to be understood as part of the context of the review. Redeterminations of disability proceeded as original determinations did, and original determinations had been deliberately designed at the time of the program's founding to be objective and impersonal. They were to rest on paper reviews of clinical evidence submitted by physicians.[38] The state examiner reviewed the record of evidence without interviewing the applicant. The impersonality of this process became over time an important basis of its differentiation from the appeals process, in which ALJs did face the applicant, and it was potentially a serious flaw in doing redeterminations, for it meant that benefits long given could suddenly cease without the recipient's ever having been seen by an administrator. An SSA task force report of 1974–75, noting that judicial rulings would require face-to-face pretermination hearings in the SSI program, seemed to suggest that the SSA institute a face-to-face hearing procedure in the disability insurance program as well, using state agency personnel.[39] However, the agency deferred action

35. *Recent Studies*, Committee Print, pp. 104–05.

36. Jerry L. Mashaw, "Disability Insurance in an Age of Retrenchment: The Politics of Implementing Rights," in Theodore R. Marmor and Jerry L. Mashaw, eds., *Social Security: Beyond the Rhetoric of Crisis* (Princeton University Press, 1988), p. 162.

37. This particular fight is analyzed in M. Donna Price Cofer, *Judges, Bureaucrats, and the Question of Independence: A Study of the Social Security Administration Hearing Process* (Greenwood Press, 1985).

38. On the role of physicians in the disability program, see Deborah A. Stone, *The Disabled State* (Temple University Press, 1984), chap. 3.

39. *Recent Studies*, Committee Print, pp. 29, 86, 120.

because litigation bearing on the issue—the *Eldridge* case—was pending before the Supreme Court. "Precipitous action at this point would make our case moot," a memo for the commissioner's office observed.[40] The agency won the case in 1976 and hence was not required to institute a face-to-face pretermination hearing.

This, then, was the condition of the disability determination process as of 1980–81, when Congress and the Reagan administration combined to set it in motion on a massive scale with orders to conduct reviews of eligibility. Redeterminations had not been differentiated procedurally from original determinations, while in practice appeals had been sharply differentiated substantively from initial decisions. This made it likely that a substantial proportion of initial decisions in redetermination would be negative—that is, many recipients' benefits would be terminated.

Carrying Out the Review

The review began in March 1981. Initially the termination rate was close to 50 percent (191,000 out of 405,000 cases reviewed up to April 1982), but it fell thereafter.[41] In keeping with the well-established pattern, the volume of appeals and reversals was also high. Just how many appeals were filed as a result of the review is not clear from official sources. The total number of requests for ALJ hearings rose from 252,023 in 1980 to 281,737 in 1981, 320,680 in 1982, and 357,200 in 1983; the increases undoubtedly reflected the effects of the review. ALJs reversed the state agency decision in 66 percent of the termination cases they reviewed in 1982 (compared with a reversal rate of 55 percent for initial determinations of disability).[42]

One might think that any review would be strongly biased in favor of the beneficiaries inasmuch as the record would show an earlier finding on their behalf, and bureaucracies no more like to admit error than do individuals. One would expect an adverse outcome only if a

40. *Recent Studies*, Committee Print, p. 120. The *Eldridge* case is discussed in chap. 8.

41. David Koitz, "Social Security: Reexamining Eligibility for Disability Benefits," Issue Brief 82078, Congressional Research Service, November 2, 1984, p. 6; and *Oversight of the Social Security Administration Disability Reviews*, Committee Print, Subcommittee on Oversight of Government Management of the Senate Committee on Governmental Affairs, 97 Cong. 2 sess. (GPO, 1982), p. 2.

42. *Staff Data and Materials Related to the Social Security Act Disability Programs*, Committee Print, Senate Committee on Finance, 98 Cong. 1 sess. (GPO, 1983), pp. 27, 35.

review revealed improvement in a beneficiary's condition. However, given the nature of the disability determination process, the agencies doing the initial review were not necessarily those that had made favorable determinations in the first place. Beneficiaries who had attained the rolls through appeals were hardest hit by the review.[43] Moreover, even though they were conducting a "review," the state agencies did not in practice consider the whole case file. Following the SSA's rules for redeterminations of eligibility, they treated each case as if it were new and solicited only current medical opinions. These were often poorly documented, if only because beneficiaries and physicians did not immediately comprehend the stakes. Beneficiaries long on the rolls, hitherto unreviewed and confident that they were qualified, did not necessarily discern the latent threat in the innocuous notice they received. In the absence of conclusive evidence of disability, state agencies decided to terminate, in effect leaving the decision to an ALJ if beneficiaries elected to appeal.[44]

There were other reasons as well for the high initial rate of terminations. The SSA had deliberately concentrated the first reviews on those classes of cases believed to have the highest incidence of ineligibility—younger recipients and those who had come onto the rolls in 1973–75, a period of rapid expansion in the program during which reviews became hurried, partly because of stresses associated with SSI. In addition, the SSA's policies in the early 1980s did not make termination depend upon evidence of improvement in the recipient's health, although for a time (1969–76) they had done so. Rather than attempt to judge whether improvement had occurred, the state agencies compared the beneficiary's current condition with current standards of eligibility and made a judgment. And the standards of eligibility had recently been revised through changes in the SSA's regulations and policy manual. For example, a section on pain had been eliminated from the manual. Whether the changes were restrictive

43. The General Accounting Office reported, on the basis of a sample, that 20 percent of terminations occurred in cases whose initial allowances were made at an appellate level, although such cases constituted only 12 percent of the sample. *Social Security Disability Insurance*, Hearing before the Subcommittee on Social Security of the House Committee on Ways and Means, 98 Cong. 1 sess. (GPO, 1983), pt. 1, p. 121.

44. For descriptions of the review, see *Oversight of Social Security Disability Benefits Terminations*, Hearing before the Subcommittee on Oversight of Government Management of the Senate Committee on Governmental Affairs, 97 Cong. 2 sess. (GPO, 1982), especially the GAO report on pp. 233–52; and *Oversight of the Social Security Administration Disability Reviews*, Committee Print, pp. 25–41. The form of the notice to beneficiaries is discussed on pp. 31–32.

or merely clarifying was open to debate, and in any case the question would be settled only through the experience of administrative and judicial application. During the review, however, the agency's critics cited the revisions to charge that recipients were being disqualified because they were being held to a newly strict standard of eligibility.[45]

Finally, whatever the regulations and policy manual said, the whole context of the time encouraged termination. Disability decisions, because of their inherent subjectivity, were highly susceptible to changes in the political context—and "crackdown" was in the air. It had been there since the late 1970s, emanating from politicians of both parties and from both the executive and legislative branches of the federal government. The Social Security Disability Amendments of 1980, which contained the requirement for the review, sought to restrain the program in various ways, above all a cap on benefits designed to ensure that no recipients could get more by qualifying for disability insurance than they had previously earned from work. The state agencies were doing what all the official cues said they should. The rate at which they allowed initial claims had fallen sharply, from 42 percent in 1978 to 29 percent in 1981. Similarly, the proportion of allowances they granted on reconsideration dropped from a range of 33 to 36 percent in 1970–75 to 15 to 19 percent in 1978–80.[46] In the four years before the Reagan administration took office, the rate of terminations in those disability cases subjected to review had ranged from 38 percent to 48 percent. Thus the difference after 1980 was not in the rate of termination, but in the much higher numbers exposed to review (436,498 cases in fiscal year 1983, compared with 83,651 in fiscal 1978).[47]

Nonetheless, the changes in context beginning in the late 1970s by no means altered the propensity of the ALJs to overturn state agency

45. *Social Security Disability Insurance Program*, Hearing before the Senate Committee on Finance, 97 Cong. 2 sess. (GPO, 1982), pp. 196–97; and "The SSI/SSDI Disability Controversy: How and Why the Social Security Administration Has Reduced the Number of SSI/SSDI Beneficiaries," prepared by State of Michigan Interagency Task Force on Disability, in *Social Security Disability Insurance*, Hearing before the Subcommittee on Social Security of the House Committee on Ways and Means, 98 Cong. 1 sess. (GPO, 1984), pt. 2, pp. 263–64.

46. *Staff Data and Materials Related to the Social Security Act Disability Programs*, Committee Print (1983), p. 27; and *Staff Data and Materials Related to the Social Security Disability Insurance Program*, Committee Print (1982), p. 146.

47. *Background Material and Data on Programs within the Jurisdiction of the Committee on Ways and Means*, Committee Print, House Ways and Means Committee, 101 Cong. 1 sess. (GPO, 1989), p. 54. Unfortunately, this source does not give rates of termination in disability reviews before 1977. Very likely, they were much lower.

denials. All the usual explanations applied: they met clients (and clients' lawyers) face to face, they reviewed the whole record, and they employed less exacting standards of eligibility than the state agencies. On top of that, the great speed with which the state agencies had been forced to act in the review meant that the factual record they bequeathed to the ALJs was even more faulty than usual.

Like SSI, the disability review severely strained the performers of basic routines—in this case the 10,000 state disability examiners and 800 ALJs who labored in the trenches of the program. It made what had long been a very bad situation suddenly and dramatically worse. State agencies, which all together had been accustomed to receiving perhaps 21,000–30,000 cases a quarter for review, now were ordered to review 100,000–150,000. As appeals to the ALJs rose, reaching 350,000 in 1983, their backlog rose at a comparable rate. By any definition, a "crisis" now occurred.

The state agencies had little time to prepare for the new task, which they described to Congress as a "nightmare," "devastating," "painful," and "ugly."[48] Although technically the disability examiners did not deal directly with clients, in practice they now faced some and feared their potential for violence; the mentally ill were disproportionately affected by the disability review. Security measures hitherto not thought necessary in the state agencies, such as guards and bulletproof glass, were added to their offices in some places.

The states fought back, motivated by a desire to protect their budgets as well as their work forces (some of those removed from the disability insurance rolls resorted to state-financed welfare programs instead). The SSA's ability to perform the disability review depended on the cooperation of these other governments in the federal system. Precisely because the states are governments in their own right, even if heavily obliged to the federal government for financial support, they have considerable bargaining power. When they withdrew from participation in the review, it was on the authority of the governors, their popularly elected chief executives.

Very likely, the governors would not have defied the SSA had they not been encouraged, and even in some instances commanded, to do so by the federal courts. The SSA's regulations for redeterminations of eligibility provided that disability benefits would be terminated when disability was not supported by current evidence. Against this

48. *Oversight of Social Security Disability Benefits Terminations*, Hearing, pp. 120–33; and *Social Security Disability Reviews: A Federally Created State Problem*, Hearing before the House Select Committee on Aging, 98 Cong. 1 sess. (GPO, 1983), pp. 105–16.

position, federal circuit courts in 1982–84 ruled in case after case that the SSA must apply a presumption of continuing disability before terminating benefits and must employ some form of medical improvement standard. In effect, the courts said that if recipients were to be removed from the rolls, it must be because *they* had changed and not because the government had changed its views about whether they were disabled.

Judicial reversals, in combination with the states' defiance, made it impossible for the SSA to carry on the review. Having lost control of the program's regulations, it could not give coherent, authoritative instructions to its field agents. The problem was dramatized early in 1984 when the secretary of HHS tried to tell the governors how to proceed with the review. The letter went out in several different versions, depending on which federal judicial circuit a state was in, whether it was under an injunction, and whether it had ceased processing terminations independently of the courts. Three months later the SSA suspended the review in order to await new legislation, which congressional action signified was forthcoming.

THE LINKS BETWEEN THE CASES

The debacles of SSI and the disability review were not random, discrete, and unrelated. In this stream of events a causal connection is discernible. The disability review would not have been thought necessary had not the number of beneficiaries and volume of expenditure risen sharply in the mid-1970s, and they would not have risen so sharply had not SSI been enacted. It contributed to the increase in several ways: by encouraging applications through outreach and enrollment efforts; by so overwhelming disability administrators that reviews of eligibility were performed less carefully; and by consuming so much administrative effort with new applications that reexaminations of eligibility failed to be performed as scheduled.[49]

49. Just how important "lax administration" was as a cause of the rise in the rolls was a matter of dispute. The analysis of Lando and Krute, "Disability Insurance," emphasized other factors. However, a 1977 report by the SSA's Office of the Actuary concluded that "administrative factors must have also played an important part in the recent increases." Cited in *Staff Data and Materials Related to the Social Security Disability Insurance Program*, Committee Print, (1982), p. 27. See also the testimony of Robert J. Myers in *Disability Insurance Legislation*, Hearings before the Subcommittee on Social Security of the House Ways and Means Committee, 96 Cong. 1 sess. (GPO, 1979), p. 4. Retired as the SSA actuary after a long career, Myers remained deeply involved in the program and an influential source of opinion. These judgments from credible sources influenced congressional thinking.

However, it is not this concretely demonstrable link that invites joining the two cases for analytical purposes. Rather, it is the possibility that they have common origins in some systemic sense. Either case considered in isolation might seem idiosyncratic. But to the extent that comparison reveals common properties, together they begin to form a basis for generalizing about the way in which policymakers approach administration.

Certainly these events bear a strong resemblance in their results. Each seriously weakened the SSA as a national administrative agency. In both instances it was left with responsibility for a fragmented, decentralized program over which it had lost its customary share of policy control. To the extent that uniform policies and practices were sacrificed (to the states in SSI, to the courts in the disability review), so was the essential character of the SSA as a national agency. Relations with employees and state agents were impaired as a consequence of their having been assigned demoralizing tasks. Relations with clients were also strained as a result of errors in performance, some that inflicted cruel hardships on innocent and vulnerable individuals and others that burdened taxpayers with unjustifiable expense.

Finally, the agency suffered a loss of prestige and self-confidence. Historically, it had had an exceptional degree of pride. It was the Marine Corps of the domestic civil service—elite and invincible.[50] It conquered new programs as the Marines conquered enemy beaches. Others thought highly of it too, so that it had limited experience of public criticism. SSI and the disability review therefore came as rude shocks, both from the evidence that the agency was not as good as it thought it was (however good nonetheless) and from the brutal criticism by Congress, press, and the courts. Whether or not pride was lost, a sense of invulnerability certainly was. After 1974, the agency wore a wounded air.

Perhaps no one could have predicted the precise effects on the SSA of what policymakers chose to do in these two cases, but in a general way administrative hazards were easy to foresee. Given the inherent difficulties of administering need-tested assistance—difficulties that were well known to every student of welfare programs—it was never likely that a federal welfare program could assume a highly simplified, streamlined form that the SSA could just put into its computers and thereafter administer painlessly. This was especially true if the SSA

50. The analogy to the Marine Corps cropped up in two interviews with current or former SSA officials in August 1989. I think it apt enough to use, although I am not sure that it would greatly appeal to the social security program's founders.

were to have responsibility for administering state supplemental payments. In addition, the fact that SSA employees had been taught for decades that their distinctive mission was administering benefits by right—and that they took particular pride in doing so—meant that they were likely to react poorly to responsibility for means-tested assistance, which they saw as a despised alternative and distinctly *not* their mission.

In the disability review, the manifest risks were more political than administrative. Removing from the rolls persons who had long been receiving benefits was likely to elicit sharp reaction. "Can the SSA do it?" was a less pertinent question than "Can it be done, given the probable outcry?" Related to that, there was a specific, foreseeable pitfall for the SSA in the review process. The GAO casually alluded to it in the report of 1981 that dramatized the alleged rate of ineligibility. "Since SSA decisions on the continued eligibility of Disability Insurance are subject to appeal," it said, "it may not be realistic to expect that all these beneficiaries would be removed from the rolls." That ALJs and federal courts often disagreed with state agencies was more than an open secret; it was an abundantly documented fact. The appeals process had been thoroughly analyzed in innumerable congressional reports. Its properties were a source of frustration but not of mystery. An astute policymaker would have paused to ask what the reaction would be if state agencies started finding large numbers of persons ineligible and ALJs and federal courts set about restoring the benefits of many of them, which was an absolutely predictable outcome. (No one, presumably, could have foreseen the horror stories—the cases of indisputably disabled persons whose benefits were terminated.)

Given that the hazards were not obscure, it is fair to ask to what extent policymakers weighed them as they designed policy change. Did they ask the elemental questions: can the SSA perform this task, and what will be the consequences if it tries? Were they so engaged in the struggle over policy change that they ignored administrative questions? Or so committed to the policy outcome that they deliberately chose to accept the administrative risks? How did they perceive those risks? Did they perhaps discount them as unimportant, on the theory that it is the duty of bureaucrats to absorb any amount of punishment?

The analysis will turn next to such questions. It will explore in turn the roles of the presidency, the Congress, and the leadership of the Social Security Administration in policymaking, with particular attention to the level and quality of their concern for administration.

Part II
Policymaking

CHAPTER 3

The Policymaking Presidency

AS THE HOLDER of "the executive power," the president has broad if ill-defined responsibility for supervising the government's executive agencies; the crucial constitutional clause is that which obliges him "to take care that the laws be faithfully executed." However, his influence on administration does not stem alone, and perhaps not even primarily, from this source. At least since the turn of the century, presidents have not personally taken much interest in the administrative function, strictly conceived. Woodrow Wilson observed in 1908 that the president's executive powers were "in commission," by which he meant that they had been delegated.[1] More important has been the role of the president in influencing what the government does. As the nation's political leader, he shapes the legislative agenda. And what the legislature enacts determines what agencies do; their tasks derive from policy choices.

This chapter will analyze how presidential policy initiatives in the cases of supplemental security income (SSI) and the disability review shaped the tasks of the Social Security Administration (SSA). I begin by arguing that both efforts originated to a considerable extent in the postelection urge of presidents and their entourages (together constituting the "presidency") to achieve transformations in domestic policy. In content, both reflected a presidential bias in favor of rationalizing the actions of government, and both betrayed an insensitivity, born of remoteness, to the practicalities of implementation in the field.

1. *Constitutional Government in the United States* (Columbia University Press, 1908; reprint, 1961), p. 67.

THE VICTORY SYNDROME

Presidents and their entourages, consisting of both immediate White House staff and appointees to the departments, arrive in Washington euphoric and impatient. Exulting in the outcome of the last election, they are already looking to the next. Victory has given them a license to act, and American political history tells them that they must do so in a hurry. There is only a fleeting moment of opportunity before the president's hard-won influence begins to dissipate. They sense that they must seize it. Otherwise there will be no record to point to, nothing for partisans, the press, or posterity to celebrate.

Both SSI and the disability review derived much of their impetus from the exertions of new administrations striving to make their mark. In August 1969 President Nixon presented to the country a welfare reform proposal conceived as the centerpiece of his domestic program. "This would be total welfare reform," the president promised, "—the transformation of a system frozen in failure and frustration."[2] The president's extreme language, which was not hyperbole but a fair rendering of the facts, referred to the administration's proposal of the family assistance plan (FAP), a federally guaranteed minimum income for all families with dependent children. Unlike aid to families with dependent children (AFDC), the fast-growing and much-disputed program that it was designed to replace, it would have covered intact families and the working poor. And it would have been federally financed and administered. Presidential adviser Daniel P. Moynihan told Nixon that he would be able "to assert with full validity that it was under your Presidency that poverty was abolished in America."[3] Under this initial proposal, state programs of support for the adult categories (aged, blind, and disabled) would have continued with increased federal aid and more stringent conditions, including national eligibility and payments standards. In the ensuing debate, which lasted until the fall of 1972, reform of the adult categories became more radical and achieved passage in the form of SSI. Reform of the AFDC program never secured a majority in the Senate, which was deeply divided on the subject.[4] As it happened, there was prolonged public

2. *Public Papers of the Presidents of the United States: Richard Nixon, 1969* (Government Printing Office, 1971), p. 648.

3. Daniel P. Moynihan, *The Politics of a Guaranteed Income: The Nixon Administration and the Family Assistance Plan* (Random House, 1973), p. 148.

4. For an analysis of FAP's demise in the Senate, see M. Kenneth Bowler, *The*

deliberation over FAP, which was not enacted, and practically none over SSI, which was.

Much as Nixon was told by his staff in the flush of victory that he would be the first president to abolish poverty, a decade later Ronald Reagan was told by his staff he would be the first "to honestly and permanently fix social security."[5] At the time—May 1981—the staff was promoting sizable cuts in the basic program of retirement insurance. This proposal turned out to be the first big blunder of Reagan's presidency, and it died quickly.[6] Its defeat, however, had no effect on a set of more modest budget-cutting measures in social security, among them an aggressive disability review that the administration had put forward in February and March. Cuts in the disability program were to account for $550 million of an estimated $40 billion reduction that the Reagan administration proposed in Jimmy Carter's fiscal year 1982 budget. Of the $550 million, $200 million was expected to come from the review and the rest from legislative changes affecting the benefit structure. Annual savings from the review were projected to rise sharply in succeeding years and to reach $1.1 billion in fiscal 1986. The cumulative total for 1981–86 was projected at $3.45 billion.[7]

Though hastily conceived and born of the postelection urge to act, neither the Nixon welfare reform proposal nor the Reagan projections of big budget savings from the disability review were concocted out of thin air. The very fact that new administrations are so eager to make fresh departures often drives them, paradoxically, to adapt prescriptions from the immediate past. The design of the Nixon welfare reforms was in large measure the work of Democratic holdovers in the Department of Health, Education, and Welfare (HEW) and the Office of Economic Opportunity (OEO). The crucial assumptions about welfare policy embodied in that design had all taken root in the 1960s; economist-planners in the OEO and HEW had begun work then on comprehensive proposals that were clear forerunners of FAP.[8] Congress

Nixon Guaranteed Income Proposal: Substance and Process in Policy Change (Ballinger, 1974), chap. 7.

5. David A. Stockman, *The Triumph of Politics: How the Reagan Revolution Failed* (Harper and Row, 1986), p. 188.

6. Stockman, *Triumph of Politics*, pp. 189–95; Lou Cannon, *Reagan* (Putnam, 1982), pp. 379–80; and Laurence I. Barrett, *Gambling with History: Ronald Reagan in the White House* (Penguin Books, 1984), pp. 155–59.

7. *Program for Economic Recovery*, H. Doc. 97-21, 97 Cong. 1 sess. (GPO, 1981), pp. 95–96.

8. Bowler, *Nixon Guaranteed Income Proposal*, chap. 4.

and the Carter administration together had fashioned legislation in 1980 to bring disability spending under control; in promising to remove ineligible recipients from the rolls, the Reagan administration was merely making aggressive use of one of the provisions of that law. In doing so, it was prompted largely by the career staff of the Office of Management and Budget (OMB), which regarded the disability insurance program as an especially promising target for reductions in spending. This staff in turn had drawn on work done by the SSA itself, by the Office of the Assistant Secretary for Planning and Evaluation in the Department of Health and Human Services, and other executive and legislative sources. Conveniently, shortly before the Reagan administration took office, the General Accounting Office circulated a draft report suggesting that as many as 584,000 recipients might be ineligible, at an annual cost to the government of $2 billion.[9] In choosing disability insurance for attention, the OMB was not in the least original.

THE EXECUTIVE AS RATIONALIZER

The aim of the presidency in both cases was to rectify error and to improve the rationality of programs that were notably in disarray. President Nixon's 1969 message spoke of the need to "modernize" welfare and to "bring reason, order, and purpose into a tangle of overlapping programs." He emphasized three anomalies in AFDC: benefit levels were unequal from one state to another; it created an incentive to fathers to desert their families; and it often provided more in support than could be earned from work, which discouraged work and was unfair to people who chose low-paying work over welfare.[10] FAP was intended to correct all three. The 1981 Reagan budget documents spoke of "huge sums" paid incorrectly in the disability insurance program to "misclassified" individuals, and promised to put an end to "misdirected" benefits.[11]

In the disability review, achieving rationalization was at least superficially simple: cases would be examined and those found ineligible would be removed. Far from a fundamental reform, the review called

9. Interview, Barry Tice of General Accounting Office, February 12, 1990. As published, the report was GAO, *More Diligent Followup Needed to Weed Out Ineligible SSA Disability Beneficiaries*, HRD-81-48 (March 3, 1981).

10. Moynihan, *Politics of a Guaranteed Income*, pp. 220–26.

11. *Program for Economic Recovery*, p. 95; and Executive Office of the President, Office of Management and Budget, *Fiscal Year 1982 Budget Revisions* (March 1981), p. 75.

merely for applying on a larger scale and at greater speed a procedure that the SSA was already supposed to be following. The Nixon welfare reform, by comparison, was the ultimate in rationalizing acts. Besides purporting to correct the inequities and perverse consequences of existing programs, it was touted as an improvement in efficiency. "The cost is not very great," Moynihan told Nixon, "*because it is a direct payment system.*"[12] The efficiency would be realized by emphasizing payments to needy individuals rather than "services," which were presumed to divert funds to the providers of service—that is, government employees. One crucial element of the wholesale effort at rationalization was centralization of administrative responsibility in the federal government.

When Nixon announced his plan for welfare reform to the country in August 1969, the accompanying background material released by the White House called for the Social Security Administration to administer the new program.[13] The logic of this choice was not spelled out at that time, but it reflected the view of welfare reform planners that public income support programs could be simplified and automated, analogous to the payment of social insurance benefits or the collection of income taxes (which the planners took to be highly routinized activities, entailing little discretion on the part of the administrators). Indeed, the designers of FAP within HEW's Office of Planning and Evaluation had proposed that administration be performed by either the SSA or the Internal Revenue Service, showing both their lack of concern about having specialists in social welfare in charge and their firm commitment to the assumption that poverty created a right to public support. A sharp distinction had previously been drawn in American public policy between income support programs based on right (social insurance) and those based on need (public assistance or welfare), but in the late 1960s the idea took root that need created a right. Some welfare reformers were more insistent than others on this notion of welfare as a right. Radicals proclaimed it in pure form, whereas the Nixon administration would have qualified it with work requirements, but all of the reform plans of this period rested on it to some extent. To those who reported poverty, the federal government would provide income. This was the grand simplification underlying presidential planning.

12. Moynihan, *Politics of a Guaranteed Income*, p. 147 (emphasis in original).

13. *The President's Proposals for Welfare Reform and Social Security Amendments, 1969*, Committee Print, House Committee on Ways and Means, 91 Cong. 1 sess. (GPO, 1969), p. 105.

To administer a program resting on such assumptions, the SSA seemed well suited by doctrine and experience. Dedicated to the belief that social security benefits belonged to the recipients by right, the SSA had trained and organized its staff to deliver them promptly and reliably. It had developed the capacity to process the masses of data from which delivery of benefits followed—automatically, it seemed. As long as welfare administration was thought to require detailed investigations and therapeutic intervention by social caseworkers—as state governments had attempted in the past, with federal encourage-ment—the SSA would obviously have been quite unsuited to it. But when welfare was reconceived by executive planners in the late 1960s, the SSA suddenly seemed a logical choice. And if the SSA had the right organizational doctrine and skills for the kind of program presidential planners were seeking to create, the corollary appeared also to be true: the kind of program they were seeking to create would not represent an unsupportable burden for the agency. To Moynihan, an "income strategy," as distinct from the provision of "services," represented a new realism because of its simplicity. Nixon planners believed that the government should "stay close to what it knew how to do, and be rigorous in judging just what that was." That the government knew how to make repetitive cash payments seemed evident from the SSA's record of success.[14]

When Secretary of HEW Robert H. Finch presented the adminis-tration's bill to the House Ways and Means Committee in October 1969, he observed that the SSA "has developed over the past 34 years an expertise in the delivery of cash payments on a regular basis to millions of Americans." It was this experience and expertise that qualified the SSA to administer FAP. In determining eligibility, he said, reliance would be placed upon detailed statements supplied by applicants. Recipients would be required to report changes in income, family composition, and other factors related to their eligibility and benefit payments. The SSA would use the reports of earnings that it regularly received to verify the applicants' declarations. In-depth verification would be done on a sample basis.[15]

By the spring of 1970, however, the administration was sounding less sure of itself in regard to the use of the SSA. Secretary Finch told

14. Moynihan, *Politics of a Guaranteed Income*, p. 150.

15. *Written Statements Submitted by Administration Witnesses Appearing before the Com-mittee on Ways and Means at Hearings on Social Security and Welfare Proposals*, Committee Print, House Committee on Ways and Means, 91 Cong. 1 sess. (GPO, 1969), pp. 23–24.

the Senate Finance Committee in April that no final decisions had been made about the administrative structure of FAP.[16] In the interim, the House Ways and Means Committee had considered the administration's proposals and expressed reservations about employing the SSA. Always protective of the social insurance program, the committee evidently wished to assure that it remain distinct from FAP, just as it had been distinct in the past from programs for support of the poor.[17] Accordingly, the committee prescribed that a new agency be established in HEW to administer FAP, and that other federal agencies inside and outside HEW "lend their support to the extent that doing so would be consistent with the performance of the duties required to carry out their own programs." As an example, it suggested that the computer equipment and other capabilities of the SSA would be utilized "to the extent it is economical and efficient to do so."[18] This left administrative questions open.

Whereas the House approved the main provisions of the administration's bill in 1970, the Senate did not. The administration thereafter continued to work with the Ways and Means Committee in the hope of producing a revision that the Senate would accept. Welfare reform remained high on the president's domestic agenda. Throughout the first five months of 1971, executive officials, led by HEW Under Secretary John G. Veneman, met steadily with the committee in executive session. Ironically, in view of the committee's doubts about assigning FAP to the SSA, it was in these sessions that the decision was made to federalize the adult categories and put the SSA in charge of them.

The decision was made after Veneman assured the committee that the SSA would be able to assume the new responsibility "with no disruption to its current functions."[19] Within the administration, Veneman and his assistant, Tom Joe, had chosen to pursue federalization of the adult categories, and Social Security Commissioner Robert M. Ball had acquiesced in their choice (see chapter 5). To support the argument that administration of the adult programs would be quite manageable for the SSA, executive officials pointed out that the aged

16. *Family Assistance Act of 1970*, Hearings before the Senate Committee on Finance, 91 Cong. 2 sess. (GPO, 1970), pt. 1, p. 186.

17. *Social Security and Welfare Proposals*, Hearings before the House Committee on Ways and Means, 91 Cong. 1 sess. (GPO, 1970), pt. 1, p. 213.

18. *Family Assistance Act of 1970*, H. Rept. 91-904, 91 Cong. 2 sess. (GPO, 1970), p. 27.

19. "Statement of John G. Veneman, Under Secretary of Health, Education, and Welfare, before the Committee on Ways and Means," February 24, 1971, copy in author's files.

and disabled were its traditional clients. (No one foresaw how much bigger and more burdensome the caseload of the disabled would soon become.)

The committee's report of a bill in May 1971 said, in effect, that what was good policy for poor families must be good policy as well for the needy aged, blind, and disabled—and would be easier to attain because the adult programs were smaller, less expensive, and more stable. Compared with FAP, which was fraught with political, conceptual, and administrative complications, federalization of the adult categories appeared to be easy. So confident were executive officials of the SSA's capacity to take over the adult programs that the committee bill offered the administrative services of the SSA free of charge to states that chose to supplement the federal payment to individuals.

After the spring of 1971, executive planning for welfare reform proceeded on the assumption that the SSA would run the adult programs, which came to be called "supplemental security income" because they were supplemental to social insurance, while responsibility for the family programs would be divided between the Department of Labor and a new agency to be created within HEW. "The establishment of a new, uniform, automated central administrative system for welfare is a vital part of welfare reform," an executive paper declared.[20] Noting that the basic benefit was to be financed entirely by the federal government, with the states reduced to a supplementary role, the paper pronounced the new programs "incompatible" with state administration. The question had become, not why federal administration, but why not?

Nixon planners operated on the assumption that federal administration was inherently superior to state administration. "State and local administration of the present Federal/State welfare programs has been characterized by a lack of public confidence, contempt from recipients, high costs, misuse of employee skills, widely varying approaches to administration, and uneven performance," the executive paper said. There was more to this attitude than Washington's customary arrogance, which derived from confidence that federal officials were more professional, more educated, more skillful, even more honest, than their state and local counterparts. More fundamentally, Nixon planners exhibited central executives' customary preference for uniformity—the rationalizing syndrome evident in any centrally planned policy initia-

20. "The Case for Federal Administration of Public Assistance Payments," enclosure to memo, Richard P. Nathan to Secretary of HEW, et al., November 16, 1971, copy in author's files.

tive. Because it was standardized, federal administration would necessarily be better. Moreover, elite opinion, which has a powerful rationalizing bias, could be counted on to support this view. As Samuel Beer has argued, scientific modernism is at the root of centralization.[21] The varied arrangements of American federalism were intrinsically unacceptable to the modernist. Thus, for example, a professor of law specializing in welfare programs could maintain that "inequity and inefficiency are inherent characteristics of a Federal grant-in-aid, State-administered system," without having to fear that any intellectually respectable critic would object.[22] No one in the community of policy analysts, whether inside or outside the administration, was likely to ask whether equity necessarily had to be achieved on a national scale, whether the persistence of interstate differences was necessarily unjust, or whether administrative efficiency necessarily increased with scale and uniformity.

Underpinning the Nixon planners' preference for federal administration were confidence in the SSA's mastery of computer technology and optimism about the application of such technology to welfare programs. Secretary of HEW Elliot L. Richardson told the Senate Finance Committee:

> When it comes to a function such as the determination of eligibility under a uniform national program, the computation of benefits, the cross-checking of income data to determine whether or not it has been accurately set forth in the application form, or the processing of checks, we think that the Federal Government has established a very good track record of capacity and, indeed, that this is a kind of function that can be performed with considerably greater efficiency on a uniform national basis, than it can be done by the States or localities.[23]

Because of computer technology, administration under federal auspices could be performed with fewer employees and with greater reliability,

21. "The Modernization of American Federalism," *Publius*, vol. 3 (Fall 1973), pp. 49–95.

22. The quotation is from Joel F. Handler, "Federal-State Interests in Welfare Administration," in *Issues in Welfare Administration: Intergovernmental Relationships*, Paper no. 5, pt. 2, *Studies in Public Welfare*, Committee Print, Joint Economic Committee, 93 Cong. 1 sess. (GPO, 1973), p. 1.

23. *Social Security Amendments of 1971*, Hearings before the Senate Committee on Finance, 92 Cong. 1 sess. (GPO, 1971), p. 119.

Richardson testified. There would be less fraud. Throughout the legislative deliberations and the SSA's preparation for implementing the law, top officials in HEW and the SSA exuded confidence about what the computers would do. "We will let the machines work for us," the SSA's director of the Bureau of Supplemental Security Income told state public welfare administrators in late November 1973, with a little over a month to go before the start of the program.[24]

By way of clinching the argument for federal superiority, Richardson appealed to the legislators' confidence in the incumbent head of the SSA, Robert M. Ball. "I would point . . . to the record of efficient administration achieved by the distinguished gentleman on my right . . . whose overhead costs in the administration [of social security] are considerably less than the overhead experienced by private insurance programs."[25]

For a long time, the Senate Finance Committee resisted the administration's proposal to federalize the adult assistance programs and make the SSA responsible for administration. However, in the late summer of 1972, after the presidential nominating conventions were over and Congress reconvened, the committee abruptly changed its position and accepted SSI. Soon thereafter the legislation was enacted.

DISTANCE FROM THE FIELD

Both in Nixon's welfare reform and in Reagan's budget cutting, presidentially driven planning displayed a notable lack of prescience about the effects of central instructions on field-level implementers and, by extension, their public clientele. Central officials failed to foresee how field staffs would respond and what the consequences of their attempts to respond would be.

In the disability review, officials at the top of the federal executive branch doubted that a large-scale purge of the disability rolls actually would occur, budget projections to the contrary notwithstanding. In the view of the OMB, the SSA and the state agencies had been very sluggish in the past about reviewing active cases; why should they be expected to change now? Besides, it was not in the nature of bureaucracy

24. "Summary of Proceedings," National Council of State Public Welfare Administrators, meeting of November 26–27, 1973, copy in author's files.

25. *Social Security Amendments of 1971*, Hearings, p. 119. The comparison of the SSA's administrative expenses with those of private insurance companies was one that federal administrators liked to make, though under critical scrutiny it would probably not have proved meaningful.

to confess error or to retract benefits once granted, no matter what GAO reports might say. Moreover, the OMB staff mistakenly believed that benefits for disability insurance recipients who were terminated would continue for as much as six months while they pursued appeals.[26] Had that been so, the review would have been less disruptive and damaging to the SSA's clientele than it was. In fact, benefits continued for only two months after a finding of ineligibility.

While OMB officials doubted the will of field operatives to cooperate, some officials in HHS doubted their capacity. One former member of HHS's budget office, a civil servant who attended a meeting early in 1981 at which HHS officials discussed the OMB's proposals for cutting their budget, recalls protesting that a review as large and as fast as the one being contemplated was an administrative impossibility. She also recalls presuming and possibly saying that large-scale cuts would not occur because the numbers of persons estimated to be ineligible and the volume of expenditures to be saved "were OMB numbers, and their numbers are never real. . . . That was the way the game was played."[27] However, Reagan appointees in HHS who attended the meeting were highly receptive to the advice of the OMB staff, as they had been receptive to the GAO report.

Subsequently, SSA budget and management staff members collaborated with HHS's budget office in preparing a rebuttal to the OMB that pointed out some of the practical difficulties in achieving a very rapid, large-scale review. State agency staffing was already supposed to increase 29 percent between the end of fiscal year 1980 and the beginning of fiscal 1982. It would be very hard to get the states to do more and impossible to impart the desirable amount of training—two months in the classroom and six to nine months on the job—to new state agency claims examiners. They also objected that the agencies of appeal—administrative law judges and the courts—would be further burdened and would probably react with heightened intensity to "what

26. Patricia E. Dilley, "Social Security Disability: Political Philosophy and History," in Arthur T. Meyerson and Theodora Fine, eds., *Psychiatric Disability: Clinical, Legal, and Administrative Dimensions* (Washington: American Psychiatric Press, 1987), p. 395. This paragraph also draws on an interview with an official source who asked to remain anonymous.

27. Interview, Patricia E. Dilley, August 30, 1988. A similar attitude seems to have prevailed within the Ways and Means Committee staff, with whom the statutory requirement for a review originated. See *Status of the Disability Insurance Program*, Committee Print, Subcommittee on Social Security of the House Committee on Ways and Means, 97 Cong. 1 sess. (GPO, 1981), which predicted (p. 4) that the Reagan administration would have trouble realizing big savings from a review.

they perceive to be a tightening of the program beyond the requirements of the law."[28] Here, as SSA officials were drawn in, genuine prescience began to be evident, informed by operational knowledge. This appeal had no moderating effect on the OMB. Reagan appointees and high-ranking officials in the OMB discounted the SSA's protest as having an organizational or programmatic bias.

In contrast to the disability review, which was intensified in the heat and haste of preparing a new president's first budget, the Nixon welfare reforms underwent an unusually prolonged effort at planning. At first this effort was sketchy and ill organized, given the uncertainty about where administrative responsibility would lie, but after the decisions taken in the Ways and Means Committee in the spring of 1971 the planning became better focused. The SSA took charge of the adult programs, and a task force of more than 200 persons, many of them on detail from the SSA, was assembled in HEW to plan FAP.

Yet despite the seemingly long lead time, the SSA too felt the pressure that is inherent in presidential policymaking. There had been virtually no opportunity within the agency to discuss the crucial decisions: that the adult programs of income support should be federalized and that the SSA should become responsible for their administration. Leading officials in Baltimore, the SSA's headquarters, were not invited to weigh at any length the pros and cons of superseding the states. The question put to them early in 1971, born of the closed sessions between Under Secretary Veneman and the Ways and Means Committee, was not whether but how. Their leader, Social Security Commissioner Robert M. Ball, was deeply involved in these meetings and brought back to the agency news of what had been decided there.[29] It was then up to the agency to rise to the expectations that the shaping of a presidential program had fostered.

At the beginning of March 1971, barely a week after Veneman had recommended to the Ways and Means Committee that the SSA be responsible for assistance to dependent adults, Commissioner Ball sent

28. HHS briefing paper, enclosure to letter, Patricia E. Dilley to author, October 12, 1988.

29. Interviews, Jack S. Futterman, retired SSA assistant commissioner for administration, August 29, 1988, and Elliot A. Kirschbaum, former SSA associate commissioner for policy, July 27, 1989. A copy of a memorandum from Kirschbaum to Glen Dehn, November 30, 1972, in the author's files, quotes or closely paraphrases what Ball said to his immediate staff on February 25, 1971. It was in this meeting that Ball delivered the news that federalization of the adult categories, including administration by the SSA, had become the Nixon administration's policy, and was being presented as such to the Ways and Means Committee.

him an extended memorandum on how the agency would perform that task. Seventeen pages long, this document became the guide for the agency's subsequent planning.[30]

The memorandum accepted the prevailing premises of welfare reform: there would be a simple application for benefits, accompanied by a routine check of SSA earnings records and possibly the records of other federal agencies; eligibility determinations would be reviewed on a sample basis; recipients would be asked to report changes that would affect their eligibility and benefit amounts; eligibility would be redetermined at periodic intervals. To these assumptions, the memo added another crucial one: "To the maximum extent possible administration of the program will be folded in with organizational arrangements currently utilized in administration of the present social security programs." Rather than being kept distant from social insurance, the new program would use social security numbers; use social security field facilities and computer and telecommunications networks; merge with social security benefit, payment, and record systems; and, most important, use social security personnel "performing comparable functions under the social security programs." In summary, "Services would be delivered as they are now delivered by Social Security from district offices."

The bulk of the memorandum outlined procedures for the new program. The rest was preface, which spelled out assumptions about program characteristics, or summary, which included a list of seven advantages of the SSA's being in charge of administration. All of the seven were of a rationalizing character:

> The organization and national process required to do the job are already in being and use of them is the one way to successfully accomplish the Federalization of the adult assistance programs in the shortest possible time.
>
> The establishment of a national roll of beneficiaries of assistance programs and its merger with the social security roll makes possible tighter administration. . . .
>
> The establishment of a national roll will close the loopholes for the commission of fraud that exist under separate State rolls. . . .
>
> The delays experienced under current programs of assistance

30. "Administration of the Adult Assistance Categories by the Social Security Administration," March 3, 1971. Copy in author's files. A handwritten note on this document says that it went from the commissioner to the undersecretary.

when people move from one jurisdiction to another . . . would no longer apply.

Information and data hard-to-come-by under the present assistance programs administrations, because much of it is not in machineable form . . . would be readily available from the national rolls of beneficiaries and recipients. . . .

The integration of the administration of assistance with the social security insurance program conserves not only overhead and enables cost benefits deriving from an enlarged scale, it would also increase the cost-effectiveness of established processes and files.

Most importantly, . . . service to the target population could be significantly improved, particularly to that segment of the target population which would be covered by both the insurance and the assistance programs. These people would have only one place to go to file claims . . . and would receive their payments in one check.

No part of the memorandum discussed the feasibility of the task, the capacity of the existing organization to perform it, or the likely effect on or reaction of the staffs in district offices. However, the arraying of "significant facts" in the preface did reveal a potentially important practical difference between the aged and the disabled or blind. Of the 5.8 million aged people expected to qualify for assistance, 5 million were already receiving social security. By contrast, about 2 million disabled and blind people were expected to qualify for assistance, of whom only about 200,000 were receiving social security. Thus federalization of programs for this group would be "an administrative task of very major dimensions"—dimensions such that "prudence and good judgment" dictated a year's delay in implementation. The takeover of the program for the aged should be accomplished first.

At various points the memorandum acknowledged that determination of need and assets would be new for the SSA. This was "the only real factor of difference" from social insurance and the one disadvantage of the takeover. But the memorandum did not dwell on it. Employees would have to be "carefully trained to make . . . determinations with skill and with the tact that would be desirable." There would need to be "a very large increase in staff and other resources," but "given the added resources, the necessary adaptations could be worked out." Except for the cautionary tone about the disabled and blind, the memorandum exuded confidence and competence.

The engagement of the SSA's own headquarters in planning for reform did not disturb or significantly refine the simplifying assumptions that had been the basis for presidential planning. The SSA commissioner's office was no more disposed than the White House or the HEW secretary's office to ask whether income support could be sharply separated from "services" for a trouble-prone, dependent population, and whether any bureaucracy having responsibility for providing such support could entirely escape the considerable burden of compensating for the deficiencies of its clients' individual competence. Was the mass of state and local regulation a product of parochial legislatures and narrow-minded, inefficient, willfully intrusive bureaucracies, as planners at the top of the executive branch in Washington assumed, or was it an inescapable product of the effort to discriminate between those who needed financial help and those who did not?

SSA headquarters did not ask whether it was realistic to suppose, as the Nixon planners did, that federal-state relations could be radically simplified through a sharp separation between the two levels of government. In their scheme the federal government was to become responsible for income support, presumed to require uniformity, while state and local governments were to retain responsibility for services, presumed to require adaptation of administrative action to particular cases. But if Congress was not willing to bear the entire cost of income support programs (and no one supposed that it was), could federal functions be sharply differentiated from state functions? Would not the states' residual, supplementary role in financial support necessarily perpetuate interdependence? The commissioner's memo referred to the states only incidentally, except for a passage in which it appealed for statutory authority to bypass state determinations of eligibility and act directly in some classes of disability cases. Finally, SSA headquarters did not ask—dared not ask, one supposes—how a field staff that for decades had been taught to take pride in administering benefits by right would react to this most fundamental revision of its mission. Would it not be affronted? And threatened?

In sum, presidential agents, including the commissioner of social security, approached Congress with plans whose assumptions were well articulated but abstract and highly simplified. Most analysts of the history of SSI have attached great significance to the fact that FAP totally overshadowed it in executive planning and subsequent debate. The implication is that if policymakers had focused on SSI they would have appreciated its complexities. However, this argument overlooks the extent to which the executive planners of 1969–72 assumed complexity away. They did so for the family welfare program, to which they gave a great deal of attention. They ended up by doing so as well for the adult categories and continued to do so even as the SSA itself was drawn in.

THE CONSTITUTION notwithstanding, faithfully executing the laws is far from the top of a president's priorities. Rather, as the nation's political leader, he is in search of policy transformations. He and his staff begin, at least, by conceiving of bold strokes—the "big fix" for "broken" government programs or features of the society. Possessing the elected chief executive's power (an extraordinary and extraordinarily enticing resource), a putative electoral mandate, and a central perspective on the government and society, they frame grand designs. Having framed them, they hope for dramatic outcomes—an end to poverty, a permanent solution to the financial problems of social security.

Transformations in policy outcomes ordinarily depend on major changes in the universe of administrative organizations—the creation of new organizations, a revision of existing missions, the alteration of routines with or without a change of mission. Such changes have costs. Presidential officials proclaim policy objectives and program designs first and leave until later the consideration of organizational arrangements with their attendant costs. How much consideration administrative questions receive is likely to depend heavily on how much time is available later. In the case of SSI there was, relatively, quite a lot of time; in the case of the intensified disability review, there was virtually none.

The relative leisure of planning for SSI did not produce insight, however. The whole effort proceeded on an extremely dubious, poorly examined administrative premise: that because the SSA had successfully administered benefits by right, in return for tax payments, it could with equal élan and efficiency administer benefits granted on the basis of need. Presidential officials assumed that putting the SSA in charge would change the character of need-tested programs more than it would change the character of the administering organization. This assumption overlooked the decades of indoctrination that the SSA staff had received in the administration of benefits by right as the agency's distinctive mission. And it overlooked signs that the agency was severely taxed by responsibilities it already had. It certainly deserved more critical examination than anyone in the government gave it. "Would the policy gains be worth the administrative costs?" was a question that no one raised for discussion. The policymaking presidency was not very concerned about the administrative costs.

The lack of extensive and critical examination of the SSI decision is accounted for in large part by the stifling effects of presidential power on policy discourse. Presidential policy initiatives, precisely because they are presidential, have a special status within the executive branch. Once a president's pursuit of a policy transformation is under way and the power and prestige of his office have been committed, the pressure on executive subordinates to cooperate is overwhelming. They cannot risk being seen to have jeopardized the president's chances of success. Chapter 5, which discusses the role of the SSA leadership in greater detail, will return to this theme.

The presidential effort in 1981 to achieve a rapid, massive review of the disability rolls also proceeded on a poorly examined, in this case unarticulated, assumption: that the SSA and its field agents would respond sluggishly to central instruction. OMB officials, who pressed for the aggressive review, anticipated very limited results from it. They failed to perceive just how effective the combined instructions of Congress and the presidency would be. They also failed to understand that adverse findings in the review would result in the prompt termination of payments to beneficiaries. In this case, lack of foresight looms larger than lack of concern as an explanation for presidential-level failures to anticipate administrative effects of policy choice.

CHAPTER 4

Congress as Legislator

WHAT THE GOVERNMENT does, and hence what administrative agencies do, depends most fundamentally on how Congress uses its legislative powers. Congressional enactments tell agencies what they are entitled or obliged to do. How Congress influences administration is, then, principally a function of the character of those enactments, which may be more or less voluminous, clear, consistent, and exacting. In this chapter I argue four main points about congressional relations with administrative agencies: Congress's interactions with the presidency tend to produce guidance that is made unclear and inconsistent by the conflicting institutional imperatives of the two branches; congressional guidance, even considered alone, is unstable, changing often as Congress reacts to the consequences of previous actions; although Congress is not deeply interested in administration for its own sake, it resorts to detailed operational commands when it has a policy or political reason for doing so; and, finally, it likes to minimize federal employment.

Congress's relations with agencies may vary greatly depending on the nature of their functions. The Social Security Administration's programs entail the use of government power to transfer income from large, inclusive classes of taxpayers (the actively employed) to large, inclusive classes of beneficiaries (principally the retired and disabled). Its programs do not involve the geographical allocation of benefits, a subject that deeply engages congressional attention. Nor do they involve the distribution of costs and benefits among groups organized by industrial sector, which occurs in programs of economic regulation and yields a distinctive politics of group conflict. Each major government activity or type of policy has its own distinctive pattern of legislative behavior and politics. Thus, were one to look at some kinds of programs other than income transfers, congressional traits in addition to those emphasized here might seem more salient to congressional-agency relations.[1]

THE EXECUTIVE-LEGISLATIVE DIFFERENCE

Policy in the U.S. government is invariably a product of interaction between Congress and the presidency, so that guidance for administrators blends the preferences of each. The blend is often poor. Congress, as the institutional embodiment of diversity, does not share the rationalizing bias of a central, unitary executive. Nor is it as responsive as the presidency to elite, cosmopolitan opinion. Its members have incentives to stay in touch with more common and provincial views.

In the disability case, such differences did not become evident at the lawmaking stage. In 1979–80 Congress and the Carter administration collaborated in preparing a bill that would contain disability insurance costs.[2] The portentous provision requiring periodic review of eligibility, indubitably a rationalizing measure, was actually contrived in Congress, which added it to the administration's bill. Only time would tell whether Congress really intended that "ineligible" persons should be removed from the rolls; in 1980 it said that it did.

In the supplemental security income case, however, executive-legislative differences very much affected the way in which the program evolved. A policy change conceived in the executive—and in conception plausibly suited to administration by a national agency—lost simplicity and uniformity as Congress went to work on it. And, once the choice had been made for national administration, no one noticed (or had the courage to point out) that the policy premises on which that decision was based were being abandoned.

The executive's belief that the SSA's responsibilities could be extended with little risk derived from the notion, prevalent within the administration, that welfare programs should be radically simplified,

---

1. Among leading attempts to categorize policy and program types and to explore their implications for both congressional behavior and political processes more generally are: Theodore J. Lowi, "American Business, Public Policy, Case–Studies, and Political Theory," *World Politics*, vol. 16 (July 1964), pp. 677–715, subsequently elaborated in Lowi, "Four Systems of Policy, Politics, and Choice," *Public Administration Review*, vol. 32 (July–August 1972), pp. 298–310; and James Q. Wilson, *Political Organizations* (Basic Books, 1973), chap. 16.

2. Edward D. Berkowitz, *Disabled Policy: America's Programs for the Handicapped* (Cambridge University Press, 1987), pp. 114–22.

nationally uniform, and rights-oriented. Being closely akin to social insurance, such programs would readily be assimilated by the SSA. Reflecting elite opinion, the executive sought to reduce intervention in recipients' lives. By contrast, Congress, consistent with a thirty-five-year pattern, held the ordinary person's less sympathetic view of welfare recipients. Reform "should make it hard to get on and easy to get off."[3] While Congress was far more sympathetic to the aged, blind, and disabled than to the "welfare mothers" on aid to families with dependent children—and hence willing in 1972 to liberalize provision for the former but not the latter—not even for the former did it produce the highly simplified, uniform, easy-to-administer program that executive planners had been assuming.

As the actual law developed, the executive's desire to simplify and rationalize yielded to the legislature's desire to constrain and control—not only because of the different political biases of the two institutions, but also because of the elemental fact that in all policymaking the path from conception to application is increasingly made rough by complexity. There were numerous examples.

One example, vivid and readily comprehensible, had to do with state residence requirements for recipients of SSI. Traditionally, state governments had required of applicants some stipulated length of residence before granting categorical public assistance. The Supreme Court had recently found residence requirements for AFDC to be unconstitutional, and they certainly had no place in the Nixon administration's plan to create a uniform national program. In its initial proposal for the adult categories in 1969–70, which would have perpetuated the grant-in-aid form but with much stronger national standards, the administration would have eliminated residence requirements. Yet Congress, making a defiant gesture toward both of the other branches, provided that states might include residence requirements in their plans for supplementation. These were plans that, under the law, the SSA could be called on to administer.[4]

Another example of the failed or perverse results of the effort at simplification was the provision of the law with regard to social security numbers. To satisfy Congress that a simplified approach to determining eligibility would not be vulnerable to abuse, executive officials had

3. The remark was made by Ways and Means Committee Chairman Wilbur Mills, and is quoted in "Statement of John G. Veneman, Under Secretary of Health, Education, and Welfare, before the Committee on Ways and Means," February 24, 1971, copy in author's files.

4. 86 Stat. 1474.

argued that a federally administered system would be superior to state administration because of the computer cross-checking that could be done at the national level among records of income tax withholding, payroll tax withholding for social security, social security benefits, unemployment compensation benefits, and other income support programs.[5] Congress perceived that to realize the benefits of all this computerized cross-checking would require reliable identification of welfare recipients, and the instrument for doing this was to be the social security number, more widely issued and more carefully controlled than in the past. The new law of 1972 directed the secretary of Health, Education, and Welfare—really, the SSA—to issue social security numbers to aliens, whether admitted to permanent residence or temporarily, and to the beneficiaries of (or applicants to) any federal or federally subsidized program. The bill also required that the SSA establish the citizenship, alien status, and identity of all applicants for social security numbers and made it a misdemeanor to furnish false information in connection with securing a social security number or to misuse a social security number.

Though not integral to SSI, these provisions regarding social security numbers significantly increased the routine administrative burden on the agency at precisely the time it received the brand-new burden of administering need-tested assistance. In reporting on the effects of the law to SSA employees, the SSA commissioner noted, even before discussing SSI, that the new law would require the SSA to double the volume of social security numbers issued in fiscal years 1973 and 1974.[6] He might have added that henceforth it would considerably complicate and delay the issuance of all social security numbers. Public complaints that the SSA takes too long to issue numbers date from the changes introduced in 1972.

More directly related to SSI—indeed, at the heart of it—were the statutory provisions defining individual applicants' income and resources. These provisions may have been simple compared with the aggregate of fifty states' definitions, but they were not simple absolutely. In establishing an applicant's monthly income, the SSA was instructed to exclude the following: $20 of any income (earned or unearned) other than income paid on the basis of need; $65 of monthly earnings and one-half above that (plus income necessary for fulfillment of plans for self-support for the blind and disabled and work expenses for the

5. *Family Assistance Act of 1970*, Hearings before the Senate Committee on Finance, 91 Cong. 2 sess. (Government Printing Office, 1970), pt. 1, p. 648.
6. *Commissioner's Bulletin*, no. 130, February 7, 1973.

blind); within reasonable limits, earnings of a student regularly attending school; irregular and infrequent earned income of an individual of $30 or less in a quarter and irregular and infrequent unearned income of an individual of $60 or less in a quarter; any amount received from a public agency as a refund of taxes paid on real property or on food purchased; the tuition and fees part of scholarships and fellowships; home produce; one-third of child-support payments from an absent parent; foster care payments for a child placed in the household by a child-placement agency; and supplementary benefits based on need and provided by a state or its political subdivision. Otherwise, all earned and unearned income was to be counted, including benefits from other public and private programs, prizes and awards, proceeds of life insurance not needed for expenses of a last illness and burial (with a maximum of $1,500), gifts, inheritances, rents, dividends, interest, and so forth. For people living as members of someone else's household, the value of room and board would be deemed to be one-third of the full monthly payment.

Individuals would be ineligible if they had resources exceeding $1,500 (or $2,250 for a couple). The following items were to be excluded from resources: the home and appurtenant land to the extent that their value did not exceed a reasonable amount; household goods, personal effects, and an automobile, not in excess of a reasonable amount; other property essential to the individual's support (within reasonable value limitations); life insurance policies, if their total face value was $1,500 or less (otherwise, insurance policies would be counted only to the extent of their cash surrender value); resources of a blind or disabled individual necessary for fulfillment of an approved plan of self-support; and shares of certain nonnegotiable stock held in a regional or village corporation by Alaskan natives. With such statutory provisions as a starting point, the SSA created a manual of guidance for SSI that quickly rivaled in thickness that of the state counterparts it was to supersede.

Just how far the law was from being simple is illustrated further by the SSA's effort to write a regulation specifying the "reasonable" value of a home. In its report of the bill, the Ways and Means Committee said that, in determining allowable limits of the value of the home, household goods, and personal effects, the secretary of HEW should generally follow the practice of the states under their existing programs. However, the practice of the states was so varied as to be inconclusive. Eighteen states had neither specified a maximum home value nor imposed liens on the homes of old-age assistance recipients. Thirty-three states had not imposed either requirement on blind recipients. Among the seventeen states that did fix maximum values for the homes of the blind, the range was very wide. Only one state, Idaho, used the concept of "reasonable" market value. An SSA planning group tried to develop a rate that would vary with housing values by region, state, or substate areas, but gave up. Nothing of the sort seemed both equitable and administrable. Instead, the group suggested fixing the allowable value of a home at $25,000, a figure defended as sufficiently low to satisfy the legislature's intent that there be an effective restriction but sufficiently high to avoid large-scale denial of eligibility.

Before the matter went to the commissioner for decision, however, the group hit on a different approach. Rather than use the value of the home as an absolute standard for determining eligibility, it proposed to use it as a guide to determine whether there should be further investigation of the individual's statement of income and resources. When the home value exceeded the specified level, the SSA would make attempts to verify other information in the application. However, this approach was rejected on the ground that it did not meet the statutory requirement for a limit.

The SSA ultimately recommended to the secretary of HEW a combined approach: a limit on home value of $35,000 and a series of tolerances that defined when further information on income and resources would be sought. This combination, an SSA document says, "seemed to meet the need for program simplicity and understanding yet contained sufficient flexibility to meet equity concerns." The secretary's office approved the dual approach but said that $35,000 was too high. Finally, the figure was set at $25,000 for the continental United States and $35,000 for Alaska and Hawaii, and formal regulations were prepared, along with operating instructions for the field.[7] Presumably the irony of this exercise was not lost on the SSA staff as they struggled to define a nationwide standard of a kind that many of the states had never had—for a program that had just been "simplified."

The crowning congressional departure from the original executive design came in the summer of 1973, eight months after SSI had been enacted and six months before it was to go into effect. At this time, Congress decided to require the states to supplement federal payments to individuals to the extent necessary to protect them from loss of

7. This account is from an unsigned memorandum, "Issue: Determination of the Reasonable Value of a Home," in the files of Beryl Radin of the University of Southern California. It appears to have been prepared by the SSA for the SSI Study Group.

benefits under the new program. The original design had been to create a nationally uniform program and induce the states to conform to it, leaving to them only the function of voluntarily adding to the federal amount. Congress chose now, however, essentially to compel perpetuation of all the old programs, except insofar as they were less liberal than the new one—and to compel the SSA to administer them. This change in the law could hardly have been more fundamental or more subversive of the executive's original intention. Then, to drive home just how little it cared for uniformity, Congress exempted one state from this requirement. Because the constitution of Texas prohibited supplementation, the law provided an exception for any state with whose constitution it was in conflict.[8]

This change happened when Congress discovered—apparently to the surprise of Russell Long, chairman of the Senate Finance Committee—that it had failed to hold individual recipients harmless. That is, nothing in the original law guaranteed that individuals would get as much under the new SSI program as they had gotten under the old, federally aided state programs. This original law encouraged but did not require the states to supplement federal payments to the needy aged, blind, and disabled. If a state chose to supplement, and also chose to have the SSA administer the supplement—an option provided by the law—the federal government would assume the costs of administration. It turned out that in about half of the states, most recipients would get more than they had been getting, but in the other half many would lose. Moreover, the federal law had confined assistance to those persons who met the eligibility standards, whereas most state laws had also made provision for "essential persons" in the household, typically spouses under the age of sixty-five. An estimated 125,000 "essential persons" stood to be adversely affected.

Once the threat to individuals became clear, having been brought to the Senate's attention by several state welfare directors who may have been hoping to delay or even derail SSI, Congress acted quickly. It amended the law to cover "essential persons" already on the rolls. Unwilling to go beyond that to use federal funds to protect individuals against harm, it in effect ordered the states to do so by threatening to withhold their medicaid grants unless they did. And it commanded the SSA to administer these mandatory supplements at a state's request, a huge increase in its administrative burden. Right away, forty of the eighty computer programs then in preparation for SSI had to be

8. 87 Stat. 157.

rewritten. New information had to be gathered from all the states, and—providing they elected administration by SSA—contracts had to be negotiated with the more than thirty states for which supplemental payments were now mandatory.[9]

CONGRESSIONAL INCONSTANCY

Above all, Congress is a busy legislature. An official of the General Accounting Office (GAO) who testified before Congress in 1983 on the administrative problems of the SSA pointed out that Congress had made ninety-two changes in the basic monthly benefit calculation since the start of the program in the 1930s. Between 1977 and 1982, members of Congress had introduced over 6,200 bills relating to the agency's programs. Of these, 66 were enacted, containing about 300 new provisions that the SSA had to implement.[10] Neither SSI nor the requirement of the disability review was a solitary legislative provision; on the contrary, both were embedded in very complex acts. The Social Security Amendments of 1972, which authorized SSI, also increased benefits to 3.8 million widows and widowers; made 1.7 million persons eligible for additional benefits by liberalizing the retirement test (which stipulates how much a beneficiary may earn without sacrificing social security benefits); extended medicare coverage to the 1.7 million beneficiaries of disability insurance; and made other important changes in medicare. The act was 165 pages long. The Disability Amendments of 1980—along with the Omnibus Budget Reconciliation Act of 1981, which followed very shortly—contained thirty new provisions, of which the requirement for the review of disability cases was but one. Turbulence in its legislative environment is the norm for the SSA, not the exception.

"The process of public administration is like an alternating current," SSA Commissioner Robert M. Ball wrote in a job description that he prepared at the request of the Nixon administration. "Out of the administration of the law and the evaluation of operations comes the

9. John J. Fialka, "Battle of the Barons," in Charles Peters and Michael Nelson, eds., *The Culture of Bureaucracy* (Holt, Rinehart and Winston, 1979), p. 95.

10. *Social Security: How Well Is It Serving the Public?* Hearing before the Senate Special Committee on Aging, 98 Cong. 1 sess. (GPO, 1984), pp. 35–63. There is an updated calculation in General Accounting Office, *Social Security Administration: Stable Leadership and Better Management Needed to Improve Effectiveness*, HRD-87-39 (March 1987), p. 26, which reports that from 1977 to 1985 Congress enacted 100 laws containing about 470 provisions governing SSA programs.

recognition of the need for change. Evaluation results flow back and lead to legislative and policy modification and to the modification of operating objectives. Then, as the modifications are put into effect, the process begins again."[11] This makes the process sound logical and orderly, as if the agency could regulate initiatives and not be subject to shocks from the alternating current of legislative modification. Yet shocks are common because forces beyond administrators' control take charge of legislation. Administrators constantly have to adapt regulations and staff routines to the changing requirements of legislative guidance.

Changes occur for many reasons. Events in the society or the economy may require adjustment of policy. Congress itself changes. Elections biennially renew the House and one-third of the Senate. Partisan alignments shift; so do the moods, perceptions, and political agendas of the membership. Sometimes Congress makes a mistake; as a maker of law and policy it discovers that it did something it never meant to do. Probably more often, it discovers that something it did, though fully intended at the time, has had unintended consequences. Sometimes these become apparent even at the policymaking stage, before a law has been fully applied. More frequently, they are revealed later. Members of Congress as providers of service, open to the appeals and complaints of individual constituents, are prone to recast what Congress the institution did as policymaker. Members collectively vacillate between the two roles, and the law undergoes revision as they do. Between them, SSI and the disability review illustrate all of these causes of the mutability of law.

Changes in the Law

In SSI the instability of congressional lawmaking seriously handicapped the SSA in the short term. Even before the program began, there was a remarkable rate of change in the fourteen-month period during which the agency was trying to make ready.

The most important change, already described, came in the summer of 1973 when Congress discovered that it had failed to hold individual recipients harmless in the original version of the act. This was a mistake. It never intended to do that—at least the Senate did not—and when Congress corrected the error, the SSA was left with an

11. "Assignment of the Commissioner of Social Security," December 14, 1972, p. 1. I am grateful to Ball for supplying a copy of this document.

incomparably more difficult administrative task. Administration officials pleaded with Congress not to make the change. "I would like to
offer my assurance that we can and will be ready to offer complete
implementation of the program by January 1, 1974," HEW Secretary
Caspar W. Weinberger told the Senate Finance Committee. "[But]
neither I nor anyone else can give you that assurance if, at this crucial
stage, you should make any basic changes in the law."[12] Congress
proceeded nonetheless.

Another change that the SSA found very burdensome was the
"rollback" amendment, also passed in the summer of 1973. Congress
became concerned about an effort by some states to move mothers
from the AFDC program to the disability assistance program so that
they would be automatically covered by SSI. This would have shifted
virtually the entire cost of supporting them to the federal government.
In order to prevent this, Congress provided that recipients of state
disability assistance could be grandfathered into SSI only if they were
on the state rolls for at least one month before July 1973 and were still
on them as of December. This meant that the SSA began SSI with a
big backlog of cases because it had to rework all of those—numbering
135,000, as it turned out—that the states had enrolled in the last six
months of 1973.[13]

Other changes made in SSI in 1973 derived less from failures of
congressional foresight. One set concerned the size of payments. It
was a time of severe inflation, a socioeconomic condition to which it
seemed necessary to make a policy response, and Congress twice
changed benefits to keep pace. In July 1973 it increased the SSI
payment level from $130 to $140 a month for an individual and from
$195 to $210 a month for a couple, effective July 1974. Then, in a bill
that the president signed on December 31, one day before SSI was to
begin, it made the change effective immediately, to be reflected in
checks starting in April. A further increase was scheduled to take
effect in July.[14]

Another set of changes addressed coordination with other programs.
Such coordination was one of the difficulties plaguing welfare reform.

12. *Supplemental Security Income Program*, Hearing before the Senate Committee on
Finance, 93 Cong. 1 sess. (GPO, 1973), p. 7.

13. *Committee Staff Report on the Disability Insurance Program*, Committee Print, House
Committee on Ways and Means (GPO, 1974), pp. 123, 406–07.

14. For a vivid description of the practical effects, see *Administration of the Supplemental
Security Income Program*, Hearings before the Subcommittee on Oversight of the House
Committee on Ways and Means, 94 Cong. 1 sess. (GPO, 1975), vol. 1, p. 20.

Would benefits under one income-support program offset those of another or be added to them? To what extent could administration of the various programs be integrated, as by using common determinations of eligibility? Even if interstate differences could have been eliminated, interprogram differences remained a source of extreme complexity and hence instability. Much tinkering followed any choice.

In 1973 the relation between SSI and the food stamp program was the leading example. Under the initial version of SSI, recipients would have been prohibited from participating in food stamp or commodity distribution programs. However, in amendments to the Food Stamp Act in 1973, Congress revised this to provide that individuals were ineligible for food stamps for a given month only if their SSI benefit, plus any state supplement, was at least equal to the amount of assistance plus the food stamp bonus they would have received under the state program of aid to the aged, blind, or disabled as of December 1973. In turn, Congress soon decided that this would be impossible to administer and would produce inequities, so in December 1973, again on the eve of the start of SSI, it repealed everything it had enacted about the relation between SSI and food stamps. "For the 6-month period beginning January 1974, the eligibility of SSI recipients for participation in the food stamp and surplus commodities programs will be determined as though P.L. 92-603 [the basic authorization of SSI] and P.L. 93-86 [an amendment to the Food Stamp Act] had not been enacted," the social security commissioner informed the SSA's employees. However, this was qualified in such a way that it did not apply in certain states, and it was also not expected to endure; Congress was going to try again to prepare legislation.[15]

This account by no means exhausts the changes that Congress made between October 1972, when the initial law was passed, and January 1974, when the SSA began its attempt to administer the program. The commissioner's listing for SSA employees of the changes of December 1973 includes such additional topics as special treatment of SSI recipients who live with AFDC families (designed to assure that where SSI and AFDC recipients were living in the same household, SSI would not result in increasing benefits for the family unit); reduction in the SSI payment by the amount of any state supplemental payment for institutional medical care; and limitations on eligibility

15. *Social Security Amendments of 1973*, S. Rept. 93-553, 93 Cong. 1 sess. (GPO, 1973), pp. 23–24; and *Commissioner's Bulletin*, no. 138, December 27, 1973, with enclosure, "Summary of the Provisions of H.R. 11333."

determinations under resources tests (a highly complex and broadly applied qualification of the grandfathering legislation of July 1973).

The agency to which such instructions were addressed was then in no condition to cope with even the least of them. In Baltimore, and far more so in the field, it had already been overwhelmed.

Fluctuations in Role and Mood

The disability review represents a different case. While Congress has made numerous changes in the law governing the disability program, more often than not for the purpose of liberalizing it, changes of role and mood are as important in this case as actual changes in statutory language. Congress's attitude toward interpreting the law has fluctuated.

On its face, the standard for determining disability is very strict. Disability consists of the "inability to engage in any substantial gainful activity" anywhere in the country. Anyone who is able to earn money through work—any kind of work existing in the national economy, whether or not it is the applicant's customary work—does not qualify. The question inescapably arises: does Congress really mean it?

Strictness is implied, too, in the procedure for determining who is qualified. The applicant's impairment must be "medically determinable." That is, it is supposed to be susceptible to objective, scientific proof. Did Congress really mean *that*?[16]

The legislation has delegated very broadly to the SSA, which must learn through experience of rulemaking and adjudication what Congress means. And one thing the agency learned soon after the program began in 1956 was that there are two Congresses: one the legislative institution that functions as policymaker for the nation, the other the collection of individual representatives of several hundred geographic constituencies and millions of individual constituents, some of whom were applicants for or recipients of disability benefits. The first of these Congresses was very strict. The second did not mean it, but was dedicated to helping individual constituents get as much as they were entitled to as quickly as they could out of an intricate, extended administrative procedure. The concerns of the second Congress were evident in oversight hearings held late in 1959; in urgent complaints

16. The disability definition is found in sec. 223(d) of the Social Security Act. See *Compilation of the Social Security Laws*, H. Doc. 93-117, 93 Cong. 1 sess. (GPO, 1973), vol. 1, pp. 170–71.

as the appeals procedures became clogged; and in the expectation of being notified in advance, before the applicant, of decisions in individual cases.[17] Congressmen often communicated directly with administrative law judges (ALJs) on behalf of constituents.

Another thing that the SSA learned was that how strict even the first of these two Congresses was depended very much on how the program was faring. The disability program was extremely vulnerable to pressures for expansion. Because the meaning of the law was problematic and application of it in any given case was highly subjective, its administration was very sensitive to exogenous forces: the demands of clients, whose expectations of entitlement grew; the pleas of their lawyers, who grew in numbers and audacity; the decisions of doctors, whose professional ethic led them to err on the side of compassion; and the decisions of courts, which were inclined to view strict application of a strict law as unreasonable. These were all in addition to the influence of Congress itself in its role as constituency server. Both Congress and the courts pushed the agency toward publication of its policies, which it had initially resisted for fear that precise public knowledge of adjudication criteria would heighten pressures on the program. If clients, lawyers, and doctors knew exactly what it took to qualify, they would adjust their claims, pleas, and evidence accordingly.[18]

By the mid-1970s, these various expansionary forces seemed to be having a cumulatively powerful effect. The program was out of control; that is, it was growing very fast and exceeding by a wide margin the costs that had been projected for it. And, as this happened, a congressional reaction set in. Even liberal Democrats shared the sense that something must be done. Members were hearing from constituents that able-bodied persons were abusing the program.[19]

17. For a revealing account of the SSA's handling of congressional inquiries, see *Recent Studies Relevant to the Disability Hearings and Appeals Crisis*, Committee Print, Subcommittee on Social Security of the House Committee on Ways and Means, 94 Cong. 1 sess. (GPO, 1975), pp. 59–62.

18. Deborah A. Stone, *The Disabled State* (Temple University Press, 1984), chap. 5; and Berkowitz, *Disabled Policy*, chap. 3. On general changes in the culture that could have affected the disability program, see Lawrence M. Friedman, *Total Justice* (Beacon Press, 1987).

19. See the remarks of Representative J. J. Pickle in *Disability Insurance Program: 1978*, Hearings before the Subcommittee on Social Security of the House Committee on Ways and Means, 95 Cong. 2 sess. (GPO, 1978), p. 15; of Senator Gaylord Nelson in *Administrative Integrity of the Social Security Program*, Hearing before the Subcommittee

Within Congress, pressure on the administration to do something came principally from Russell B. Long, chairman of the Senate Finance Committee, and from the House Ways and Means Committee, which had a staff member, Frederick B. Arner, who was a specialist in the disability program and was dedicated to bringing it under control. The House Appropriations Committee also joined in the effort. Since enactment of SSI, which was financed with general revenues (as distinct from the earmarked payroll tax that supported social insurance), the Appropriations committees had increased their scrutiny of the SSA's budget. Now, with a little prodding from the Ways and Means Committee—and with a keen sense of concern about the financial condition of social security and of the federal government generally—the House Appropriations Committee began asking the SSA what it was doing to get disability spending under control. In the spring of 1980, when presenting the agency's budget for fiscal year 1981, Commissioner William J. Driver told the committee that "in response to [your] concerns" major increases had been requested, including an additional $47 million for conducting reviews of the eligibility of persons already on the rolls.[20] Congressional pressure to control the program did not subside even in the face of signs that the administration was achieving improved control without legislation. The allowance rate (the proportion of new applications that were approved), after peaking at 47 percent in 1975, fell to 28 percent by 1980. Growth in the rolls stopped in 1978.[21]

In Social Security Act amendments in 1980, Congress as policymaker provided that the disability program should be more strict. Signifi-

on Social Security of the Senate Committee on Finance, 96 Cong. 1 sess. (GPO, 1979), p. 3; and of Representative Bill Gradison in *Social Security Disability Insurance*, Hearing before the Subcommittee on Social Security of the House Committee on Ways and Means, 98 Cong. 1 sess. (GPO, 1983), p. 4. Joseph A. Califano, who served Jimmy Carter as secretary of HEW, writes that Carter heard the same thing from voters during the 1976 campaign, and came to believe that the disability program was being "ripped off" and that drug addicts and alcoholics were filling the rolls. Joseph A. Califano, Jr., *Governing America: An Insider's Report from the White House and the Cabinet* (Simon and Schuster, 1981), p. 384.

20. *Departments of Labor, Health, Education, and Welfare, and Related Agencies Appropriations for 1981*, Hearings before a Subcommittee of the House Committee on Appropriations, 96 Cong. 2 sess. (GPO, 1980), pt. 5, p. 281. See also the exchange between Driver and Representative Robert Michel, p. 366.

21. *Staff Data and Materials Related to the Social Security Disability Insurance Program*, Committee Print, Senate Committee on Finance, 97 Cong. 2 sess. (GPO, 1982), pp. 20–25.

cantly, though, these amendments made no change in the most salient feature of the law—the definition of disability. Unable and unwilling itself to abide consistently by the strict standard it had set, Congress was also unable to devise a statutory alternative. Obstacles inhered both in the legislature, which could not agree definitively on whether it wished the program to be strict or lenient, and in the program itself, which defied the formulation of an objective standard of eligibility. Because the law conveyed so much discretion to the agency—some on the face of the law and some barely hidden beneath superficially strict terms—and because the stakes of the program were so large, the SSA as administrator became the object of a broadly encompassing and increasingly bitter political contest. A wide array of institutions and interests fought over how the agency should behave. In the disability review of the early 1980s, the contest erupted visibly, in an acute form. Characteristically, Congress was on both sides, at first instructing the agency to be tougher, then chastising it severely for having become too tough (as chapter 8, on congressional oversight, will show).

INDIFFERENT YET IMPERIOUS

On the face of it, Congress is not very interested in administration. Members are extremely busy. Electoral pressures compel them to give priority to matters that promise political rewards or threaten political costs. Questions of administrative performance and feasibility rarely do that. Thus members of Congress are not receptive to objections that something they want to do is not administratively feasible. Staff members or executive officials who work with them on legislation learn that if a proposal threatens an agency with an onerous administrative burden, their best approach is not to register a direct protest on administrative grounds, but to devise an alternative that is equally or more appealing politically. As long as their political objectives are served, members of Congress will allow discretion as to administrative means, but they will not hear suggestions that political objectives should be compromised for the sake of administrative ones.[22]

Lack of interest in administration per se does not, however, imply lack of action on administrative subjects. If administrative performance directly or indirectly gives rise to a political issue—for example, if the

22. Interviews, Michael Stern, former staff director, Senate Finance Committee; Lawrence Thompson, assistant comptroller general of the United States; and Joseph Delfico, associate director, GAO Human Resources Division, July 21, 1989.

disability caseload is judged to be out of control in part because the SSA has become lax in administration—members of Congress do not hesitate to seek correction with detailed commands. They give instruction in matters that one might expect to be left to administrators' discretion.

The statutory provision of 1980 requiring the SSA to review every three years those cases in which disability was not classified as permanent was a congressional prescription. Although the SSA leadership promised to invest more effort in reviews, it did not welcome a statutory requirement.[23] The Carter administration's legislative proposals for improving administration of the disability insurance program, shaped by the executive's perspective, were confined to enhancing the position of the SSA in relation to the state governments and the courts. While granting much of what the administration asked, particularly in regard to SSA authority over the states,[24] Congress also took the occasion to impose controls of its own over the SSA.

Besides compelling the periodic review, Congress also instructed the SSA to resume reviews of state disability determinations. At one time, the SSA staff, as distinct from the administrative law judges, had routinely reviewed a high proportion of state disability allowances, but these reviews were virtually eliminated in 1972 as the SSA searched for ways to cut administrative costs. In 1980 Congress required the SSA to restore them progressively, by reviewing 15 percent of allowances in fiscal year 1981, 35 percent in 1982, and 65 percent thereafter. Also in 1980, Congress required the SSA to review decisions rendered by ALJs in disability cases (it did not say how many or what

23. In the spring of 1979, in response to written inquiries from the Ways and Means Committee about its plans for reviewing the rolls, the SSA said that it intended to "establish a goal of reviewing all nonpermanent disability cases at least as frequently as every 3 years." It also said, "We believe it would be desirable to avoid the rigidity of putting a mandatory reexamination procedure in the law, and would prefer the flexibility to develop the most cost-effective program for reexamining cases where improvement seems likely." *Disability Insurance Legislation*, Hearings before the Subcommittee on Social Security of the House Committee on Ways and Means, 96 Cong. 1 sess. (GPO, 1979), p. 78. What the agency had proposed as a goal Congress chose to enact as a command.

24. The law authorized the secretary of HHS to promulgate regulations governing state agency conduct "in such detail as he deems appropriate." The state governments retained no shred of independence. 94 Stat. 454. In regard to judicial review, the law limited the scope for introducing new evidence in cases before the courts. In effect, it provided for closing the record after the administrative law judge had ruled. 94 Stat. 458. The administration had sought a much broader provision, limiting judicial review to issues of constitutional and statutory interpretation (as distinct from a review of the facts).

proportion) and to report findings.[25] In 1977, when Congress had to raise a great deal of new social security revenue in order to keep the program solvent, the Ways and Means Committee had warned that it would return to the subject of disability insurance, which it had been unable to address at that time.[26] Three years later Congress made good on that promise and embedded numerous administrative controls in law.

By definition, law is binding; the nature of it is to embody command. Thus, when Congress passes a law containing numerous new provisions, all equally require implementation. The legislature does not stipulate priorities. It does not say, "If you must choose, do this before that." It cannot, without diluting the force of its acts, acknowledge that such choices may be necessary. In the process of creating administrative tasks, it operates without any evident sense that organizational capacities are finite, and that therefore it should make choices. When expenditures are clearly involved and program activities wear price tags, Congress is constrained through the (imperfect) discipline of the budget process to make trade-offs. It chooses more of this and less of that, in the recognition that it cannot have everything it wants. But there is no budget of administrative capacity, no currency with which to compare the magnitude of various tasks of implementation, and thus no decisionmaking mechanism with which to discipline Congress's desire for the performance of administrative acts, except indirect limits posed by budgetary constraints that may limit the enlargement of spending programs.

Not ordinarily as a guide to its priorities, but rather to make sure that its commands are obeyed, Congress is prone to prescribing statutory deadlines. The fourteen provisions of the Social Security Disability Amendments of 1980, for example, had lead times ranging from twenty-three days to eighteen months.[27]

With a large number of assignments and finite capacity, the agency typically cannot work as fast as Congress tells it to in the wake of new laws. Implementation of laws ordinarily requires preparation of regulations and redesign of computer software, as well as revision of internal operating instructions. The SSA often has fifty to sixty regulations in preparation at once. They must be preceded by research

25. 94 Stat. 456. The report ("the Bellmon report") appears in *Staff Data and Materials Related to the Social Security Disability Insurance Program*, Committee Print, pp. 133–86.

26. *Social Security Financing Amendments of 1977*, H. Rept. 95-702, 95 Cong. 1 sess. (GPO, 1977), pt. 1, pp. 20–21.

27. GAO, *Stable Leadership and Better Management Needed*, pp. 27–28, 126.

and internal coordination; publication of a notice of proposed rule-making in the *Federal Register*; analysis of public comments, which are often voluminous; revision and republication, possibly with another round of comment; and clearance with the Department of Health and Human Services and the Office of Management and Budget. The procedures are not within the SSA's discretion, but for the most part are prescribed by the Administrative Procedure Act and executive orders.

In a tally of five social security laws that were passed between 1980 and 1984, the GAO identified eighty provisions that required a regulation, but in only two cases of the eighty was the agency able to produce one by the time the law took effect. For SSI, the agency began publication of proposed regulations in the *Federal Register* in early August 1973, about ten months after the law was enacted, and essentially completed its initial framing of a body of regulation a year later, eight months after the law took effect. This represented a very large volume of work in a relatively short time.

The situation is similar with respect to the redesign of computer software. The GAO identified forty-three provisions of law between 1980 and 1984 that required the SSA to modify its computer systems, but in only eight of these cases was the agency ready on time. The effort to be ready has led to shortcuts such as frequent patching of software and inadequate validation, which in turn increase the risk of error and make subsequent legislative changes more difficult to implement.[28] Computer software performs most reliably when it comes in discrete, self-contained packages. When it is changed piecemeal, errors increase. This means that computer technology and U.S. policy processes are very much in tension with each other. Most policymaking is patchwork. Laws are constantly changed incrementally, in detail, compelling data processing staffs to respond in kind. And even when, as with SSI, policy comes in whole new pieces rather than as patchwork, insufficient time is allowed for preparation of the corresponding data processing system. Besides, no sooner was the whole act enacted for SSI than the policy patching set in.

In SSI, the lack of sufficient time to develop data processing systems was critical. SSI depended far more heavily on automatic data processing than the SSA's established programs did. It entailed a

---

28. GAO, *Stable Leadership and Better Management Needed*, chap. 10. The problem of heavily patched software is by no means confined to the SSA or to public agencies. See Paul B. Carroll, "Patching Up Software Occupies Programmers and Disables Systems," *Wall Street Journal*, January 22, 1988, p. 1.

completely new system, which was not ready when the program began. To administer SSI required one hundred separate software programs, with nearly 1 million individual instructions, making it one of the largest and most complex computer operations in the country.[29] It took several more years to bring the system to a satisfactory standard of performance.

The effect that statutory deadlines had on the disability review is more open to debate. The law, which became effective in June 1980, stipulated that the requirement for periodic review would take effect on January 1, 1982. This was a long lead time as statutory lead times go. The law also provided that all cases subject to review should receive it every three years. Thus, review of the entire caseload of 2.8 million (minus those judged to be permanently disabled, a figure initially set at 675,000) was to be completed by the end of 1984. That meant that the work load of the state agencies would sharply increase in the short run. SSA officials started the review early, in the spring of 1981, in order, they said, to spread a heavy work load over a longer period.[30] Their critics disbelieved them, inferring that the rapid start was intended to speed the realization of budget savings. Depending on which side one credits, the statutory deadline either compelled precipitous action, as a necessary accommodation to administrative capacities, or provided the excuse for it, on the part of those who cared above all about reducing government spending.

Deadlines per se are often unavoidable, of course. If Congress is to define a new responsibility, as it did with SSI, as a practical matter it has to name an effective date. The public cannot be told that the new program will begin "whenever the agency is ready to do it." Underlying Congress's habitual choice of tight deadlines is probably an assumption that any other kind would have no effect. Proximate dates maximize pressure on the agency to perform; they are tantamount to stipulating implementation "as soon as possible," and they often result in faster performance than the agency has felt able to promise. Under pressure,

29. For a discussion of its complexity in the context of SSA computer programs generally, see SSI Study Group, "Report to the Commissioner of Social Security and the Secretary of Health, Education, and Welfare on the Supplemental Security Income Program," January 1976, pp. 195–96. Reproduced in *Oversight of the Supplemental Security Income Program*, Hearings before the Subcommittee on Oversight of the House Committee on Ways and Means, 94 Cong. 2 sess. (GPO, 1976), pp. 244–45.

30. Testimony of Paul B. Simmons, *Social Security Disability Insurance*, Hearing before the Subcommittee on Social Security of the House Committee on Ways and Means, 98 Cong. 1 sess. (GPO, 1983), pp. 50–57; and interview, Fred Schutzman, former acting deputy commissioner of social security, August 2, 1989.

the agency surpasses its own expectations. However, the inability to conform and the strenuous effort to do so nonetheless often have high costs in chaos and inefficiency.[31]

COST CONSCIOUSNESS

As a general rule, Congress likes to keep bureaucracy lean and cheap, although it does not necessarily cut agency administrative budgets very much. The SSA has generally gotten about what the president's budget has asked for it, and in the disability case even came under pressure to ask for more. One of the ways in which Congress signaled its desire for closer scrutiny of the disability rolls in the late 1970s was to ask the SSA commissioner why he was not requesting more appropriations for that purpose.[32]

Congress's preference for economy in administration has been manifested instead in its choice of techniques that harness the administrative capacities of state governments or private organizations, thereby minimizing direct federal employment. The SSA has been distinctive in that its core function, administration of retirement and survivors' insurance, is done directly, with no reliance on state governments or private contractors. Only in the disability program, in which it depends on state agencies to make initial determinations of eligibility, and in medicare, in which it depended on private contractors, has the SSA had to practice "government by proxy," as Donald F. Kettl has termed it.[33]

So strong has been Congress's preference for proxy arrangements that its choice of a purely national administration for SSI in 1972 is profoundly puzzling. Whereas Congress ordinarily relies on state governments to be federal agents, here it turned the customary arrangement upside down and offered the administrative services of the SSA, free of charge, to those states that engaged in supplementation.

31. See GAO, *Stable Leadership and Better Management Needed*, pp. 126–29, for a discussion of the toll that unrealistically short deadlines take in computer efficiency.

32. *Departments of Labor and Health, Education, and Welfare Appropriations for 1980*, Hearings before a Subcommittee of the House Committee on Appropriations, 96 Cong. 1 sess. (GPO, 1979), pt. 6, pp. 231–32.

33. *Government by Proxy: (Mis?)Managing Federal Programs* (CQ Press, 1988). See also Frederick C. Mosher, "The Changing Responsibilities and Tactics of the Federal Government," *Public Administration Review*, vol. 40 (November–December 1980), pp. 541–48. (The Health Care Financing Administration, newly created in 1977, assumed responsibility for medicare from the SSA.)

In a case study of SSI, it is essential to understand why it made this anomalous—and to the SSA, very costly—choice.

Congress chose federalization initially for the family programs, perceiving that the costs of AFDC were out of control and apparently believing that a thoroughgoing federalization both of substance (eligibility and payments standards) and of administration was necessary to contain them. As of 1969–70, AFDC, even though shared with the states, was no bargain from the federal point of view. Spending on assistance had soared, and Congress's effort to contain it with grant-in-aid conditions had failed. In 1967 Congress had required states to refer able-bodied adult recipients of AFDC for work and training. Some states cooperated but others did not. "We were quite disappointed," Chairman Wilbur Mills told his House colleagues. The committee had been particularly disappointed in New York, which has "got us under the present program . . . like the fellow who has the bear by the tail going downhill." Mills's Republican counterpart on the committee, John W. Byrnes, shared this view. "The present system is completely open ended," he told the Rules Committee, referring to the fact that the federal government was obliged to support whatever number of recipients qualified for assistance under state law. "The Congress and the Federal Government are at the mercy of the States." As examples, he cited New Jersey along with New York as states where welfare payments exceeded the federal government's officially defined poverty level.[34] Mills and Byrnes hoped that a thoroughgoing federalization would reduce costs by enhancing Congress's control.[35]

Having chosen a thoroughgoing federalization for the family program, Congress then decided to do the same for the adult programs. It was encouraged to do this by executive officials, who conceived the proposal and testified that the SSA would be able to handle administration.[36] In its report of a welfare reform bill in late May 1971, largely

34. *Family Assistance Act of 1970*, Hearings before the House Committee on Rules, 91 Cong. 2 sess. (GPO, 1970), pp. 106, 136, 157.

35. In addition to the primary sources already cited, see M. Kenneth Bowler, *The Nixon Guaranteed Income Proposal: Substance and Process in Policy Change* (Ballinger, 1974), pp. 110–12.

36. M. Kenneth Bowler indicates that Mills took the initiative in federalizing the adult programs. (*Nixon Guaranteed Income Proposal*, pp. 92–93.) Because Bowler, as a congressional fellow of the American Political Science Association, had access to transcripts of the Ways and Means Committee's executive sessions, his interpretation is entitled to much credence. However, Robert M. Ball, who was intimately involved in

written by SSA staff members, the Ways and Means Committee said that it had become convinced "that successful administration of [SSI] could be achieved by utilizing the administrative structure of the Social Security Administration." On the one hand, the committee seemed satisfied that the SSA, with which it had close and respectful relations, had been given a role. On the other hand, it seemed apprehensive about mixing insurance with need-tested assistance, which SSA officials had long told them was unwise. The committee said it "emphasizes strongly its position that while a single agency might administer the programs, there is no intent to merge the new assistance program with the existing social insurance program. Each is to maintain its unique identity."[37]

The Senate Finance Committee was initially dubious. In hearings early in 1972 a few members, especially Gaylord Nelson of Wisconsin, questioned administration witnesses about the wisdom of abandoning state administration. Why did the administration favor turning manpower programs almost completely over to the states while itself choosing to take charge of welfare? Nelson asked. "All big bureaucracies become inefficient in direct ratio to their size," he observed.[38] Through June, the committee opposed a federal takeover of state administration, but after the members returned to Washington from their summer recess, they relented without public explanation.[39]

In late summer, the committee chairman, Russell B. Long, suddenly invited executive officials to propose ways to end poverty among the elderly. He was responding, apparently, to a partisan challenge or opportunity. It was a presidential election year. In a speech accepting renomination at the Republican national convention in late August, Richard Nixon had implored—or promised—his national audience to

---

the committee's deliberations, is "90 percent sure" that the idea came from HEW Under Secretary John G. Veneman and his assistant, Tom Joe. Joe confirmed that it did not come from Mills. Interview, December 30, 1988. According to Ball, "Mills and Jack Veneman developed a very close and trusting relationship. . . . They were seeing each other all the time. The ideas of one became the ideas of the other." Interview, October 31, 1988. No doubt, it is true that *within the committee*, Mills sponsored the idea.

37. *Social Security Amendments of 1971*, H. Rept. 92-231, 92 Cong. 1 sess. (GPO, 1971), pp. 157, 158.

38. *Social Security Amendments of 1971*, Hearings before the Senate Committee on Finance, 92 Cong. 1 sess. (GPO, 1971), p. 118.

39. The committee's positions may be found in *Social Security and Welfare Reform, Summary of the Principal Provisions of H.R. 1 as Determined by the Committee on Finance*, Committee Print, 92 Cong. 2 sess. (GPO, 1972), pp. 53–56; and *Social Security Amendments of 1972*, S. Rept. 92-1230, 92 Cong. 2 sess. (GPO, 1972), p. 384.

"quit treating our senior citizens in this country like welfare recipients."[40] This was an objective that appealed to Long. While he had no sympathy for AFDC recipients—partly for that reason, FAP died in the Senate in 1972—he favored generous public support for the aged. From a list of several alternative proposals that Robert Ball prepared overnight, Long chose federalization of aid to the aged, blind, and disabled—an element of the Nixon welfare reform measure, H.R. 1, that had already passed the House. Of the alternatives, it was the one that executive officials preferred. HEW Under Secretary John G. Veneman and Ball pushed for it. With the additional support of Long, who dominated the Finance Committee, it now became part of the Social Security Amendments of 1972.[41] It passed the Senate with very little attention on the floor or in conference.[42]

The ultimate administrative outcome, which not only required the SSA to administer SSI but also compelled it to administer a large volume and variety of state supplements, was not anyone's original intention or even deliberate choice. Congress arrived at that result in a series of steps, none of which alone pointed to that outcome. The suddenness of the Finance Committee's conversion to federalization may help explain why Long failed to detect the fact that the bill did not hold individual recipients harmless—a discovery that led in turn to a drastic increase in the SSA's burden of administering state supplemental payments. Long himself testified in 1973 to the committee's inadequate grasp of what it had done. "It is not the bill that we would have drafted if we had known then what we know now," he remarked.[43]

From the SSA's point of view, there was an underlying consistency in Congress's actions in both SSI and the disability review. In both, Congress's desire to get spending under control caused it to limit the SSA's autonomy. In the disability review, it did so directly, by telling the agency in detail how to carry out its business. In SSI, it did so in a far more convoluted and haphazard way. Assuming that welfare costs could be better controlled by direct federal administration (the motive of Mills and Byrnes for choosing federalization of the family programs, which then set the pattern of policy change), it uncharac-

---

40. *Public Papers of the Presidents of the United States, Richard Nixon, 1972* (GPO, 1974), p. 790.

41. Ball interview, October 31, 1988.

42. Bowler, *Nixon Guaranteed Income Proposal*, pp. 142, 147; and Vincent J. and Vee Burke, *Nixon's Good Deed: Welfare Reform* (Columbia University Press, 1974), chap. 9.

43. *Supplemental Security Income Program*, Hearing, p. 10.

teristically opted for that; but it also, quite characteristically, relied on state governments as a source of financial help in sustaining program costs. The result of these combined decisions was to sacrifice the autonomy of the SSA to the state governments, whose supplemental payments it was now obliged to administer. The fact that the form of federal-state sharing in this instance was extremely unusual does not vitiate the general point, for federal-state sharing in some form is very common and is usually the product of Congress's desire to limit the federal government's costs by taking advantage of the presence of other governments in the federal system.

CONGRESS, like the president, gives first priority to policy and political objectives. When considerations of administrative practicality threaten appealing policy choices, it turns a deaf ear. Thus it ignored administrators' pleas not to recast SSI so as to hold all individual recipients harmless against elimination of the old state public assistance programs. Correspondingly, Congress does not hesitate to give detailed commands about administrative conduct when it believes that doing so may secure a policy objective. Thus, it ordered by law a regular and comprehensive review of disability insurance cases in the hope of containing the program's costs. To assure that it gets its way, it has a propensity for setting statutory deadlines—and for setting them unrealistically on the short side.

Unlike the president, however, Congress is not by nature inclined to shape policy on a comprehensive scale. It does not value rationality and consistency as presidential policymakers do. It does not do grand designs. Rather, it is an improviser, for only in that way can it reconcile the interests of its many members. It reacts to the president's proposals, to proposals generated by its own members, to pressures of constituency opinion and organized interests—in short, to whatever political forces develop in a vast and varied society. And this means that its actions are unpredictable. Exactly what policies it chooses depends on complex political contests whose outcomes are hard to foresee. Each one is unique. Neither scientific analysis nor political experience enables anyone to predict the results with accuracy—perhaps not even in gross terms, and certainly not in the degree of detail that an administrative agency would require were it to be well prepared in advance for its tasks. The agency cannot know exactly what it will be obliged to administer until congressional action is complete.

Moreover, action is *never* complete. Constantly changing in composition, torn always between its roles as policymaker for the nation and representative of particular constituencies and constituents, responsive by nature to a society that itself constantly changes, Congress engages endlessly in lawmaking. And in doing so, it displays little independent interest in anticipating the administrative consequences of its enactments. As a habitual improviser, always ready to legislate and to revise previous legislation, it appears to lack both the capacity and the felt need to calculate administrative consequences in advance.

Insofar as an agency's environment is shaped by Congress, that environment is unstable and unpredictable. As a policymaker, Congress is bound neither by presidential advice nor its own past choices. It has a will of its own, as its extensive recasting of SSI illustrates. Yet it has an inconsistent will, illustrated by its vacillation on disability policy. Always needing to balance competing political forces and values, it is perpetually in search of the "right" compromise.

To respond to congressional guidance, an agency needs to be highly versatile—that is, capable of undertaking a variety of tasks, entailing varying degrees of discretion. It also needs to be adaptable—that is, capable of devising new routines or altering old ones very quickly. Finally, given Congress's preference for lean and cheap bureaucracy, it must be able to carry out its tasks in cooperation with other organizations, including some in the state governments.

CHAPTER 5

Agency Leaders

THE PRESIDENCY and Congress are political, in the pure sense that they respond to the electoral connection, either as imperative or opportunity. There is not much incentive for either the president or Congress to attach high importance to administrative feasibility. I now look at that part of the government where one would expect administrative considerations to be paramount—the leadership of an executive agency. There, one might expect the role of leadership to be highly contingent on the nature of the incumbent—whether newly appointed or long experienced; whether a careerist from within the agency or a political appointee from outside it; whether a managerial generalist or a program specialist.

As it happened, the nature of agency leadership was strikingly different in the two cases being analyzed, but the practical results were similar. In neither case did agency leaders insist on injecting administrative considerations into policy deliberation.

ABSENT LEADERSHIP: THE DISABILITY REVIEW

In regard to the disability review, the main thing to be said of SSA leadership is that there was none. "I wasn't there at the time," the Reagan administration's first social security commissioner, John A. Svahn, testified to Congress at the end of 1981, referring to the decision in the spring of 1981 to expedite the review.[1] The Carter administration's last commissioner, William J. Driver, had left office on January 19, 1981. President Reagan announced the choice of Svahn to succeed him in early March, and Svahn was sworn in early in May.

1. *Administration of the Social Security Program*, Hearing before the Subcommittee on Social Security of the House Committee on Ways and Means, 97 Cong. 1 sess. (Government Printing Office, 1982), p. 22.

In the interim, there was an acting commissioner: Herbert Doggette, a career civil servant who had begun with the SSA as a mail and supply clerk in 1958 and had risen to be deputy commissioner for operations. He was hardly in a position to talk back to the combined forces of Congress and the new administration, nor did anyone invite him to do so. He was not included in meetings of administration officials at which the SSA's budget was discussed.

The agency leadership during the Carter administration, when disability legislation was being framed, had asked the House Ways and Means Committee *not* to include a requirement for periodic review in the law. HEW Secretary Joseph A. Califano promised that the SSA would increase the volume of reviews, but Social Security Commissioner Stanford G. Ross, in a written elaboration of the agency's position, specifically asked for flexibility in doing so.[2]

Surprisingly, Wilbur Cohen, a former secretary of Health, Education, and Welfare who was the very personification of the social security establishment even if long out of office,[3] had spoken of the requirement with positive enthusiasm:

> I strongly support section 17 in the bill for the periodic review of the disability determination. In this bill, they provide that you ought to reexamine every person at least every 3 years. . . .
>
> Now, if you were willing to add the personnel, I would make that periodic review every year. I think the reason . . . they made it every 3 years, is because obviously, it means adding more staff.
>
> . . . if I were doing it to save money in disability, I would have more frequent periodic review of disability, and you could save more money.[4]

Cohen was testifying on behalf of Save Our Security, an organization formed in the late 1970s to lobby against cuts in social security.

Any incoming commissioner in the spring of 1981 had no choice other than to accede to a review. As a member of the Reagan administration, Svahn was bound to embrace it as a welcome gift. The General Accounting Office had issued its report recommending that

2. *Disability Insurance Legislation*, Hearings before the Subcommittee on Social Security of the House Committee on Ways and Means, 96 Cong. 1 sess. (GPO, 1979), pp. 50, 78.

3. Martha Derthick, *Policymaking for Social Security* (Brookings, 1979), pp. 52–55.

4. *Social Security Act Disability Program Amendments*, Hearings before the Senate Committee on Finance, 96 Cong. 1 sess. (GPO, 1979), p. 152.

the review be expedited, and the Reagan transition team had seen this report even before its formal release. The Heritage Foundation, a conservative think tank, had published a massive set of transition reports for the new administration, including one on the Department of Health and Human Services that called attention to the need for the disability review. It charged that the SSA had failed to make public its finding that 20 percent of the recipients were ineligible.[5]

As a prospective appointee and a veteran of earlier Republican administrations, Svahn was present for the transition and was aware of these recommendations. Despite the claim that he "wasn't there," it is very likely that he did participate in the decision to expedite the review. At the same time, much else was going on with respect to social security. The disability review was neither the most urgent nor the most controversial item on the incoming commissioner's agenda. The financial condition of the whole program claimed top priority— there was danger that it would soon go bankrupt—and the agency's data processing systems ("potentially catastrophic," the Heritage Foundation report said) also demanded attention. Once in office, Svahn became much more deeply engaged in these subjects than in the disability review.[6]

VIGOROUS LEADERSHIP: SSI

When the supplementary security income program was developing in 1969–72, the Social Security Administration could not have had more engaged leadership. Robert M. Ball had worked on building the social security program the whole of his adult life, had in effect been its chief executive since the early 1950s, and had been commissioner since 1962. He had excellent relations with Congress, especially the Ways and Means Committee, and was respected by the Republican executives in the Department of Health, Education, and Welfare, who favored keeping him in office when the Nixon White House might have preferred otherwise. After the 1972 election, the Nixon White House prevailed and Ball left in March 1973, but this was after SSI had been enacted. He was very much present while planning and enactment took place.

5. Charles L. Heatherly, ed., *Mandate for Leadership: Policy Management in a Conservative Administration* (Washington: Heritage Foundation, 1981), pp. 295, 300–01.

6. Interviews, Louis D. Enoff, deputy commissioner of social security, July 28, 1989; and Fred Schutzman, former acting deputy commissioner of social security, August 2, 1989.

In the past, Ball as commissioner had shown no great interest in having responsibility for need-tested assistance. Indeed, in 1963, shortly after he became social security commissioner, at his instigation the Welfare Administration was made an independent organizational entity within HEW separate from the SSA. This was a change from the historic arrangement, under which separate bureaus for public assistance and old-age and survivors' insurance had coexisted within the SSA. Ball often cited this as evidence that government bureaucrats are not necessarily imperialistic. It might just as plausibly have been cited as evidence that shrewd government executives do not like to be in charge of programs that are unpopular, hard to administer, and rapidly increasing in cost, all of which described welfare in the 1960s. But whatever the explanation of Ball's interest in giving up jurisdiction over welfare in 1962, it is hard to see why he would have changed his mind in the next decade. Between 1962 and 1972 welfare became more controversial and more costly.

Why, then, did Ball accept jurisdiction over SSI? Did he have no choice? Did the SSA try to stop SSI at the legislative stage? If ineffective or unwitting there, did it try later at least to buy time, delaying some or all of the program until it could get ready? And why, in negotiation with the states in 1973, did it make concessions that considerably complicated its own task?

Legislative Planning

Ball had no illusions about the difficulties of administering means-tested income support. On August 5, 1969, three days before President Nixon delivered his speech on welfare reform, Ball sent a memorandum to Secretary of HEW Robert H. Finch on the subject of administering the proposed family program, which was the centerpiece of Nixon's plan. He warned that administration would be very difficult:

> The program will be a very complicated one to administer. I do not think it is possible to develop an acceptable program of this kind that would be semi-automatic and therefore simple to administer.
>
> Some of the complications would be similar to those inherent in almost any public assistance program. . . . One major consideration is whatever plan is devised must be sensitive to frequent fluctuations in income. Probably a high proportion of the recipients who would have other income would be those who have occasional work at

varying rates of pay and with frequent changes of employer. Moreover, the earnings might often come from casual employment, which would be hard to reconstruct; there might not even be any record of the earnings.

At best, I believe there will be a fairly high rate of ineligibles on the rolls but I believe it is worth quite a bit to keep the rate as low as possible. Therefore, I believe it would be unwise to argue that administrative costs will be low. If we are to do a reasonably adequate job of paying only the right people the right amounts administrative costs will be quite high.[7]

Despite such concerns, Ball argued that if there were to be direct federal administration, the SSA, not the Internal Revenue Service, should be in charge. "It seems quite important," he wrote, "that the program be administered by an agency which is concerned with social policy issues, which has a service orientation, and which is primarily directed toward making money payments to people." He acknowledged that if the SSA were to be in charge there would be "some disadvantage to the existing social security program" because the public would tend to confuse the two no matter how strenuously the government tried in its public presentations to keep them distinct. Leaders of the social security program had always insisted on maintaining a distinction between the wage-related insurance program, in which workers "earned" benefits through "contributions," and means-tested assistance, in which it was necessary to prove dependency. In this difference, they believed, lay the great popularity of "insurance." Thus it was the potential confusion of the two activities in the public's mind, not the prospective administrative burden on the SSA, that was of most concern to Ball.

For the next several months, executive officials, including Ball, proceeded on the assumption that the SSA would administer the family assistance plan (FAP), and Ball made presentations to the Ways and Means Committee on how that would be done. The agency set up a task force late in 1969 to begin planning. Nearly twenty years later, Ball denied that he was responsible for the Ways and Means Committee's decision in 1970 to limit the SSA's role in FAP, but he acknowledged breathing a sigh of relief when it happened.[8] He was apprehensive about administering FAP, and it seems likely that the committee detected his doubts, however subtly they may have been conveyed.

7. Memo, Robert M. Ball to the secretary of HEW, August 5, 1969, author's files.
8. Interview, October 31, 1988. Subsequent quotations from Ball in this chapter are from this interview, unless otherwise cited.

Ball was much less reluctant to accept responsibility for administering SSI, but that too was not his idea. The Nixon administration's planning for welfare reform came to be dominated by John G. Veneman, the under secretary of HEW, and Tom Joe, an assistant whom Veneman had brought with him to Washington from California. Both were very liberal.[9] "They got very anxious to include the aged, blind, and disabled categories," Ball said later. The original administration proposal had called merely for strengthening the conditions attached to federal grants-in-aid to the states, a relatively cautious incremental step. "Veneman and Joe called me in," Ball recalled, "and said, 'This is what we want to do and SSA ought to administer it—what do you think?' "

Ball had mixed feelings about this proposal. As policy, he was for it. As he explained to a congressional committee several years later, SSI represented an important advance because it provided a federally guaranteed minimum income as a right, free of home liens or relative responsibility provisions such as some of the states had employed, and freed the recipients from the stigma of going to an office patronized solely by the poor.[10] In his long career at the SSA, Ball had been above all a program builder, an expounder of concepts, and designer of legislation; and SSI as conceived in the Nixon administration suited his vision of social policy.[11] From a policy point of view, it would have been incongruous, even perverse, for him to resist this nationalizing, liberalizing initiative of a Republican administration. On the other hand, he was reluctant to have the SSA take on the administration of means-tested assistance, and he anticipated that field employees would dislike doing so.

9. See Martha Derthick, *Uncontrollable Spending for Social Services Grants* (Brookings, 1975), chaps. 5, 6.

10. *Administration of the Supplemental Security Income Program,* Hearings before the Subcommittee on Oversight of the House Committee on Ways and Means, 94 Cong. 2 sess. (GPO, 1976), vol. 5, pp. 2–4.

11. In 1972, at the request of the Nixon administration, Ball wrote an essay describing the functions of the social security commissioner. He said that the principal assignment was to "manage" the agency's statutory programs, and that inherent in this basic function were the following five responsibilities: "(a) recommendations for changes in the programs themselves, (b) policy interpretation of the existing laws, (c) the setting and modification of standards of service, (d) the interpretation and explanation to the public of the philosophy and meaning of the programs, and (e) modifications in the administering institution—its methods, personnel, organizational structure, physical plant, and system of values." "Assignment of the Commissioner of Social Security," December 14, 1972. It is probably no accident that administration strictly conceived is fifth and last in this list.

Despite his reservations, Ball raised no objections, at least in public. Joe recalls his saying that the SSA was already overwhelmed, that administration of SSI would be very difficult, and that there was danger of causing a good thing to collapse. If Ball had said absolutely that the SSA could not do such a thing and if he had said it publicly, "then we couldn't have done it," Joe said years later, "but he didn't." Joe, though not unaware that means-tested assistance was very hard to administer, credited Ball's expertise and banked heavily on his administrative skill as head of the SSA—as did other participants in the planning of welfare reform. "How many of us, other than Ball, had large-scale organizational experience?" he asked rhetorically, in retrospect.[12]

Assuming federalization of the adult categories, which Veneman and Joe wanted, the logical argument for the SSA's accepting responsibility appeared compelling. As the administrator of social insurance, the SSA was already serving much of the new program's clientele; thus it would not make sense for the federal government to create an entirely new agency. Moreover, it was hard to define a defensible ground for objection. "You can't stop a program on the ground that the agency will have difficulty. You have to try to cope with it," Ball later said.[13] Besides, he had already testified that the SSA could cope with FAP. Therefore he could hardly protest that it could not handle SSI, which was much less daunting. Ball had a very high estimate of the organization's capacities. Even FAP, he believed, lay "at the outer limits" of those capacities rather than beyond them. Finally, Nixon administration officials, in promoting a presidential initiative, expected cooperation, and Ball, as the administration's appointee, owed it to them. "We couldn't say at the stage that [FAP and SSI] came to us that the president was off his rocker," Ball said in retrospect.[14]

In presenting the plan for SSA administration of SSI to the Ways and Means Committee early in 1971, Ball stressed the close complementarity of social insurance and SSI among the aged population. He testified that, while the SSA would need a much larger staff, on the

12. Interview, December 30, 1988.
13. Interview, October 31, 1988.
14. It is unlikely that the president personally ever considered SSI, but in Joe's memory the president's domestic policy staff was at least briefly involved. He recalls being summoned to the White House on a Saturday morning to be put in a room with Charles Hawkins, a veteran legislative liaison man at HEW, to write the legislative language for SSI. SSI lacked the elaborate planning process that underlay FAP, with its 200-man task force. "The only process I remember," Joe said, "was Charlie, me, Wilbur Mills, and Jack Veneman."

whole the new program "could be handled . . . on an integrated basis without major distortion of the present social security processes as long *as the broad outlines of the program are kept uniform and simple."* To be simple, it would have to be free of attempts to adapt to variations in individuals' circumstances such as local costs of living or housing status (that is, owning, renting, or residing with relatives). He proposed a gradual assumption of responsibility by the SSA, whereby it would first receive applications from persons made newly eligible. Only later, and then state by state, would it become responsible for persons already on the rolls. He drew a sharp distinction between the program for the aged and that for the disabled and blind, among whom there was much less overlap with SSA's existing clientele. There the transition would involve a "tremendous" initial work load, making it necessary "to phase this program in over a considerable period of time." It might be necessary to consider changes in the process of hearings and appeals, which was already very cumbersome and which, if simply extended to a much larger clientele, "might well create quite unmanageable appeals loads." He recommended that assumption of responsibility for the disabled and blind be undertaken only after the transition had been completed for the aged.[15] This was consistent with the recommendations that Ball had made to Under Secretary Veneman a week earlier.

As it turned out, Congress almost completely ignored his advice about the need for simplicity and phasing. Except for a provision that permitted the states to continue administering assistance during a transitional year, there is no trace in the law of his recommendations about timing. In 1976, Ball conceded that the executive branch had acceded too readily, "without argument," to many of the complications that Congress introduced in order to define the eligible population in equitable fashion. In the Senate, he had had to wage a fight even to gain the limited amount of time the SSA was given:

> During the consideration of this legislation, particularly in the Senate, we had to try very hard to get as long as 14 months. It just seemed way too long to most of the Senators who are involved in

15. "Notes for Presentation for the Ways and Means Committee on Administration of Adult Categories of Assistance by the Social Security Administration," enclosure to memo, Commissioner of Social Security to Secretary, HEW, March 9, 1971, author's files (emphasis in the original). I have no confirmation that Ball made this presentation. The committee's transcripts, which would reveal what he actually said, are closed to the public.

this. . . . We were fortunate to persuade them to have as much as 14 months.[16]

Once Congress decided to do a liberal thing for the aged, blind, and disabled, it wished to do it all at once and in a hurry.[17]

Administrative Planning

If Ball had any reservations about the wisdom of accepting responsibility for SSI, they were not conveyed to his executive subordinates at agency headquarters. As near as they could tell, he was strongly for it—and so, therefore, were they. From the start, the attitude at headquarters was that this was something the agency very much wanted to do. Discussion revolved around how. Even as difficulties mounted, there was no hesitation. "In this business," one official later observed, "you say you can do it or you lose it. He [Ball] didn't want to lose it."[18] Partly out of fear that the new program could in some sense be "lost," the agency managed to suppress or deny that any serious problems of implementation were impending. If flags of administrative warning had been raised, some part of the policy change might have been shot down.

In enacting the law, Congress had given the SSA an option of a year's delay during which the states might continue administration under interim agreements. Despite its early preference for a phased approach, the SSA leadership firmly rejected any such notion once the law was enacted. Rather, it committed the agency unequivocally to meeting the January 1, 1974, deadline and then worked as hard as was humanly possible to do so.

James B. Cardwell, a career civil servant who became commissioner in October 1973 and bore the brunt of defending the agency's actions to congressional overseers in 1974–76, found the explanation for this stance in pride and a sense of public obligation:

Here you had an agency, SSA, that had a proven record of

16. *Administration of the Supplemental Security Income Program*, Hearings, vol. 5, p. 6.

17. Ball recalled that he had not pressed for the proposals for phasing. "Nobody was very sympathetic to it." Even Ball's own deputy, Arthur Hess, took the view "that we might as well go ahead and do it. Art took the view that long lead times didn't help much."

18. Interview, Elliot Kirschbaum, former SSA associate commissioner for policy, July 27, 1989. Kirschbaum's recollection is supported by other veterans of the agency.

success, that represents the largest concentration of computer equipment and expertise in this Government—in this country, probably, and probably in the world—and the attitude was, "If anybody can do it, we can do it."

Second, you have a group of people who were conditioned to give their very best to try to get something done, and that is what they were doing. They were trying to satisfy a requirement of law. They are conditioned to carry out a complicated law. And, by hook or by crook, they were going to make it work.[19]

Reinforcing these attitudes was the commitment to SSI as progressive social policy, the latest challenge of many that the agency had faced in building a structure of social protection. "I know SSA will succeed in this next important stage of social security development," Ball wrote to employees in his last bulletin as commissioner. "I have great confidence in your capacity to carry on to new heights of achievement."[20]

In his last months as commissioner, Ball, along with his deputy, Arthur Hess (who became acting commissioner for six months in 1973 until Cardwell took over), set to turning all of the many wheels that decades of administrative experience told them must be turned. Late in January 1973 these innumerable actions were summarized in a thirty-two-page, single-spaced document that probably was prepared to inform and impress a new secretary of HEW, Caspar W. Weinberger. They included, for example, the creation of a new Bureau of Supplemental Security Income, which had just been formally approved by Weinberger's predecessor, Elliot L. Richardson, as one of his last acts in that office. It was a superbly competent document, clear and well organized, with an impressive array of decisions made and deadlines pending. It conveyed the impression of a superbly competent organization fully mobilized to meet an unalterable deadline. While the document acknowledged that the law contained the possibility of a year's delay, it dismissed this as "a last resort," adding that "all present schedules point to SSA's completing necessary activities and assuming full administration of the new program by January 1, 1974."[21] It would have been very hard for a new secretary to decide otherwise.

19. *Future Directions in Social Security*, Hearing before the Senate Special Committee on Aging, 94 Cong. 1 sess. (GPO, 1975), pt. 12, p. 989.

20. *Commissioner's Bulletin*, no. 130, February 7, 1973.

21. SSA, "Strategy for Implementation of the Supplemental Security Income Program for the Aged, Blind, and Disabled," files of Professor Beryl Radin of the University of Southern California.

Soon after this document was prepared, SSA officials met with the new HEW secretary to brief him. It must have seemed a delicate occasion. Hess spoke for the SSA in lieu of the departed Ball, whose ouster by the Nixon White House after so many years of distinguished service had shaken the agency. Weinberger, though serving the same president as his predecessors, Richardson and Finch, who had helped plan welfare reform, nonetheless represented a new regime. The second Nixon administration was more exacting in regard to the loyalty of agency heads and possibly less committed to the success of SSI. The new appointees in HEW came largely from California, where, as associates of Governor Ronald Reagan, they had opposed liberalization and federalization of welfare programs. They had a rival prescription, which would have reduced the rolls by tightening eligibility standards and reversed the trend toward nationalization. Whatever their reservations about SSI, though, they recognized it to be the law. Robert B. Carleson, who had administered the Reagan reforms in California and now was Weinberger's special assistant for welfare, acknowledged that the law left no choice.[22] The meeting in February confirmed that the SSA should proceed at full speed, pursuing the January 1 deadline. Hess had made an eloquent statement in support of doing so.[23]

In May 1973, talk of postponement arose from the states. In late April the Council of State Welfare Administrators recommended that the states continue to administer the adult programs for one year with federal reimbursement. Any state wishing to proceed with conversion would be free to do so. Some state welfare directors complained of the SSA's slowness in making policy decisions that would affect the states' choice of whether to supplement and, if so, whether to rely on federal administration. The HEW secretary's office, likewise showing impatience, prodded the SSA with a memorandum asking it to confidentially identify the states that might be interested in opting to continue administration for a year.[24] The SSA did not waver. This hint from the states that it might fail, premised on the certain knowledge that

22. Karen E. DeWitt, "Complexities and State Pressures Could Delay Welfare Responsibilities Shift to U.S.," *National Journal*, May 12, 1973, pp. 671, 674. Hess remembered Carleson as a "fifth-wheel" or "monkey wrench" because so much had to be cleared with him, but not as a saboteur. Interview, October 27, 1986.

23. Interview, Sumner G. Whittier, September 11, 1986. Whittier attended the meeting as director-designate of the new Bureau of Supplemental Security Income. A former lieutenant governor and Republican gubernatorial candidate in Massachusetts, he had been suggested for the job by Secretary Richardson, who likewise had been a Republican officeholder in Massachusetts.

24. DeWitt, "Complexities and State Pressures," p. 674.

the task was far more difficult than federal officials had been assuming, only intensified its determination to succeed. And it would argue that, no matter what some welfare directors said, the governors and state legislatures were expecting a federal takeover in January. That was the federal promise, from which there could be no turning back.[25] Weinberger insisted in two strongly worded letters to the Senate Finance Committee that there could be no delay.[26]

In addressing SSA employees in 1973, the commissioner's office showed the same confidence it showed in addressing Congress and the HEW secretary's office. A bulletin in mid-August described the progress that had been made, which was in fact impressive. Between October 1972 and July 1973, the SSA had hired about 9,000 people to administer SSI, and it was starting to hire another 6,000 permitted by the new budget. The Bureau of District Office Operations was opening branch offices at a record rate—139 in the first seven months of 1973. The Bureau of Data Processing had opened a new data input center in Albuquerque. A new IBM System 370 Model 165 had just been installed in Baltimore. An agreement had been signed with the General Services Administration to develop a high-speed telecommunications network to serve SSI by connecting district offices with the central computer complex. Minicomputers that were a critical part of this system had already been installed at two regional locations. And much more, all of which would "help millions of people in need to supplement their income and live with dignity."[27]

In addressing the states, agency headquarters likewise demonstrated confidence, even bravado. There was a meeting with state public welfare officials in late November 1973, with only a month to go before the start of the program. Sumner Whittier, director of the Bureau of Supplemental Security Income, came wearing a lapel pin that promised "we can do it." Describing the many preparations that had been made, he offered no warning of problems except to concede that unknown "land mines out there" would have to be defused by the common sense and good will of local staffs. In particular, he noted that expanded computers and a new telecommunications system were in place, and affirmed that the SSADARS system (see chapter 2) would be in place.[28]

25. See *Supplemental Security Income Program*, Hearing before the Senate Committee on Finance, 93 Cong. 1 sess. (GPO, 1973), pp. 1–7.

26. Weinberger to Russell B. Long, May 8 and June 13, 1973, author's files.

27. *Commissioner's Bulletin*, no. 136, August 14, 1973.

28. A summary of the proceedings of this meeting is in the author's files.

In short, at no point between October 1972 and January 1974 did the agency leadership reconsider its commitment to prompt, full implementation.

Negotiating with the States

As critics would later point out, the SSA would have had a much easier time with SSI if it had not agreed, as a matter of policy, to administer numerous variations in state supplements. These included variations among categories of recipients, three geographical zones within a state, and five different living arrangements. It then negotiated agreements individually with the states, which led to a different result in each one. California ended up with seventeen variations, Iowa with fifteen, and Massachusetts with twelve; a typical number was between five and nine.[29] Why did the agency compound the difficulty of its task in this way? The answer, paradoxically, sheds light on the leadership's intense commitment to achieving a national program for which the SSA would bear full administrative responsibility.

The intent of the law had been to create a program that, if not nationally uniform, would be at least essentially uniform insofar as the SSA was responsible for administering it. States could opt for federal administration of their supplements, if any, but in return were required to provide supplements to all beneficiaries and to abide by such rules as the secretary of HEW "finds necessary . . . to achieve efficient and effective administration."[30] The report of the Ways and Means Committee on H.R. 1 provided the following interpretation:

> Your committee believes . . . that the responsibility of the Federal Government in administering a State program of supplemental payments should generally be limited to administration of a basic uniform payment which does not vary according to [special needs of individual beneficiaries] and is the same throughout the State. . . .
>
> In general, it is anticipated that the same rules and regulations would be applied to both Federal [payments] and State supplemental

29. This was as of January 1983. Renato Anthony DiPentima, "The Supplemental Security Income Program: A Study of Implementation," Ph.D. dissertation, University of Maryland, 1984, p. 86. A congressional source reported that in 1976 there were eight variations in California, nine in New York, and fifteen in Massachusetts. *The Supplemental Security Income Program*, Committee Print, Senate Committee on Finance, 95 Cong. 1 sess. (GPO, 1977), p. 70.

30. 86 Stat. 1474.

payments with the only difference being the level of such payments. However, the Secretary could agree to a variation affecting only the State supplemental if he finds he can do so without materially increasing his costs of administration and if he finds the variation consistent with the objectives of the program and its efficient administration.[31]

Thus both the law and the committee report contained clear language with which the SSA could protect itself against state variations if it chose to do so. It failed to protect itself because it very much wanted the states to choose federal administration of their supplements; it wanted them to make that decision quickly, well in advance of the program's January 1, 1974, starting date; and it lacked sufficient bargaining power to induce them to do so on its own terms. As a result, it largely accepted their terms.

The SSA wanted the states to choose federal administration because the law and all of the executive's planning for effectuation of the law presumed that they should; because agency leaders believed that a national program, with the SSA in charge, was correct social policy; and because the agency's own pride and prestige were at stake. Nobody likes to be refused when offering a favor. Here the federal government was offering to perform administration better and cheaper, as the planners of welfare reform earnestly believed. For the states to decline would undermine the nationalizing objectives inherent in the law and embarrass the SSA.

In the federal-state negotiations, the states had the upper hand because the crucial choice was theirs to make, and they could make it whenever it suited them to do so. The law stipulated no deadline for their decision. States were in this favorable position because they retained prerogatives as governments in a federal system. The federal government could offer rewards and apply sanctions to induce the behavior it sought; Congress had become accustomed to doing a great deal of both. But it would have been inconsistent with the prevailing customs of federalism simply to command them to accept federal administration of their expenditures.

The SSA feared that if the states did not choose federal administration of supplements—and if they succeeded in getting Congress to

31. *Social Security Amendments of 1971*, H. Rept. 92-231, 92 Cong. 1 sess. (GPO, 1971), p. 200.

order a year's delay, during which they would administer the program with federal reimbursement—the whole effort at federalization of administration might be jeopardized. The delay might persist and even become permanent. The outcome then would be a program that was federally financed but state administered, which would have been the worst possible outcome from the SSA leadership's point of view. The SSA became very eager to avert this threat, even if at the cost of concessions to the states.[32]

Given this general set of circumstances, the SSA entered into negotiations with the states in a fundamentally disadvantageous position. Moreover, it turned out that the combination of rewards and sanctions that had been devised to induce the states to accept federal administration of their supplements was not very effective. The states had been promised that the federal government would bear the administrative costs of supplementation and that they would be "held harmless" against having to spend more than their 1972 level of spending for public assistance. Abiding by federal rules of eligibility, in other words, would not increase their costs above the existing level. This was not a good enough bargain to get them to go along. They were looking for *savings* from SSI. They were also looking for policies that would minimize disruption of their current distribution of benefits. To achieve these objectives, they sought variations in supplemental payments. This was their way of improving the bargain.

The SSA was well aware that variations would be burdensome. An internal account says, "As the number of variations increased, so too did the amount of processing time increase, training needs were greater, computer systems were more complex, less administrative control was possible, costs would increase and more staff was needed."[33] Nonetheless, it gave in. The agency's intense desire to achieve a nationalized program resulted, contrary to its own operating convenience, in a program that was largely nationalized administratively but remained quite decentralized substantively. The states developed benefit levels closely paralleling what they had had before.[34] Although this outcome was on its face perverse and contrary to the spirit of the law, it met at the time with no objection from either the HEW secretary's office

32. Kirschbaum interview.

33. "Issue: State Variations in SSI Supplementation under Federal Administration," unsigned and undated memo prepared for the SSI Study Group, files of Professor Beryl Radin of the University of Southern California.

34. DiPentima, "Supplemental Security Income Program," p. 171.

or Congress, which made no effort to buttress the SSA's basically weak negotiating position and were not showing much respect for the spirit of the law themselves.

The secretary's office no longer contained the planners of FAP and SSI, but rather was populated by new arrivals from California who thought nationalization of welfare was a mistake. Whereas their predecessors at the top of HEW had talked of uniformity, they talked of flexibility. They urged the SSA to grant variations, including those sought specifically by the state from which they had just come. Doubting their good faith, some SSA officials suspected them of preferring state administration of the new federal program.

Congress, having belatedly confronted the distressing fact that some individual beneficiaries could lose from welfare reform, decided to threaten the states with a severe sanction, loss of medicaid grants, unless they supplemented sufficiently to hold all individuals harmless— a measure that indubitably had the effect of perpetuating the old state programs. In effect, Congress mandated its own version of variations.

In one respect, Congress's decision to require supplementation was a help to the SSA. States that had been trying to decide whether to supplement now were effectively deprived of the option not to. And, once they were compulsorily engaged in supplementation, they were likely to choose federal administration of the supplements. Nonetheless, the SSA still felt the necessity of inducing the choice quickly and still made concessions to obtain it.

In addition to variations, these concessions also extended to the application of the law's provisions holding states harmless. At stake here was determination in each state of an "adjusted payment level," which under the law was the benchmark by which a state was to be held harmless. The higher its level, the better for the state. The adjusted payment level was derived from assistance payments made under the old programs, but the calculation was complex and contained many discretionary elements. Hence the level became a subject of negotiation between state officials and the SSA. A Senate Finance Committee staff report in 1976 accused the SSA of bending the law governing the levels to the states' advantage.[35]

Negotiations were decentralized, and states that were not doing as well as they liked with SSA regional officials might go over their heads

35. *Supplemental Security Income Program*, Committee Print, pp. 71–72; and Sydney E. Bernard and others, "The SSI Conversion in Michigan," Michigan Department of Social Services, Studies in Welfare Policy, no. 7, August 1975, pp. 81ff.

to the national headquarters or to HEW. According to the subsequent account of an SSA official:

> As time went on and the situation became critical, some states responded while others held out in hopes of pressuring SSA to accept certain variations which SSA had been resisting. These states gambled that it was too late for SSA to turn down their proposed variations and that SSA would not want to sustain the bad publicity and recipient fury of not getting the checks out. They continued to delay in giving SSA their variations decisions in an effort to extract further concessions, and when SSA threatened to cancel all agreements, they, in turn, threatened to tell the press and recipients that it was SSA's fault that supplement checks would not be issued on time, since SSA reneged on its agreements. Finally, on December 18, 1973, with only two weeks left before the first checks under the new program were due, SSA made certain concessions, the last of the states made its final decisions, and the checks ultimately went out on time.[36]

The last of the states to conclude an agreement—the one that reached its decision two weeks before SSI started—was California, which had been known to HEW officials for many years as a hard bargainer in intergovernmental relations, and in this case had the advantage of being the home of numerous high-ranking political appointees in HEW, including the secretary.

AGENCY LEADERSHIP that is absent, as was the case at the SSA in the transition between the Carter and Reagan administrations, is self-evidently unable to balance administrative considerations against policy goals. However, not even a thoroughly competent and effective leadership, as was that of the SSA in 1969–72, was aggressive in pressing administrative considerations on the presidency and Congress. Universally admired as articulate, Robert Ball did not do much talking back.

This was not because Ball had illusions about the inherent difficulty of administering means-tested assistance. He carefully explained some of these difficulties to Nixon officials in the earliest stages of their planning of welfare reform.

36. DiPentima, "Supplemental Security Income Program," pp. 172–73.

Ball may have had some illusions about the capacities of the organization he led. Perhaps because their experience had been so favorable for so long, the SSA's highest officials in the early 1970s had extremely optimistic expectations of the agency's ability to perform additional tasks, even ones recognized in advance to be difficult. Pride in the organization's history of accomplishment would have discouraged a dispassionate analysis of organizational strengths and weaknesses even if there had been time or an invitation from political superiors to engage in one. Such optimism, indeed, may be a prerequisite to leadership. Career officials do not rise to the top of their organizations by becoming adept at explaining to political superiors why assignments cannot be accomplished.

Yet the SSA leadership's early plan for phasing in SSI was quite astute from an administrative point of view. Had it been followed, SSI presumably would have had a smoother start. Had the agency begun by taking on responsibility only for the aged, leaving the disabled for later, and had it begun by assuming responsibility only for new applicants, leaving to the states the incumbent caseload, its tasks would have been far more manageable in the short run and there would have been time to learn and adjust. Ball did not press hard for that approach, however, perhaps because it lacked political appeal, perhaps to avoid raising doubts about the SSA's ability to do the job. In general, although he made statements of administrative caution, they were private, circumspect, and not sustained.

The leadership of the SSA took on the administration of SSI because it had no choice. It could not say "no" to a major policy initiative of the incumbent administration whose leader had acquired the right to give instructions by winning a free, competitive election. There was no way to tell him he was "off his rocker" without by implication challenging his legitimacy as head of the executive branch and without seeming to assert the superiority of administrative ends to policy and political goals. There was no way to insist on administrative objections to the plan without putting a major presidential policy initiative at risk. Agency heads do not do any of these things; rather, they "cope." Simply to function as advocate and protector of the agency as an organization is a luxury that agency heads in the U.S. government cannot afford and some might not even enjoy. In a political environment, policy objectives override administrative considerations, and the head of an executive agency who cannot accept that fact will not remain its head for very long.

At the same time, it is true that policy considerations overrode administrative ones even at the pinnacle of the agency. The SSA leadership accepted responsibility for SSI willingly, believed strongly in its correctness as social policy, and gave priority to the basic policy goal—achieving a liberalized, nationalized program—without regard to the cost in administrative convenience. In the end, the continuing power of the states in the federal system and a lack of support from the second Nixon administration and from Congress contributed to making the costs in administrative convenience very high, as the original goal of uniformity was sacrificed to the realities of federalism and to Congress's insistence that no one should lose from the policy change.

Part III
Oversight

CHAPTER 6

The Administrative Presidency

THE PRESIDENT'S powers as chief administrator are ambiguous but undeniably important. They are ambiguous because under the constitutional system of separated powers Congress and the president share control over the agencies and compete for dominance. The president derives very broad authority from the Constitution's grant of "the executive power." But nothing in the Constitution prevents Congress from passing laws that constrain the use of such power. The Constitution obliges the president "to take care that the laws be faithfully executed," but this may be construed either as a very broad grant of administrative authority or as a command to strictly respect the acts of Congress. Although the dominant strand of administrative theory in this country has tended to portray the executive branch as a hierarchy with the president as its head, in practice his right to direct the agencies is ill defined and persistently open to dispute.[1] Congressional enactments have created the principal agencies and defined their authority.

The president's powers of supervision derive from two well-estab-

1. Among numerous sources that might be cited, I have found the following to be especially helpful: Hugh Heclo, "One Executive Branch or Many?" in Anthony King, ed., *Both Ends of the Avenue: The Presidency, the Executive Branch, and Congress in the 1980's* (Washington: American Enterprise Institute for Public Policy Research, 1983), pp. 26–58; Herbert Kaufman, *The Administrative Behavior of Federal Bureau Chiefs* (Brookings, 1981), pp. 45–78; Richard M. Pious, *The American Presidency* (Basic Books, 1979), chap. 7; Herman Miles Somers, "The President, the Congress, and the Federal Government Service," in Wallace S. Sayre, ed., *The Federal Government Service* (Prentice-Hall, 1965), pp. 70–113; and James L. Sundquist, "Congress as Public Administrator," in Ralph Clark Chandler, ed., *A Centennial History of the American Administrative State* (Free Press, 1987), pp. 261–89.

lished functions. One is budgeting. Since passage of the Budget and Accounting Act of 1921, he has been responsible for preparing the government's budget, although Congress asserted a counterclaim with passage of the Congressional Budget and Impoundment Control Act of 1974. Since 1939 the executive agency with responsibility for budgeting (initially called the Bureau of the Budget and known since 1970 as the Office of Management and Budget) has formed the core of the president's permanent staff. It gives guidance to the agencies on what their budgets should include, reviews their budget submissions, and advises the president on how to respond to those submissions. Complementing its budget review functions are functions of legislative review and regulatory review, designed to ensure that the agencies do not make legislative proposals or issue regulations that are inconsistent with the president's preferences, but the budget functions have been the most stable and effective of the OMB's powers. Budget review is more penetrating and thoroughly routinized than legislative review and less controversial than regulatory review. Moreover, it has greatly increased in importance as deficits have grown and reduction of spending has seemed more exigent. The OMB has become more and more a policymaker.

The president's other important source of supervisory power is the appointment of executive officers, explicitly given to him by the Constitution. Many of his nominations must be submitted to the Senate for its advice and consent, but as a general rule it defers to his choices of executive agents. The presumption is that he can have whomever he wants in his own administration and that his appointees ought to be loyal to him. Given the dispersion of authority and power in American government, others may also make claims on their loyalty, but the president has an advantage. Constitutional tradition holds that he can remove whomever he has appointed except in the independent regulatory commissions.[2]

The presidency as supervisor of administration—the administrative presidency, as I will call it—seeks to make the agencies' actions serve

2. On the evolution and use of the appointment power, see Edward S. Corwin, *The President: Office and Powers, 1787–1957* (New York University Press, 1957), pp. 69–79; Wilfred E. Binkley, *President and Congress*, 3d rev. ed. (Vintage Books, 1962), pp. 170–77; William M. Goldsmith, *The Growth of Presidential Power: A Documented History* (New York: Chelsea House, 1983), vol. 1, pp. 157–239, and vol. 3, pp. 181–89; G. Calvin Mackenzie, *The Politics of Presidential Appointments* (Free Press, 1981); and Richard P. Nathan, *The Administrative Presidency* (Macmillan, 1983).

the president's policies. It is an instrument of control. Drawing once more on the cases of supplemental security income and the disability review, I will develop two themes in this chapter: first, that the administrative presidency's effort at control through the budget process is in tension with the policymaking presidency's urge to innovate, so that an agency must struggle to reconcile the presidency's inconsistent expectations; and, second, that the use of the appointment power to achieve control has destabilizing effects directly on agency leadership and indirectly on other attributes of the organization. In closing, I will attempt to show how, to the extent that the administrative presidency achieves its objective of control, the policymaking presidency and other external actors can realize potential opportunities to manipulate an agency's agenda.

In focusing on presidential controls, this chapter conforms to the book's purpose of analyzing the performance of the major governmental institutions in administrative matters, but it should not be mistaken for a complete account of central constraints on agency conduct. Agency hiring practices are supervised by the Office of Personnel Management; acquisition of space by the General Services Administration; and acquisition of data processing equipment by the GSA and OMB combined. In the SSI case, the Social Security Administration's relations with the GSA had an added wrinkle. Formerly the principal user of a governmentwide teletype system run by the GSA, the SSA wanted a communications system exclusively its own in order to administer SSI and had to fight with the GSA for several months to get it. These subjects will be touched on here only incidentally or not at all, even though SSA officials both at headquarters and in the field believed that constraints imposed by the various regimes of central supervision adversely affected the agency's ability to administer SSI.[3]

---

3. For a general discussion of the adverse effect of central administrative controls on federal agencies, see National Academy of Public Administration, *Revitalizing Federal Management: Managers and Their Overburdened Systems* (Washington, November 1983). For a brief discussion of the SSA's own situation in particular, see "The Social Security Administration: Management Reforms as a Part of Organizational Independence," a report of the National Academy of Public Administration in *A Plan to Establish an Independent Agency for Social Security*, Committee Print, Congressional Panel on Social Security Organization, 98 Cong. 2 sess. (Government Printing Office, 1984), pp. 69–119. A field manager told a reporter in 1977: "If you were to ask me what are the largest barriers you have to overcome in order to do an efficient job . . . you know what my answer would be? The Civil Service Commission and the General Services Administration. . . . They do not serve us. . . . It's like they're in business for themselves. And

BUDGETING

Whereas the presidency as policymaker impels innovation, the administrative presidency imposes restraint, especially in its role as budget manager. The two forces are not always and completely in opposition, however. When policy initiation takes the form of an effort to reduce expenditure, as was true in the case of the disability review, the tendencies merge: the two presidencies have acted in concert, both saying "try harder to do (and thus spend) less." Yet even in such a case, there is a lingering tension, for the administrative presidency tends to expect that the agency will try harder *with* less; one of its main goals is to limit federal employment.

In the case of SSI, the tension between these two forces was acute. Paradoxically, the policymaking presidency was sponsoring a major new assumption of responsibility by the federal government while the administrative presidency was simultaneously insisting on a reduction of federal employment. Toward the close of 1971, less than a year before SSI was enacted, the Office of Management and Budget ordered that federal employment be reduced by 5 percent by June 30, 1972, and that federal agencies reduce the average grade level of their employees. Although the president's staff never expected the SSA to take on the task of administering need-tested income assistance with *no* added staff, in various ways presidential influence worked to keep the numbers artificially low.

Perhaps in an effort to satisfy departmental and presidential expectations, the SSA made the highly implausible assumption that SSI cases would take the same amount of staff time as retirement insurance cases. The SSA estimated that developing an initial SSI claim would take an hour of work; in fact, it turned out to take more than four. Redeterminations of eligibility were expected to take about half an hour; experience showed that they required more than two hours. The SSA expected that one out of five recipients would come to a district office during the year for a postentitlement action; experience showed that one out of three did so. The SSA also erred in supposing that the program would serve mainly aged recipients, who were expected to

---

their sole preoccupation is to keep themselves in power without rendering service." The reporter encountered "one horror story after another" about problems in hiring workers and getting office equipment and space. Haynes Johnson, "Days of Endless Struggle, Drowning in a Sea of Paper," *Washington Post*, March 27, 1977, p. 1.

constitute three-fourths of the caseload. Instead the disabled were predominant among new claimants and recipients of new awards, and they would soon become predominant in the total caseload. This was important, because they were a harder population to serve than the aged.[4]

The executive branch's initial request to Congress was for 15,000 additional SSA employees to administer SSI. At this point the influence of the OMB is immediately visible. The secretary of Health, Education, and Welfare had supported an SSA request for 18,000 additional persons, 15,000 of them in fiscal year 1973 and the remaining 3,000 in 1974. After meetings with the OMB, the request was scaled back to 15,000: 9,000 to be added in 1973 and the remaining 6,000 in 1974.[5] This was about half the number of employees being used by the states for comparable purposes, but no one in the federal executive branch seemed to find it implausible that a federal agency would or should be twice as efficient. This reflected a general hubris as well as the stringency normally imposed by the OMB.

After SSI began, it soon became apparent that the 15,000 new staff members were far less than the SSA would need, but the OMB's reluctance to authorize new staff inhibited a response. In mid-1974 the SSA submitted a request to HEW for authority to hire 12,000 more permanent employees. Several months of negotiations within the executive branch culminated in a decision in mid-December 1974 to permit 10,000 new positions on the condition that they be temporary. The OMB was unconvinced that the SSA would need so many employees for the indefinite future. The administrative troubles of SSI persisted, negotiations continued, and in March 1975 the SSA received permission to hire 4,000 persons as temporaries and 6,000 as "term" employees, meaning that their appointments would be limited to two

4. *The Supplemental Security Income Program*, Committee Print, Senate Committee on Finance, 95 Cong. 1 sess. (GPO, 1977), p. 39. In an interview more than fifteen years later, Millie Tyssowski, who had been the SSA's budget officer at the time, recalled "considerable pressure" from departmental and OMB officials. She believed, without having a distinct recollection, that the SSA had made allowance for the need-based nature of SSI, contrary to what the Finance Committee's staff report said. Interview, August 26, 1988.

5. *Future Directions in Social Security*, Hearing before the Senate Special Committee on Aging, 94 Cong. 1 sess. (GPO, 1975), pt. 12, pp. 991–92; *Administration of the Supplemental Security Income Program*, Hearings before the Subcommittee on Oversight of the House Committee on Ways and Means, 94 Cong. 2 sess. (GPO, 1976), vol. 3, pp. 20–21; and Robert M. Ball, "Assignment of the Commissioner of Social Security," December 14, 1972, p. 36 (copy in author's files).

years. That made them temporaries of longer than usual duration. The presidency was clinging to its original hope that SSI could be made simple to administer and persisting in its determination to limit federal employment.[6]

Having to rely on temporary employees made it hard for the SSA to develop proficiency. Candidates for federal employment were reluctant to apply for these jobs in the SSA, or they left quickly in favor of permanent jobs, taking with them whatever skills they had managed to acquire. Although term employees could convert to permanent status as vacancies opened up, turnover rates ran around 40 percent as of 1976.[7] Worse, sometimes trained temporary or term employees did not leave voluntarily, but were terminated at the insistence of the Civil Service Commission (predecessor to the OPM) because their appointments had expired, to be replaced by new, untrained temporaries.[8] Even veteran employees of the SSA suffered from lack of training. In the initial crush of the program, there was insufficient time for it. The heavy reliance on temporary employees compounded this underlying deficiency.

Eventually, the OMB became persuaded that much of the SSA's need was genuine and enduring, and in January 1976 the agency was given permission to convert term employees to permanent status provided that they were legitimately available from a civil service register. (The Civil Service Commission insisted that their experience should give them no competitive advantage, and again persons with experience were terminated.) The authorized number of the agency's permanent employees rose from 72,000 to 80,000 between 1976 and 1977.[9] Thus the SSA received half of what it asked for after a wait of more than two years—years that were critical in the founding of the program.

The effort of the administrative presidency to economize on personnel is interwoven with the whole history of the two cases and links them. Pressure to reduce federal employment in 1972 led to the SSA's decision to greatly reduce the practice of "postadjudicative" review of disability cases. Initially it had employed a case-by-case review of all

6. *Supplemental Security Income Program*, Committee Print, p. 40; and *Future Directions in Social Security*, Hearing, pt. 12, p. 993.
7. *Administration of the Supplemental Security Income Program*, Hearings, vol. 3, pp. 14, 20.
8. *Supplemental Security Income Program*, Committee Print, p. 41.
9. *Supplemental Security Income Program*, Committee Print, p. 42.

disability determinations by the state agencies. Gradually it allowed the proportion of reviews to drop as the program grew and its supervisory relation with the state agencies matured, so that by 1972 the proportion planned for review was down to 60 percent from 100 percent. Then, under the combined pressure of heavy work loads and the OMB's insistence on reducing employment, the agency switched to a 5 percent sample, a change that congressional analysts would later conclude was one contributing cause of the sharp rise in the disability caseload in the mid-1970s.[10] In the Disability Amendments of 1980, Congress mandated a phased restoration of the earlier level of review.

As the postadjudicative review fell victim to the combined effects of rising work loads and rising pressures for economy, so too did routine redeterminations of eligibility for disability insurance. Under the impact of SSI, the SSA and the state disability determination agencies fell behind in their schedule of reviews. In particular, there was a sharp drop-off in reviews in 1974. Noting this, the House Ways and Means Committee began to urge a restoration of effort as one way of controlling disability costs. In turn, the SSA, responding to the rising pressure from the committee, included in its proposed fiscal 1980 budget a request to hire more staff for use in reviews of disability eligibility. The OMB sharply reduced this request.[11] After Congress in 1980 mandated periodic reviews, the SSA estimated that this would require the addition of 1,000 state agency employees at federal expense. States would soon complain that the federal government had failed to make the necessary commitment of funds.[12] Moreover, in numerous states, governors and their budget offices, which shared the economizing perspective of the president and the OMB, had imposed moratoriums on hiring.[13]

10. *Departments of Labor and Health, Education, and Welfare Appropriations for 1973*, Hearings before a Subcommittee of the House Committee on Appropriations, 92 Cong. 2 sess. (GPO, 1972), pt. 5, pp. 61–62; and *Committee Staff Report on the Disability Insurance Program*, Committee Print, House Committee on Ways and Means, 93 Cong. 2 sess. (GPO, 1974), pp. 27–30.

11. Statement of William J. Driver in *Social Security Financing Issues*, Hearings before the Subcommittee on Social Security of the House Committee on Ways and Means, 97 Cong. 1 sess. (GPO, 1981), p. 163.

12. *Status of the Disability Insurance Program*, Committee Print, Subcommittee on Social Security of the House Committee on Ways and Means, 97 Cong. 1 sess. (GPO, 1981), p. 39.

13. *Oversight of Social Security Disability Benefits Terminations*, Hearing before the Subcommittee on Oversight of Government Management of the Senate Committee on Governmental Affairs, 97 Cong. 2 sess. (GPO, 1982), p. 197.

APPOINTMENTS

The president appoints the commissioner of social security, subject to confirmation by the Senate. Assuming that presidents use the opportunity latent in the appointment power, one would expect commissioners to change at least as often as party control of the presidency changes. Beyond that, one might expect change with any change in presidents regardless of party, on the supposition that a president would want to name his own commissioner to assure personal as well as partisan loyalty. One might even expect change at least every four years, on the supposition that a president who won reelection would want to renew his administration with fresh appointments. Any of these assumptions, however, would considerably understate the amount of change that took place in the period embracing the two cases under analysis here.

Between October 1972, when SSI was authorized, and October 1984, when Congress passed a law that closed the most turbulent phase of the disability review, the leadership of the SSA was constantly in flux. There were nine commissioners or acting commissioners (not counting an acting commissioner who served only two days).

Commissioner	Took office	Left office
Robert M. Ball	4/17/62	3/17/73
Arthur Hess (acting)	3/27/73	10/4/73
James B. Cardwell	10/24/73	12/12/77
Don Wortman (acting)	12/12/77	9/27/78
Stanford G. Ross	10/5/78	12/31/79
Herbert Doggette (acting)	1/1/80	1/3/80
William J. Driver	1/3/80	1/19/81
Herbert Doggette (acting)	1/19/81	5/6/81
John A. Svahn	5/6/81	9/12/83
Martha A. McSteen (acting)	9/14/83	6/26/86

The practical result of the presidential appointment process was not so much to supply leadership to the SSA as to deprive it of any. Assuming that an appointee is new for a year, the SSA had a new leader or no formally approved leader for well over half the time in the twelve-year period of this analysis. Voids occurred predictably following an election. An acting commissioner was named while the newly elected administration searched for an appointee, and this meant that the agency lacked experienced and authoritative leadership at precisely the time when the momentum of policy change was greatest. David Stockman, who as director of the OMB masterminded the

Reagan administration's budget cutting in 1981, later wrote that his success within the executive branch was due in large part to vacancies in the agencies: "[The] White House personnel operation was overwhelmed with several thousand slots to fill. As a result there were empty desks all over Washington. Most cabinet secretaries hadn't even yet gotten their top policy deputies approved."[14] However, the voids were by no means limited to these periods of postelection transition.

Frequent changes in leadership are likely to mean changes in kind of leadership. Some of the eight persons who were named, formally or informally, to head the agency between 1973 and 1984 were political appointees in the sense that they had had careers in the private sector and earned appointment through activity on behalf of a party or individual politician; others were career civil servants without being specialists in social security; others, predominant though not universal among the acting commissioners, were career civil servants with backgrounds in the SSA. At least one was deliberately chosen from outside the SSA "to take a hard look at the program," in the words of the HEW secretary who recommended him to the president.[15]

Frequent changes in leadership are also likely to mean frequent changes in the leadership's immediate subordinates. Commissioners appoint other executives, and the instability at the very top in this period was reproduced just below the top. It is hard to measure how fast incumbents in particular offices changed, however, because offices themselves were rapidly redefined through reorganization. In combination with appointments, commissioners were using changes in organizational structure in an effort to improve their control over the SSA.

Historically, the major subunits within the SSA were focused on benefit programs. The core unit was the Bureau of Old Age and Survivors Insurance (BOASI, later renamed Retirement and Survivors Insurance, or BRSI). After disability insurance was enacted in 1956, a Division of Disability Operations was created within the BOASI, headed by an assistant bureau director to whom the director delegated much of the responsibility for the disability insurance program.

14. Stockman goes on to explain that as a result cabinet secretaries were forced to rely on veteran civil servants for support in budget discussions, and he illustrates how, tactically, the Reagan White House was able to limit the influence of these career officials. *The Triumph of Politics: How the Reagan Revolution Failed* (Harper and Row, 1986), p. 110.

15. Joseph A. Califano, Jr., *Governing America: An Insider's Report from the White House and the Cabinet* (Simon and Schuster, 1981), p. 393.

Divisions of program analysis, claims policy, personnel, training, accounting operations, and field operations, among others, were subsumed within this basically program-oriented bureau. Later, disability insurance became the responsibility of a separate bureau, as did health insurance after the enactment of medicare in 1965, but in the short run, the increase in the number of program-oriented units only reinforced the basic organizational principle. Each of these bureaus was responsible for policy development and evaluation and management of operations for its particular program. A record-keeping and data processing unit served all three program units, as did a single field organization. Also located in the commissioner's office were crosscutting staff units for agencywide program evaluation and planning, research, actuarial analysis, public affairs, and administration, but the program-oriented bureaus were the center of gravity, and most employees identified strongly with them.[16]

When SSI was enacted, a program-oriented unit was once again created: the Bureau of Supplemental Security Income (BSSI), which was theoretically in charge of that program, but it was weak, poorly integrated with the overall organization, and unable to take the lead in support of the new activity. From the perspective of the field offices, the result was chaos. The Bureau of Data Processing, not BSSI systems staff, dominated planning for data processing; Bureau of District Operations planners, rather than those in the BSSI, made decisions about field operations; the BOASI and Bureau of Disability Insurance staff similarly dominated where their interests intersected with those of the BSSI. Because the White House and HEW, prime movers in welfare reform, continued for some months to take an interest in planning for SSI, the bureau director, Sumner G. Whittier, as a political appointee, looked to them as well as to the SSA commissioner for guidance.[17]

The program-oriented structure did not survive the 1970s. In 1975 a commissioner appointed from outside the SSA submerged the separate program bureaus under a new unit, the Office of Program Operations, and so reduced them in size that they lost much of their capacity for independent functioning. The aim, he explained to Congress, was to

16. This discussion of organization is based almost entirely on Jack S. Futterman, "Report to the National Commission on Social Security: The Social Security Administration's Recent Reorganizations and Related Administrative Problems," July 28, 1980 (copy in author's files).

17. Jack S. Futterman, "A Two-Level Review: SSA Organization for Administering SSI; SSA's Organization as a Whole," March 1, 1974, pp. 22–24, copy in author's files.

deprive the separate programs of their separate managements and to put all cash benefit programs under unified direction.[18]

Before this reorganization had been fully effectuated and absorbed, another followed in 1979. President Carter's first secretary of HEW, Joseph A. Califano, upon taking office in 1977, was strongly committed to curbing fraud, waste, and abuse, to proving that the department and its various components could be managed, and specifically to restoring "program and fiscal integrity to social security," which at the time was threatened with financial insolvency.[19] One of the first major pieces of domestic legislation the Carter administration had to deal with was Social Security Act amendments in 1977, which rescued the program with the largest peacetime tax increase in the country's history. This experience heightened Califano's interest in achieving control of the agency, and reorganization was one of the means his choice for commissioner, Stanford G. Ross, used to that end.

Ross broke up what remained of the program-oriented subunits and organized the agency into functionally designated parts, under associate commissioners for public affairs, governmental affairs, policy, management, budget and personnel, assessment, systems, and operational policy and procedures. A majority of these units, including both the Office of Assessment and the Office of Policy, were placed under persons who were not career officials in social security. One goal was to force issues up to the commissioner for decision.[20]

This organizational turbulence, besides being traceable to the turnover in the commissioner's office, was largely a consequence of the SSA's troubles in administering SSI. One of the main purposes of the first reorganization was to improve the integration of SSI with other cash benefit programs and to fix a locus of responsibility for it. Subsequently, as the financial troubles of the program deepened, the effort at reorganization evolved (in combination with use of the

18. *Departments of Labor and Health, Education, and Welfare Appropriations for 1976*, Hearings before a Subcommittee of the House Committee on Appropriations, 94 Cong. 1 sess. (GPO, 1975), pt. 4, p. 373.

19. Califano, *Governing America*; Robert Sherrill, *Why They Call It Politics: A Guide to America's Government*, 3d ed. (Harcourt Brace Jovanovich, 1979), p. 204; and *Disability Insurance Legislation*, Hearings before the Subcommittee on Social Security of the House Committee on Ways and Means, 96 Cong. 1 sess. (GPO, 1979), p. 46.

20. Futterman, "Report to the National Commission on Social Security," pp. 18–22; and General Accounting Office, *Social Security Administration: Stable Leadership and Better Management Needed to Improve Effectiveness*, HRD-87-39 (March 1987), pp. 56–57. The GAO report describes the SSA's current organizational structure and criticizes the emphasis on function.

appointment power) to emphasize the administrative presidency's purpose of attaining control over all of the SSA's activities, especially policy development and evaluation. This effort at control helped produce the administrative debacle of 1981–84.

THE SSA AGAINST ITSELF

It is a remarkable fact that the finding of very high error rates for the disability insurance program in 1980–81—rates on which the Reagan administration eagerly seized in its search for big and quick budget savings—came not from the GAO, whose report broadcast the data and was typically cited as the source, but from the SSA. These were the first returns from pilot studies that the SSA did in an effort to create a quality control procedure for disability insurance.

Historically, the SSA had not systematically produced, let alone disseminated, data on its own errors. The program-oriented bureaus were charged with assessing their own activities. Sophisticated quality control activity, complete with published error rates, arrived at the SSA in the mid-1970s via the back door of SSI. In conjunction with administration of welfare grants, in the early 1970s HEW had imposed on state governments a quality control program, employing a case-sampling procedure, that was designed to reveal errors in payments. The premise was that if the states failed to attain an acceptable standard, HEW would penalize them by reducing their grants.[21] When, with passage of SSI, the SSA became an administrator of welfare programs, superseding the states for that purpose in the "adult" categories, it too was impelled to employ the quality control procedures. Ironically, this was done largely at the insistence of the states. Many of them, at the federal government's invitation, were using the SSA to administer their supplemental payments, and they insisted that they would not reimburse the federal government for any such payments that the SSA made in error, for example, through faulty determinations of eligibility. "What is sauce for the goose, I think, is sauce for the gander," Commissioner James B. Cardwell explained to Congress, summarizing the states' position.[22]

21. "Controlling AFDC Error Rates," Kennedy School of Government Case Program, C14-80-302 (Harvard University, 1980).

22. *Oversight of the Supplemental Security Income Program*, Hearings before the Subcommittee on Oversight of the House Committee on Ways and Means, 94 Cong. 2 sess. (GPO, 1976), pp. 27–28; *Administration of the Supplemental Security Income Program*, Hearings, vol. 3, pp. 17–18; and *Supplemental Security Income Program*, Committee Print, pp. 49–53.

What was sauce for the goose of SSI then turned out to be sauce as well for the gander of the insurance programs. The publication of error rates for SSI highlighted the absence of such data for retirement and survivors' and disability insurance. In the mid-1970s oversight agencies in both the executive branch (the HEW Inspector General's Office) and the legislative branch (the General Accounting Office) began charging, somewhat incongruously, that there were huge but unknown amounts of waste, fraud, and abuse in the SSA's programs. A report in 1979 by the newly established Office of the Inspector General was especially important. Its suggestion that as much as $1.6 billion was misspent annually by the SSA was picked up by newspapers, notably the *Los Angeles Times*, which rounded the figure to $2 billion annually.[23]

Commissioner Ross responded that the SSA did not know how much it might be misspending but was determined to find out. "It is my belief that we should not be afraid to discuss our shortcomings openly," he told Congress. He explained that one of the major purposes of his reorganization was to bring a number of hitherto fragmented quality assessment activities together into one "inspector-general type" operation of the SSA's own. The purpose of this unit, the Office of Assessment, would be to ferret out mistakes. It would begin by developing basic data on error rates in the programs of retirement and survivors' and disability insurance, an effort for which planning had begun in 1976–77.[24] To head this office as associate commissioner for assessment, Ross chose Fred Schutzman, not a career SSA employee but an engineer recruited from the private sector in the mid-1970s for

23. The HEW Inspector General's office originated in Congress, but it was the first inspector general and the secretary who appointed him, Joseph A. Califano, who decided in the spring of 1977 that the office's first report would be an inventory of fraud, waste, and abuse in HEW's programs. Developed independently by the inspector general and released to Congress without the secretary's having had a chance to review it, the report got more publicity than either of them initially anticipated. This story is recounted in "Fraud, Abuse, and Waste at HEW," Kennedy School of Government Case Program, C14-80-337 (Harvard University, 1980). The HEW Inspector General's office has not consistently been an important source of oversight for the SSA. For a GAO report of the period, see General Accounting Office, *The Social Security Administration Should Provide More Management and Leadership in Determining Who Is Eligible for Disability Benefits*, HRD-76-105 (August 1976).

24. *Administrative Integrity of the Social Security Program*, Hearing before the Subcommittee on Social Security of the Senate Committee on Finance, 96 Cong. 1 sess. (GPO, 1979), pp. 8–9; and *Staff Data and Materials Related to the Social Security Disability Insurance Program*, Committee Print, Senate Committee on Finance, 97 Cong. 2 sess. (GPO, 1982), p. 41.

his management skills. His first appointment in the SSA, in 1976, had been as director of the Office of Financial Management.

In 1979 and 1980 the SSA's Office of Assessment conducted a pilot study of the disability insurance program based on 3,154 cases randomly selected from all cases active as of April 1979. It concluded that in more than 20 percent of these cases the recipients were either ineligible or were receiving benefit payments higher than they were entitled to. As the term "pilot study" suggested, this was a first attempt at data gathering—a trial run that was to precede establishment of a routine procedure.[25] Limitations in the data were acknowledged, but the report imperfectly acknowledged—indeed, by its very existence denied—the biggest limitation of all, which lay in the extreme procedural and substantive confusion surrounding the criteria for determining eligibility. Any report on eligibility rates was bound to be misleading if it did not make clear that there had developed *two* systems for determining eligibility: that employed by the state agencies, using the SSA's policy manual as guidance and written submissions as sources of evidence, and that employed by the administrative law judges, which used more general criteria of law and regulation and drew on personal testimony of the applicants, often accompanied by lawyers, in addition to written submissions. The caseload contained so many persons who qualified through the second, more permissive, of these two systems that it was bound to show a high rate of error if judged by a review procedure that in effect replicated only the first of them, as did the pilot study.

Development of an assessment staff that was truly independent of operating units divided the agency internally and put program operators on the defensive, with a whole series of ramifications in the disability case. It meant that the agency generated data for consumption and dissemination by external critics, the GAO preeminently on this occasion. The evaluators told the outside world that the operators were doing a bad job. The GAO then transmuted the findings of the evaluators into its own findings. Program operators then made an exaggerated response, different in character from what would have been made to purely internal signals. "When you get a report from GAO that says over 20 percent of the people on the rolls don't qualify, it suggests you'd best get moving," SSA's deputy director of disability programs told a reporter.[26] Memories of congressional and press criticism when SSI began were still fresh at agency headquarters and probably heightened the sensitivity; officials did not wish to undergo another public flogging for waste and error.

There were dissenters who argued the defects of the data in the pilot study and warned that by succumbing to frenzy the SSA was risking the well-being of its clients and its own reputation. The issue was not whether to conduct a review—the law left no choice about that—but the dissenters would have done it more cautiously. The law left the agency some discretion, in that it prescribed review of those cases not classified as permanently disabled. The agency could define the group that would be subject to review more or less broadly. It began by defining it very broadly and undertook a narrowing only as the review ran into trouble.

No matter how operating officials responded to external criticism, the presence of a rival, critical perspective *within* the agency heightened its potential responsiveness to political overseers in search of cost savings. Schutzman, whose Office of Assessment had produced the findings about the rate of ineligibility, was serving as acting deputy commissioner for operations in the spring of 1981. From that position, he argued for aggressive implementation of the review. Even if the 20 percent figure for ineligibility was too high, even if the rate was only half or one-fourth as much, the review still needed to be done in a comprehensive and expeditious way, he contended. In March he signed the crucial memo giving regional commissioners instructions about the accelerated review.[27]

The SSA had indeed created its own inspector-general-type activities, had indeed been candid and self-critical, had indeed been made accountable and responsive to the administrative presidency. The result was the headlong plunge of 1981 into the disability review. Significantly, the large scale and rapid speed of the review were not forced on an unwilling agency, despite the existence of dissenters. There was enough support for the review from career officials to give the Reagan

26. Morrow Cater, "Trimming the Disability Rolls—Changing the Rules during the Game?" *National Journal*, September 4, 1982, p. 1513.

27. *Oversight of Social Security Disability Benefits Terminations*, Hearing, p. 151. The memorandum spoke of a "large scale effort" that was intended to produce "large savings to the trust fund." My account of the SSA's internal reactions to the disability review draws mainly on interviews with Schutzman and with Nelson Sabatini, former deputy commissioner of SSA for management and assessment, on August 2, 1989, and on the agency's comments in General Accounting Office, *More Diligent Followup Needed to Weed Out Ineligible SSA Disability Beneficiaries*, HRD-81-48 (March 3, 1981), app. 2.

administration all the cooperation it could have wanted. Some of this cooperation stemmed from career civil servants' sense that it was proper, or prudent, to follow political direction, but to a considerable extent the foundations of it had been laid by political executives through reorganizations and appointments designed precisely to make the agency more responsive to such direction.

THERE IS A GAP in American government between what agencies are asked to do and the resources they are given to do it. This gap begins, so to speak, "at home," in the executive branch. Whereas the policymaking presidency impels innovation and hence enlargement of tasks, the administrative presidency, embodied in the OMB, works to contain budgetary costs. Especially in the case of SSI, the conflict between the two presidencies was acute. The SSA was strained to reconcile the two forces.

Nonetheless, the two presidencies tend to reinforce each other tactically. To the extent the administrative presidency succeeds in achieving control over an agency through appointments and ancillary tactics such as reorganization, it creates opportunities for the policy-making presidency to act, as in the disability review, by exposing causes for action.

Less obviously, there is a reciprocal effect. The initiatives of the policymaking presidency, to the extent they enlarge agency missions, are likely to reduce agency autonomy. The more the agency does, the more attention it is likely to get from other actors and the more opportunities arise for them to involve themselves in its activity. Additional activities promoted from outside the agency, as by the policymaking presidency, are more likely than those promoted from within to prove incompatible with existing missions and to destabilize the prevailing pattern of agency relations with other actors, producing losses of the agency's control over its affairs.

SSI had a profoundly destabilizing effect on the SSA. The agency's poor initial performance and its permeability in this program to the influence of the state governments invited and facilitated intense scrutiny from the administrative presidency. The effects then spilled over into all of the agency's other activities—and were powerfully reinforced, as it happened, by the financial shortages that began to afflict social security generally in the mid-1970s. These shortages had themselves been deepened by SSI, insofar as it contributed to the unexpected explosion of the disability insurance program.

CHAPTER 7

The Courts

THE POTENTIAL for conflict between courts and agencies is great because their functions are similar. Martin Shapiro has argued that appellate courts, at least, are very difficult to distinguish in function from the administrative bureaucracy. Both supplement general statutes with explanatory rules in order to provide adequate guides for the making of myriad specific decisions in individual cases. Except that judges are generalists, ignorant of any particular policy area, while administrators are expert specialists in their programs, Shapiro detects little significant difference between them.[1]

The more filling in of statutes that the courts do, the greater the costs to the administrative agency in uncertainty, disruption of routines, more exacting standards of performance, adverse publicity, and added assignments—often with deadlines—for which appropriations may not be available.[2] Also, because courts are numerous (there are ninety-three federal district courts and twelve circuit courts), their rulings may be uncoordinated and thus difficult to manage for an agency that seeks to have uniform policies.

In addition to their filling in of statutory law, courts engage in constitutional interpretation. Especially important for administrative agencies is their interpretation of the Constitution's guarantee that individuals may not be deprived of life, liberty, or property without due process of law. The scope of an agency's duties is likely to depend heavily on judicial definitions of due process.[3]

1. Martin Shapiro, *The Supreme Court and Administrative Agencies* (Free Press, 1968), pp. 44–95.
2. For an extended, well-documented account of the costs to one agency (the Environmental Protection Agency), see R. Shep Melnick, *Regulation and the Courts: The Case of the Clean Air Act* (Brookings, 1983).
3. Jerry L. Mashaw, *Due Process in the Administrative State* (Yale University Press, 1985).

In their role as interpreters of statutory and constitutional law, courts significantly enlarged the administrative burden of supplemental security income on the Social Security Administration, while in the disability review the agency ended up virtually in judicial receivership. In this chapter I analyze the agency-court interactions that bore most directly on the initial implementation of SSI and the conduct of the disability review. This is by no means an exhaustive account of relations between the federal courts and the SSA even in regard to SSI and disability insurance, let alone more generally.[4]

DUE PROCESS REQUIREMENTS IN SSI

Enacted late in 1972 and initiated on January 1, 1974, SSI came in the wake of *Goldberg* v. *Kelly*, a landmark case of constitutional and administrative law that the Supreme Court decided in 1970.[5] The case arose out of the program of aid to families with dependent children in New York. Its core finding was that the due process clause of the Fourteenth Amendment requires that public assistance recipients have the opportunity of an evidentiary hearing *before* termination of their benefits. The city of New York (Goldberg was the city's commissioner of social services) contended that constitutional requirements of due process were met by the opportunity for a hearing after termination occurred and by the informal pretermination review of the case. In rejecting this argument, the Supreme Court laid down a very exacting standard of agency performance, closely approximating judicial procedures. The *Goldberg* requirements included an impartial decision-maker; timely and adequate notice to claimants; their right to be represented by an attorney; the opportunity to confront adverse witnesses, to present oral arguments and evidence, and to cross-examine adverse witnesses; disclosure of opposing evidence; a statement of reasons for the agency's determination and of the evidence relied on; and reliance on the legal rules and evidence adduced at the hearing as the basis for the determination.

In the short run—as long as state governments remained responsible

4. For a comprehensive analysis of judicial relations with the SSA in the disability program, see Susan Gluck Mezey, *No Longer Disabled: The Federal Courts and the Politics of Social Security Disability* (Greenwood Press, 1988); and Jerry L. Mashaw and others, *Social Security Hearings and Appeals: A Study of the Social Security Administration Hearing System* (Lexington Books, 1978), chap. 5.

5. 397 U.S. 254 (1970); see the discussion in Lief H. Carter, *Administrative Law and Politics: Cases and Comments* (Little, Brown, 1983), pp. 125ff.

for administering means-tested assistance—*Goldberg* v. *Kelly* had no effect on the SSA, but when SSI was enacted, it had the incidental effect of bringing the rights revolution home to the federal agency. Falling heir to state public assistance programs, the SSA also fell heir to *Goldberg* standards.

The SSA's rules regarding reduction or termination of SSI benefits, while conforming generally to the *Goldberg* criteria, provided for three exceptions to the requirement of advance notice and an evidentiary hearing. The usual procedure need not be followed, they said, when the decrease in benefits resulted from: (1) a change in federal law; (2) clerical or mechanical error, or (3) facts supplied by the recipient, provided they were complete and not subject to conflicting interpretations. These exceptions were challenged, and in 1975 the district court in the District of Columbia struck all of them down in *Cardinale* v. *Mathews*, finding that they violated the constitutional requirement of due process as interpreted in *Goldberg* and its successors.[6] The court's opinion shows how much judicial reasoning was at odds with executive reasoning, specifically that of the presidential planners of SSI. The judiciary would not tolerate or trust the simplified, automated program that they intended to create.

One of the principal arguments for adoption of SSI was that it would take advantage of economies of scale and of the superior data processing capacities of a national agency, making administration more efficient. More specifically, it would facilitate the coordination of income support programs through computer interfaces. For example, if recipients of SSI received an increase in social security benefits (and well over half of them were social security recipients), computers would automatically reduce their SSI payments by a corresponding amount. The SSA's rules exempted such reductions from *Goldberg* requirements because they were not inherently problematic and in order to realize the newly created potential for efficiency. The SSA told the court that to interject *Goldberg* rights into such benefit adjustments would make the computers useless and require manual handling of each claim. The court was completely unsympathetic to this argument. It responded that the SSA had no right to implement an across-the-board change in benefits "without . . . explaining [itself] to every recipient," and that the agency had overlooked the possibility

6. The full text of *Cardinale* v. *Mathews* is in *Administration of the Supplemental Security Income Program*, Hearings before the Subcommittee on Oversight of the House Committee on Ways and Means, 94 Cong. 2 sess. (Government Printing Office, 1976), vol. 3, pp. 98–110.

that its automatic, computerized adjustments might err in individual cases. To preclude this result, the full *Goldberg* procedure must apply.

The court was not more persuaded of the legitimacy of the SSA's other two exceptions. If machine malfunctions and keypunching errors sometimes caused the SSA to err in determining benefits, there was no reason to suppose that the attempts at correction would not themselves err, it said. One of the functions of *Goldberg* was to protect the individual from factual mistakes. Finally, the court concluded that even where the agency acted on the basis of facts supplied by the beneficiary, there was no legitimate ground for an exception to *Goldberg*. That facts came from the beneficiary did not necessarily make them accurate, it said. Besides, in the absence of elaborate due process requirements, there was no guarantee that the agency would not misapply the law to the facts.

The SSA was reduced to pleading with the court to at least allow it to stop one check in cases where it was erroneously sending two and to let it reduce payments to the maximum legal amount. Thus, for example, if $157.70 a month were the legal maximum for an individual payment, the SSA asked to be allowed to reduce payments it discovered to be above that amount. The court acceded to the first of these requests on condition that the lower of the two checks be discontinued. On the second point, it met the SSA only part way. Extremely high payments that resulted from technical errors could be corrected in part. For example, erroneous payments involving mandatory state supplementation could be reduced, but not below $200 per month.[7]

The *Cardinale* decision was but one among many. A report of the Senate Finance Committee staff early in 1977 said that legal services attorneys had brought 143 suits against the SSA on behalf of SSI recipients, 105 of them as class actions. In the early stages of the program the SSA had operated under forty-one temporary restraining orders or preliminary injunctions, of which twenty-six involved class actions. The plaintiffs' objections had ranged from the wording of notices to the statute's exclusion of Puerto Rico. A district court had taken jurisdiction over the content of notices and ordered the use of a full-page description of the SSI appeals process, covering all the various forms that it might take. Reviewing this record of litigation, the

---

7. *Administration of the Supplemental Security Income Program*, Hearings, p. 11; and *The Supplemental Security Income Program*, Committee Print, Senate Committee on Finance, 95 Cong. 1 sess. (GPO, 1977), p. 101. The original regulation may be found at 40 Fed. Reg. 1510 (January 8, 1975). For the post-*Cardinale* revisions, see 42 Fed. Reg. 2079 (January 10, 1977) and 43 Fed. Reg. 18167 (April 28, 1978).

committee staff observed that "each of the Nation's district courts apparently has the capacity to intervene in the administration of the program and dictate changes in policy and procedure according to its lights."[8] The role of the judiciary in SSI was nonetheless minor by comparison with what it was to be in the disability review.

THE DISABILITY REVIEW AND "NONACQUIESCENCE"

In the case of SSI, the courts had been for the SSA no more than an additionally troublesome presence in a generally troubled situation. There was no quarrel in spirit with the *Cardinale* decision, Commissioner James B. Cardwell testified. The SSA had concluded without judicial prodding that SSI was basically subject to the requirements of *Goldberg*.[9] By contrast, the disability review touched off a major battle between the agency and the courts over who was to run the program, with the SSA the loser. In order to reach an accommodation with the circuit courts, it compromised its long-standing position that there must be a uniform national program. Before making this compromise, it was humiliated by the widespread refusal of the state governments, which are its administrative agents, to continue cooperating with it, a position that they would have been unlikely to take without judicial encouragement.

Even before the disability review occurred, the courts were extensively involved in the disability program, for they were the last of the several stages of appeal of initial disability determinations. As of 1979, about 19,000 disability cases were pending in the courts and new filings were running at a rate of about 8,000 to 9,000 a year. Social security filings, originating mainly in the disability program, constituted 7 percent of all civil actions commenced in the federal courts in fiscal year 1976 and nearly 25 percent of all actions in which the United States was a party.[10]

On the whole, the SSA had fared reasonably well in these cases. As late as the 1970s, its rate of reversal ordinarily did not exceed 10 or 11 percent.[11] The law gave it an advantage, in that courts were

8. *Supplemental Security Income Program*, Committee Print, pp. 101–02.

9. *Administration of the Supplemental Security Income Program*, Hearings, vol. 3, p. 10; and *Supplemental Security Income Program*, Committee Print, p. 101.

10. Mashaw and others, *Social Security Hearings and Appeals*, p. 126.

11. Mashaw and others, *Social Security Hearings and Appeals*, report that reversals between 1970 and 1975 ranged from a low of 8.8 percent in 1972 to a high of 16.1

obliged to uphold its decisions when they were supported by "substantial evidence." When courts did overturn the agency, almost without exception they did so on the basis of their review of the facts. Cases rarely turned on statutory or constitutional interpretation.[12]

Even when a court did challenge the SSA's interpretation of the statute—and circuit courts occasionally did so in significant ways—the judicial challenge did not necessarily have much effect. Mashaw and his collaborators concluded in the late 1970s that the SSA's Bureau of Hearings and Appeals made little effort to adhere to judicial precedents. It lacked, they judged, either a policy of compliance or one of disregard. Correspondingly, it lacked institutional mechanisms for internalizing judicial decisions.[13] Only once had the SSA formally acquiesced to a judicial holding in the disability program. That was in respect to the *Kerner* doctrine, enunciated by Judge Henry J. Friendly in 1960.[14] The doctrine requires that, once a claimant makes a showing of inability to engage in his or her prior work, the agency show that there are substantial numbers of jobs in the local or national economies that the claimant could perform; the burden of proof shifts to the government. After the general counsel's office in Health, Education, and Welfare failed to persuade the U.S. solicitor general to appeal to the Supreme Court in this case, the SSA published the *Kerner* decision, distributed interpretive materials to the state agencies, and created a nationwide group of vocational experts to provide testimony in hearings on disability determinations.[15]

In general, the agency had been upheld in the Supreme Court. The Supreme Court did not review a disability case until 1968. In the next

percent in 1970, and for the five-year period stood at 11.5 percent (p. 129). Similarly, a reversal rate of around 10 percent for most of the decade, but a slight rise toward the end of it, is shown in a graph in Social Security Administration, Litigation Strategy Task Force Report, "Need for a Shared Strategic Vision" (June 1988), p. 6.

12. Statement of Stanford Ross, social security commissioner, in *Veterans Act of 1979, S. 330,* Hearing before the Senate Committee on the Judiciary, 96 Cong. 1 sess. (GPO, 1979), p. 3.

13. Mashaw and others, *Social Security Hearings and Appeals,* pp. 110–15, 140–46. For a historical account of judicial challenges to the agency, see Frederick B. Arner, *A Model Disability Structure for the Social Security Administration,* Report to the Alfred P. Sloan Foundation, Grant B 1988-38 (September 1989), pp. 74–81.

14. 283 F.2d at 916 (2d Cir. 1960).

15. Mashaw and others, *Social Security Hearings and Appeals,* p. 142. See also Jerry L. Mashaw, *Bureaucratic Justice: Managing Social Security Disability Claims* (Yale University Press, 1983), pp. 185–90. Mashaw's work is indispensable for understanding the relation between the agency and the courts in the disability program, and indeed for understanding the program's administrative processes generally.

twenty years, it heard approximately one such case a year, ruling in favor of the agency much more often than not.[16] Notably, it declined in 1976 to apply *Goldberg* standards to the termination of disability insurance benefits. The case was *Mathews* v. *Eldridge*.[17] District and circuit courts had ruled that Eldridge, a recipient of disability insurance, was entitled to a pretermination hearing that met the standards of *Goldberg* v. *Kelly*. However, the Supreme Court found that the SSA's procedures satisfied constitutional due process standards, which it said could be less exacting when benefits were independent of a means test, and it gave weight to the government's and the public's interest in "conserving scarce fiscal and administrative resources." The benefits of additional safeguards to the individual had to be weighed against the costs, it said.

It seems possible that the result in *Mathews* v. *Eldridge*, compared with the very different result in *Goldberg* v. *Kelly*, reflected the bias of the federal courts in favor of the federal government as litigant. The United States generally wins its cases before the Supreme Court and generally fares much better than state governments do.[18] In this instance, the result may have lulled the SSA into a false sense of security. At any rate, winning a victory in *Eldridge* did nothing to help prepare it for the crushing judicial reaction to the large-scale termination of disability benefits that came in the review.

Important though it was, *Mathews* v. *Eldridge* did not protect the SSA from the threat of judicial reversal of disability determinations in new cases. This threat grew in the late 1970s as the volume of appeals to the courts rose. As part of an encompassing effort to contain the growth of the disability caseload, the Carter administration proposed to change the law so as to confine the courts' review of disability cases to constitutional and statutory interpretation. The agency's findings of fact would have ceased to be reviewable.[19] From the agency's point of view this change would have done more than simply spare it from the

16. Mezey, *No Longer Disabled*, pp. 95–100.

17. 425 U.S. 319 (1976). For a case study, see Phillip J. Cooper, "Mathews v. Eldridge: The Anatomy of an Administrative Law Case," in Felix A. Nigro and Lloyd G. Nigro, *Readings in Public Administration* (Harper and Row, 1983), pp. 340–76.

18. Robert Scigliano, *The Supreme Court and the Presidency* (Free Press, 1971), pp. 177–82; and Reginald S. Sheehan and Donald R. Songer, "Parties before the United States Courts of Appeals in the 1980s," paper prepared for the 1989 annual meeting of the Midwest Political Science Association.

19. *Veterans Act of 1979*, Hearing, p. 3; and *Social Security Act Disability Program Amendments*, Hearings before the Senate Committee on Finance, 96 Cong. 1 sess. (GPO, 1979), p. 85.

courts' practice of conducting a de novo review of the facts. Because administrative law judges were sensitive to the views of federal judges and fearful of being overturned by them, it would also have tended to reduce the large and growing disparity between the decisions of state agencies and those of the ALJs.[20] Congress did not accept this proposal, however, so the courts' powers of review were intact when the disability review began.

The Start of the Review

There were unmistakable signs, as the review began, that some judges would not view it favorably. In a way, the review of disability insurance cases had a trial run in 1979–80. In response to a General Accounting Office report of 1978 that criticized its failure to remove ineligible persons from the SSI rolls, the SSA had been engaged in a review of disabled persons on SSI; the shift to disability insurance occurred after the GAO observed that "the magnitude of the Disability Insurance problem and the greater savings from correcting it now require that SSA give more priority to reevaluating this caseload."[21] As the SSA began to switch its attention to insurance, the judicial results of its efforts in SSI were becoming apparent. The Ninth Appellate Circuit, based in San Francisco, was raising objections. In *Patti* v. *Schweiker*, it ruled early in 1982 that the SSA must show that the condition of a disability recipient in SSI had improved before it could determine that disability had ceased.[22] Invoking the language of the Social Security Act—language that arguably was not relevant to the crucial issue—the court held that medical evidence relied on by

20. On the relation between ALJs and the federal courts, see *Social Security Appeals and Case Review Process*, Hearings before the Subcommittee on Social Security of the House Committee on Ways and Means, 97 Cong. 1 sess. (GPO, 1981), p. 245; and *Oversight of Social Security Disability Benefits Terminations*, Hearing before the Subcommittee on Oversight of Government Management of the Senate Committee on Governmental Affairs, 97 Cong. 2 sess. (GPO, 1982), p. 128.

21. General Accounting Office, *More Diligent Followup Needed to Weed Out Ineligible SSA Disability Beneficiaries*, HRD-81-48 (March 3, 1981), p. ii. At the urging of the GAO, the Reagan administration in the spring of 1981 had secured permission from Congress to use for review of disability insurance cases funds that had initially been appropriated under Carter for review of SSI cases. See the testimony of Paul B. Simmons in *Social Security Disability Insurance*, Hearing before the Subcommittee on Social Security of the House Committee on Ways and Means, 98 Cong. 1 sess. (GPO, 1983), pp. 54–55.

22. 669 F.2d 582 (9th Cir. 1982).

the SSA to deny Patti's eligibility did not comprise "substantial evidence" of a change in her condition since the previous determination of disability.

Not long before, the same court had ruled in *Finnegan* v. *Mathews* that a recipient of SSI who had been "grandfathered" (that is, had qualified initially under the old state-run program and had then been automatically covered when SSI was enacted) could not be terminated without proof of improvement in his condition or of the commission of a clear and specific error in the initial state determination of disability.[23]

These decisions were a fundamental challenge to the SSA's rules, which provided that disability would terminate when it was not supported by "current medical or other evidence." They did not require that the recipient's medical condition have improved. The SSA had employed a medical improvement standard to govern termination decisions between 1969 and 1976, but had abandoned it as too hard to administer.[24] Confident that its rules were sufficiently grounded in law, the agency met the court's challenge with a defiant response. It issued formal rulings of "nonacquiescence" in both the *Patti* and *Finnegan* cases. The SSA disagreed with "the court's conclusion [in *Patti*] that medical improvement . . . . is required." Noting that the court had not even referred to the SSA's regulations and that other circuit courts had not required a showing of improvement to terminate disability benefits, it proclaimed that "Patti does not provide a judicial interpretation of the disability regulations which should be followed." Of *Finnegan*, the SSA said that the standard laid down by the court would be impossible to administer and that the correct standard was contained in its own regulations.[25] It pointed out that many grand-fatherees such as Finnegan had been on the state disability rolls for years and that the evidence on which they had originally been found eligible might not even exist. The SSA could not be expected to apply a medical improvement standard in such cases. The proper and feasible approach was to find such recipients ineligible if they were not disabled according to current evidence.

23. 641 F.2d 1340 (9th Cir. 1981).
24. On the history of the SSA's use of a medical improvement standard, see *Social Security Disability Insurance*, Hearing, pp. 47, 127–28; and Mezey, *No Longer Disabled*, pp. 74–76.
25. SSR Rulings 82-10c and 82-49c, *West's Social Security Reporting Service, Rulings 1975–1982* (West Publishing Co., 1983), pp. 951–65.

Confrontation

If other appellate courts had not in general come to agree with the Ninth Circuit, the SSA's defiance might have succeeded. Instead it became the start of a full-scale fight. By the end of 1984 all the circuits had ruled that the SSA must apply some form of medical improvement standard or a presumption of continuing disability before benefits could be terminated; the Ninth Circuit had enjoined the agency to abide by its rulings in *Patti* and *Finnegan*; motions or threats of motions to hold the secretary of Health and Human Services in contempt numbered in the hundreds; and judges all over the country were berating the SSA from their benches.[26] Nonacquiescence, a member of the Ninth Circuit said, was like the "pre-Civil War doctrine of nullification, whereby rebellious states refused to recognize certain Federal laws within their boundaries." The SSA had flouted "some very important principles basic to our American system of government—the rule of law, the doctrine of separation of powers embedded in the Constitution, and the tenet of judicial supremacy."[27] As a result of rulings in the Ninth Circuit, the agency had been given sixty days in which to send notices to all persons in that circuit who had been terminated without a finding of medical improvement—a total of nearly 29,000—telling them that they could reapply for benefits.[28]

Before Congress, the SSA defended nonacquiescence by arguing that courts were not suited to make policy because, short of the

26. Katharine P. Collins and Anne Erfle, "Social Security Disability Benefits Reform Act of 1984: Legislative History and Summary of Provisions," *Social Security Bulletin*, vol. 48 (April 1985), p. 31; and Louis D. Enoff, acting deputy commissioner for programs and policy, memo to all SSA executive staff, "Litigation Management Project—INFORMATION," August 27, 1984, in author's files. Mezey, *No Longer Disabled*, chap. 6, gives citations for decisions of each of the circuits and analyzes the courts' reasoning.

27. Robert Pear, "U.S. Flouts Courts in Determination of Benefit Claims," *New York Times*, May 13, 1984, p. A1.

28. *Lopez v. Heckler*, 713 F.2d 1432 (9th Cir. 1983). Further, the agency was ordered to immediately reinstate benefits to all of these persons retroactively. HHS appealed and won a partial stay from Supreme Court Justice William Rehnquist, sitting as circuit justice. Rehnquist held that, pending appeal, the agency need not reinstate benefits. He ruled that the injunction "significantly interfere[d] with the distribution between administrative and judicial responsibility for enforcement of the Social Security Act which Congress has established." 463 U.S. 1328-38 (1983). The history of this significant case is recounted in Mezey, *No Longer Disabled*, pp. 136–39. Among the issues it posed was the constitutionality of nonacquiescence. The Supreme Court agreed to hear arguments in the case, but remanded it after Congress enacted the Disability Benefits Reform Act of 1984 (see chapter 8).

Supreme Court, they could not produce uniform results, and that individual disability cases, which constituted the courts' raw material, were poor vehicles for policymaking because each turned on a particular set of facts.[29] It also tried to convey the magnitude of the practical problems it would face if policy differed among the circuits:

> There would be enormous practical problems with circuit-by-circuit acquiescence since we would need to keep track of applicants as they move through the decisionmaking process, determine which circuit law should apply, and separately handle claims by jurisdiction. Special problems could arise where there are conflicting decisions within a single circuit, or a claimant or beneficiary changes residence while a decision on appeal is pending.[30]

The underlying premise—that policy must be nationally uniform—was not in the least contrived for the occasion. It was contained in law, Congress having stipulated in 1980 that administration of the disability insurance program be "uniform . . . throughout the United States."[31] Just as important, it had long been at the core of the agency's operating code. Besides reflecting the nature of bureaucracy, with its universalistic, rationalizing bias, this code had been reinforced in the SSA's case by the particular historical circumstance that its programs and administrative style were a reaction against the features of American federalism. For the SSA's programs to develop regional differences would be more than a monumental inconvenience to the agency; it would constitute a humiliating retrogression to the time when state governments dominated domestic functions and citizens were treated differently depending on where they happened to live. The SSA's very existence rested on the belief that such differences were unfair.[32] Finally, to compromise the principle of uniformity would concede

29. On the first point, see *Oversight of Social Security Disability Benefits Terminations*, Hearing, pp. 30–31; on the second, see *Social Security Disability Insurance Program*, Hearing before the Senate Committee on Finance, 97 Cong. 2 sess. (GPO, 1982), p. 168.

30. *Social Security Disability Insurance Program*, Hearing before the Senate Committee on Finance, 98 Cong. 2 sess. (GPO, 1984), p. 106.

31. 94 Stat. 454 (1980).

32. A semiofficial history lists seven basic principles of social security, of which one is that "Social Security is to be administered by a single federal agency applying its principles uniformly throughout the nation." Rufus E. Miles, Jr., *The Department of Health, Education, and Welfare* (Praeger, 1974), p. 90.

control over the SSA's several hundred administrative law judges to the courts.

The legal merits of the SSA's position on nonacquiescence were open to debate. The agency did not contend that it had a right to ignore a court's decision in a particular case. It restored benefits to Patti and Finnegan, but denied that circuit court doctrines in those cases were otherwise binding, even within the circuit. This flouted a conventional view that decisions of circuit courts should prevail within the circuit. Yet no Supreme Court decision specifically addressed that subject, and even judicial opinion about the practice of nonacquiescence, though generally adverse, was not absolutely uniform. The SSA was not alone among federal agencies in using the practice. The Internal Revenue Service, the only agency comparable to the SSA in the scope and impact of its operations, and the National Labor Relations Board also had employed nonacquiescence with some frequency, while other federal agencies did so on rare occasions.[33] The SSA had used the practice at least since the 1960s—sometimes formally, with an announcement of nonacquiescence, but more often informally, by silently ignoring court decisions.[34] The Mashaw report, produced in the late 1970s by a Yale professor of administrative law along with eminent collaborators, did not criticize the agency's use of nonacquiescence per se, but strongly recommended a formalization of responses to judicial decisions. It urged the agency to acquiesce or not, on the record.[35] This recommendation may have encouraged the renewed use of formal nonacquiescence in the early 1980s, following a lapse in the 1970s. On this interpretation, the formal nonacquiescences of the early 1980s represented, rather than lawlessness, the agency's good-faith effort to

33. "Administrative Agency Intracircuit Nonacquiescence," *Columbia Law Review*, vol. 85 (1985), pp. 582–610. On the legal issues, see also Miriam R. Rubin and Karen Ann Naughton, "Government Nonacquiescence Case in Point: Social Security Litigation," *West's Social Security Reporting Service, Cases*, vol. 15 (West Publishing Co., 1987), pp. 768–92; the exchange between Anthony Lewis and Paul M. Bator in *New York Times*: "Respect for Law?" June 18, 1984, p. A19, and "Disability: No 'Lawless' Government Stance," June 28, 1984, p. A26; and Statement of Carolyn B. Kuhl, deputy assistant attorney general, in *Social Security Disability Insurance Program*, Hearing (1984), pp. 113–23. There is a comprehensive analysis of the issues, along with a description of federal agency practices, in Samuel Estreicher and Richard L. Revesz, "Nonacquiescence by Federal Administrative Agencies," *Yale Law Journal*, vol. 98 (February 1989), pp. 679–772.

34. Estreicher and Revesz, "Nonacquiescence," report that between 1966 and 1982, the SSA issued ten rulings of nonacquiescence—one each in 1966, 1967, and 1968, two in 1980, two in 1981, and three in 1982 (pp. 694–95n).

35. Mashaw and others, *Social Security Hearings and Appeals*, pp. 110–15.

implement, at least procedurally, the advice of a respected group of law professors.

Yet if the SSA's position was not nakedly indefensible, it came to be much weakened in this instance by two related circumstances: the high degree of agreement among circuit courts that the agency was in error, and the executive's failure to carry appeals to the Supreme Court. Because the justification for nonacquiescence rested crucially on the agency's obligation to maintain a nationally uniform program, agency practice became harder to defend as court decisions became more widespread and consistent. Although the different circuits used different rationales to arrive at their results and the results differed in details, the circuit courts were virtually unanimous as of mid-1984 in granting plaintiffs in the disability review cases a presumption of continuing disability and in requiring the agency to show that some change had occurred, in the plaintiff's medical condition or otherwise, to warrant termination.[36] Moreover, if uniformity was what the SSA sought, critics said, then the executive should have attempted to elicit a ruling from the Supreme Court.

Collapse

Publicly and in court, the secretary of HHS, on behalf of the SSA, sought to meet the judicial challenge by arguing the prerogatives of the executive as a coequal branch of the government. The department took refuge in the separation of powers. Not being part of the judicial branch, HHS denied that it was bound by *stare decisis*, the doctrine that binds courts to their own precedents and the decisions of superior courts.[37]

The Department of Justice, as the lawyer for executive agencies, helped formulate these arguments and displayed a good deal of public sympathy for the SSA's position. Opposing a proposed extension of judicial review to decisions of the Veterans Administration, a member of the department testified to Congress in 1983 that judicial review had not worked well in the social security disability program:

Judicial review in an analogous area—social security benefits decisions . . . has greatly increased the length of time and expense

36. The cases are analyzed in Mezey, *No Longer Disabled*, pp. 111–15.

37. Rubin and Naughton, "Government Nonacquiescence Case in Point," pp. 777–78, citing "Defendants' Memorandum Concerning Instruction to Administrative Law Judges," filed in *Steiberger* v. *Heckler*, 615 F. Supp. 1315 (S.D.N.Y. 1985).

involved in processing social security cases, from the standpoint of both the claimant and the Social Security Administration. The scope of review established for these cases has varied widely from court to court. The lack of familiarity of the generalist federal judges with the social security system has created inefficiency and even confusion in the way cases are handled. . . . One result of the participation of the federal judiciary has been a lack of conformity of the rules applied in different sections of the country and the need to endure time-consuming appeals up to the Supreme Court to resolve these conflicts. If one of the chief objectives of a fair benefit determination system is uniformity of result, the social security system certainly proves that provision for judicial review does not ensure consistency.[38]

Privately, nevertheless, officials in Justice were alarmed and discomfited by the rising confrontation between the SSA and the courts. They saw that their client was in very deep trouble—and not just with the courts, but with Justice's own field staff. U.S. attorneys' offices, which handle the bulk of disability cases, were complaining to headquarters that their credibility in the courts was being undermined. The U.S. attorney for the Southern District of New York, Rudolph W. Giuliani, virtually apologized for the SSA's position in a letter to the judges in his district.[39] Also, Justice feared that the agency's aggressive posture on nonacquiescence could elicit legislation or judicial decisions that would adversely affect the litigating choices of the government generally. "The government cannot automatically appeal all adverse decisions," a department witness explained to Congress, "but must retain the flexibility to accept some defeats, while refusing to acquiesce in the rule of law they establish pending the resolution of future test cases."[40] Above all, Justice wished to avert a finding that nonacquiescence was unconstitutional. Privately, therefore, it was urging the agency to use restraint.[41]

38. Statement of Carolyn B. Kuhl, deputy assistant attorney general, in *Judicial Review of Veterans' Claims*, Hearings before the Subcommittee on Oversight and Investigations of the House Committee on Veterans' Affairs, 98 Cong. 1 sess. (GPO, 1983), pp. 143–44.

39. On the role of U.S. attorneys in disability cases and their reaction to the review, see Jack B. Weinstein, "Equality and the Law: Social Security Disability Cases in the Federal Courts," *Syracuse University Law Review*, vol. 35 (1984), pp. 916, 929–30. A copy of Giuliani's letter to the judges, dated June 25, 1984, is in the author's files.

40. Statement of Carolyn B. Kuhl, in *Social Security Disability Insurance Program*, Hearing (1984), p. 114.

41. Interview, Carolyn B. Kuhl, July 7, 1989.

In view of the intercircuit agreement and the lack of strong backing from the Department of Justice, there was no prospect whatever of the SSA's reaching the Supreme Court in order to test the circuit courts' insistence on a medical improvement standard. The solicitor general, who decides what cases the United States will appeal, does not lightly attempt to appeal one to the Supreme Court. In 1982 the Solicitor General's Office had rejected a request from the Office of the General Counsel in HHS to pursue an appeal in *Patti* v. *Schweiker*. HHS and Justice officials then settled upon a ruling of nonacquiescence in that case as an alternative to pursuing an appeal. Thereafter, the prospects for appeal became steadily more remote as adverse judicial decisions mounted and the possibility of a legislative resolution developed. The agency was forced therefore to confront the fact that it was in a losing fight with a powerful adversary. An internal memorandum in the summer of 1984 acknowledged that the agency was experiencing a "crisis" in litigation and that its credibility before the courts was "at an all-time low."[42]

The disability review had of course caused a sharp increase in the number of cases that were eligible for appeal. Denials by the Appeals Council, the fourth and last administrative stage of the disability determination process, rose from 45,997 in 1981 to 78,642 in 1983. The review also sharply increased the rate at which challenges to these decisions were filed in federal district courts. In 1981, 19.7 percent of the administrative denials were contested; in 1984, 41 percent.[43] As the volume of litigation soared, the SSA was unable to cope with it. Processing times lengthened, files were lost, filings of briefs failed to meet judicial deadlines, and the briefs consisted more and more of boilerplate rather than being tailored to the cases. The agency's reversal rate, which stood at 19 percent in fiscal year 1980, soared to nearly 60 percent in fiscal 1984, both because of these failures of performance and because of the vulnerability the courts found to inhere in agency policies governing the review.[44] Given the conflict between the agency and the circuit courts, such a result was inevitable; while HHS might deny being bound by *stare decisis*, no one could deny that the district courts were bound.

As the agency lost cases, it also lost face. The courts were coming to perceive that it would defend any case no matter how poor the facts

---

42. Enoff, "Litigation Management Project—INFORMATION."

43. SSA, Litigation Strategy Task Force Report, "Need for a Shared Strategic Vision," p. 4.

44. Data supplied to the author by the Office of General Counsel in HHS.

or faulty the record. The extraordinary rate of reversals was only the most evident source of embarrassment. Others included the sharply critical tone in which court orders were cast, and the fact that the courts were beginning to award sizable amounts of compensation to private litigants in response to complaints that the SSA's position was "not substantially justified."[45] Still another was the fact, revealed by congressional publication of an internal agency memorandum, that the SSA was unwilling to contemplate appeal in the *Finnegan* case because it too believed, after reviewing the record, that Finnegan was disabled.[46] As the courts suspected, the agency was finding it hard to discriminate among the cases in its huge load of litigation; thus it often defended cases that were indefensible even on the facts. Acknowledging that the *Finnegan* case was too weak to take to the Supreme Court did not make it look very strong as one piece of the foundation for the practice of nonacquiescence.

How far, how long, and with what result the SSA could pursue its defiance of the courts depended very much on how other institutions reacted. Besides the Department of Justice and Congress, these included, crucially, the state governments, on which the SSA depended to be administrative agents. In 1983, when the state governors, taking cues or outright commands from the courts, began declining to collaborate in the disability review, the SSA's position became increasingly untenable. In theory, the executive branch might have responded to the governors' defiance by federalizing the administration of disability insurance. The Disability Amendments of 1980 required the secretary of HHS to assume the disability determination function from a state agency if it substantially failed to make determinations in a manner consistent with SSA guidelines. This course of action seems not to have been seriously contemplated, however. In contrast to the Nixon administration's position on SSI, Reagan administration officials eschewed any intention of replacing the states in disability administration.[47]

---

45. The statute on which these awards were based was the Equal Access to Justice Act, in effect between 1980 and 1984, when President Reagan vetoed an extension of it. As of 1984 courts had awarded $723,000 in SSA cases and an additional $1,299,000 was pending. "Administrative Agency Intracircuit Nonacquiescence," p. 608; and Enoff, "Litigation Management Project—INFORMATION."

46. *Social Security Disability Insurance Program*, Hearing (1982), pp. 482–84.

47. See, for example, *Social Security Disability Insurance Program*, Hearing (1982), p. 77. The *National Journal* quoted a congressional staff aide as saying that for the federal government to take over administration was "out of the question" because "no President in recent history has been willing to hire 10,000 new federal employees all at once."

Congress could settle the dispute between the SSA and the courts insofar as it was able to agree on how to do so. Substantively, it allied itself on the whole with the courts. In the Social Security Disability Benefits Reform Act of 1984, passed late in the year, it enacted a qualified medical improvement standard.[48] It was unable to agree on statutory language prohibiting nonacquiescence. The House would have compelled the agency to treat circuit court decisions as binding within the circuit; the Senate refused to concur; and they compromised on a statement in the conference report urging that nonacquiescence be employed only when the executive intended to carry an appeal to the Supreme Court or to seek a legislative remedy. Arguing that the constitutional issues could be settled only by the Supreme Court, the report urged the administration to seek such a resolution.[49]

By settling the immediate policy issue, which revolved around the standards to apply to redeterminations of disability, Congress reduced the intensity of the jurisdictional dispute, but in the aftermath of the new law the SSA and the courts continued to spar over a set of class actions that Congress said should be remanded to the agency. The Justice Department's explanation of the situation to Congress highlighted tensions between the agency's desire for uniformity and the judicial appellants' quest for individualized justice. A deputy assistant attorney general testified:

> SSA . . . worked very hard to try to develop some notice procedures . . . that would be uniform throughout the country as far as possible, with regard to these class actions. And we felt that the very quickest way to handle all of these numerous individuals was to do it insofar as possible on a uniform basis.
>
> The plaintiffs in many of these class actions . . . have all kinds of ideas about special procedures that they wanted or toll-free numbers they wanted set up. . . . What they were trying to do was

Linda E. Demkovich, "Administration About-Face on Disability Could Be a Political Blessing in Disguise," April 28, 1984, p. 824. According to Frederick B. Arner, the OMB "shot down" a possible SSA takeover of disability administration in Wisconsin that had been under consideration in 1980–81. *A Model Disability Structure*, pp. 29–30. To add significantly to the federal payroll was too high a price to pay to improve control over administration even when the stakes of control had risen very high. To this extent, the administrative presidency was in tension with the policymaking presidency, even in the disability review.

48. 98 Stat. 1794. See chap. 8 for details of the medical improvement standard.

49. *Social Security Disability Benefits Reform Act of 1984*, H. Rept. 98-1039, 98 Cong. 2 sess. (GPO, 1984), pp. 37–38.

to persuade the court to make relief as individualized as possible, which we were saying . . . would have slowed matters down. That was the basis of those disputes.[50]

Surrender

The courts and the agency also sparred over the SSA's policies regarding nonacquiescence, with the result that the agency surrendered by stages to judicial supervision. In June 1985 the secretary of HHS announced a new policy that sought to reconcile the SSA's conflicting needs to achieve a nationally uniform program and to abide by the decisions of an ill-coordinated judicial system.[51] Under the new policy, the initial stages of disability determination would continue to be guided by the SSA's rules. The 10,000 state disability examiners and their initial reviewers in the state agencies and the SSA would be instructed to take their cues from the SSA. Officials at later stages of decision—the administrative law judges, the Appeals Council—would be instructed to abide by circuit court decisions in case of a conflict. Nonacquiescence would be employed only if the executive determined that it should pursue appeals. The SSA undertook to issue "acquiescence rulings" identifying court decisions at variance with its policies. Each ruling would explain how the agency would apply the adverse decision in the circuit that rendered it.[52]

Although this policy might have reduced the SSA's overt conflict with the courts, it could hardly be said to have resolved the underlying

50. *Implementation of the Social Security Disability Amendments of 1984*, Hearing before the Subcommittee on Social Security of the House Committee on Ways and Means, 99 Cong. 1 sess. (GPO, 1985), pp. 24–25.

51. A vivid example of lack of intercircuit coordination in the 1980s—albeit one that was resolved by the Supreme Court—had to do with SSA regulations governing the severity of an impairment. The regulations require applicants to prove that they have an impairment that "significantly limits" their capacity for performing "basic work activities." Four circuit courts upheld the regulation, but five found it to be inconsistent with the statute, which requires that age, education, and work experience be considered in determining the severity of impairments. The Supreme Court upheld the agency, although not without criticism. Mezey, *No Longer Disabled*, pp. 104–05. The Supreme Court's decision was rendered in *Bowen* v. *Yuckert*, 107 S. Ct. 2287 (1987).

52. Robert Pear, "U.S. Will Drop Efforts to Halt Aid to Disabled," *New York Times*, June 4, 1985, p. A1; Rubin and Naughton, "Government Nonacquiescence Case in Point," pp. 784ff.; and Estreicher and Revesz, "Nonacquiescence by Federal Administrative Agencies," p. 696.

tension between them. Rather, it threatened to make the disability determination process permanently and formally a hostage to that tension. There were to be two disability determination processes—one bureaucratically controlled and nationally uniform in application, the other judicially controlled and potentially varying among the circuits. In truth there had been two processes for some time, but the SSA had been struggling to make them one. It had been trying to consolidate the rules governing the two, to induce the ALJs to conform to those rules, and to fend off, with nonacquiescence, the discordant effects of judicial review. This had been a very costly effort, and the new policy statement constituted an admission that the SSA was giving it up.

Six months later, this policy in turn was revised to provide that under certain circumstances acquiescence would extend to all four administrative levels. A policy statement issued in January 1986 contemplated two different types of acquiescence rulings—those that would apply only at the ALJ and Appeals Council levels and those that would apply at lower levels as well. Although the first of these alternatives laid the basis for continuing differences with the courts, the agency declined in practice to invoke it. All of the acquiescence rulings that it subsequently published applied to all administrative levels.[53] An internal SSA task force concluded that "nonacquiescence is *not* an effective way for SSA to maintain its national policy. Courts can (and do) respond to nonacquiescence by certifying circuit-wide classes and enjoining the agency from following its policy."[54] Late in 1988, the agency published a new set of proposed regulations under which it promised to acquiesce in circuit court rulings with which it disagreed unless the government pursued an appeal.[55] This was a complete capitulation.

Nonacquiescence had been designed to contain the impact of court decisions by limiting them to single cases, but litigants and courts were able to combat it with class actions. Judges in the 1970s and 1980s were increasingly willing to certify such actions, and the Supreme

53. Estreicher and Revesz, "Nonacquiescence by Federal Administrative Agencies," pp. 698–99, report the issuance of thirty-three acquiescence rulings between January 1986 and March 1988, all applying acquiescence to all levels of administrative decision. The SSA's Litigation Strategy Task Force Report, published in June 1988, likewise found not a single instance in which the agency had chosen the option of limited acquiescence that it had defined for itself.

54. SSA, Litigation Strategy Task Force Report, "Need for a Shared Strategic Vision," p. 3.

55. 53 Fed. Reg. 46628 (November 18, 1988).

Court in 1979 had sanctioned their application to the Social Security Act.[56] Between 1980 and 1988 approximately one hundred class actions had been filed against the SSA over disability insurance issues, roughly half of which challenged the standards used in the review. By 1988, these actions had become a major arena of court-agency interaction, and the SSA was trying to come to grips with the fresh administrative challenges that they posed. They were very costly. The SSA estimated that in the nineteen medical improvement classes covered by the Disability Benefits Reform Act of 1984, it spent $853,400 to identify 217,109 potential class members, another $4,350,000 to screen them so as to define the actual class (54,307 members), and another $61,638,445 to readjudicate those cases, which resulted in 46,700 decisions favorable to the claimants. A class action brought by the State of New York and challenging the weight the agency gives treadmill results in adjudicating cardiovascular cases had a potential class membership of 150,000 and was expected to require two years of manual screening simply to identify members of the class.[57] However, the lack of systematic information about the costs of class actions made it hard for the SSA to budget for them in advance or to argue to the courts that they were excessively burdensome.

The agency's critics continued to charge that it "nonacquiesced" in court decisions by ignoring some decisions and interpreting others to be consistent with its own policies when in fact they were not. Both SSA policies and judicial decisions were ambiguous enough that there was always plenty of room for debate about degrees of consistency. But by 1988 the agency was anything but defiant. An internal task force that studied litigation strategies concluded: "Now that the courts are actively overseeing SSA's implementation of [its] policy formulation role . . . , SSA must adjust its decisionmaking procedures accordingly."[58] Among the adjustments it called for were clearer agency

56. Mezey, *No Longer Disabled*, p. 101. The case was *Califano* v. *Yamasaki*, 442 U.S. 682.

57. SSA, Litigation Strategy Task Force Report, "Need for a Shared Strategic Vision," p. 16. The report notes that the SSA "may have to do an enormous amount of manual screening in *State of New York* because it has no database which would identify cardiovascular cases with treadmill results in New York—or elsewhere, for that matter. In addition, SSA lacks the hardware or software to perform an ongoing, systematic compilation of class action data which would support statistical and cost analyses" (p. 17).

58. SSA, Litigation Strategy Task Force Report, "Need for a Shared Strategic Vision," p. 6. This group developed a proposed policy statement providing that the SSA would generally acquiesce in adverse circuit court decisions but attempting to

policies, better explained in court and more consistently applied—hardly a combative stance.

By the late 1980s, the agency's relations with the courts were settling down. The volume of pending cases was slowly declining, though at 33,000 in mid-1989 it was still well above the level of 18,000–19,000 that prevailed between 1978 and 1981, immediately preceding the review. The reversal rate was down to 28 percent in the first half of 1989, half of what it had been in the record year of 1984, yet still much higher than it had been in the late 1970s. How far judicial supervision of the disability program will ultimately reach remains to be seen. There are limits to the ability of courts to control administrative behavior.[59] There can be no doubt, however, that the disability review fundamentally altered the SSA's relation to the courts, making the agency much more submissive.

COURTS ARE an active overseer of agency action. While it is tempting to conclude that they do not in general defer to agency judgment or attach much weight to administrative costs, it would probably be wrong to make sweeping inferences from the necessarily partial history presented here. Evidence from even this history is mixed, given the Supreme Court's support for the agency in *Mathews* v. *Eldridge*, and it is clear that the circumstances in both SSI and the disability review made the agency unusually vulnerable. Policy changes originating in the political branches positively invited judicial intrusion. Furthermore, the judicial system itself, with the decision in *Mathews* v. *Eldridge*, had failed to send signs of its potential level of interest in disability redeterminations. The agency was delivered down the garden path.

One of the numerous unanticipated consequences of the SSA's inheriting the state-run public assistance programs was that it also inherited the exacting judicial standards that had been applied to the state governments in *Goldberg* v. *Kelly*. When the SSA acquired responsibility for SSI, the rights revolution wrought by the federal judiciary reached home, engulfing one of the federal government's own social agencies. The agency's well-publicized difficulties in administering SSI then heightened its vulnerability. The court that decided *Cardinale* lacked confidence in the SSA.

define the circumstances under which relitigation of an issue within the circuit should be pursued.

59. See Mashaw, *Bureaucratic Justice*, p. 189.

In the disability review, the effects of presidential and congressional policymaking were more direct. When the rolls exploded in the mid-1970s, policymakers in the political branches made a sharp response, and when the SSA implemented their commands, the judiciary made a sharp response in turn. Evident flaws in the agency's performance, both as administrator and as litigant, again heightened its vulnerability; it went naked down the garden path.

If these cases presented special circumstances, they also dramatized structural tensions in agency-court relations. The agency's clash with the courts over nonacquiescence was rooted in its quest for uniform national standards. A decentralized court system, which is one of the institutional reflections of federalism, has the potential for frustrating that quest.

At bottom, nonacquiescence was a purely jurisdictional dispute. The issue was whether the SSA or the courts should make the rules for the SSA's programs. But when the SSA asserted what it saw as its prerogatives, using tactics that challenged the courts' authority, the only place to turn for an assessment of their legitimacy was the very institution being challenged. Courts are excellently situated to have the last word. When the Department of Health and Human Services revised its position on nonacquiescence, an official in the OMB explained that this had been done in order to restore the SSA's credibility with the courts.[60]

The courts are overwhelmingly important in their own right, and no agency can afford to be consistently at odds with them, liable to constant reversal. Moreover, they are held in high esteem by third parties whose cooperation or good opinion the agency needs. In the disability review, the costs of nonacquiescence were not confined to the courtroom. They extended to the SSA's relations with the state governments, on which the agency depended for execution of its administrative routine. And, as the next chapter will show, these costs extended as well to the agency's portrayal on the front pages of the nation's newspapers.

60. Pear, "U.S. Will Drop Efforts to Halt Aid to Disabled."

CHAPTER **8**

Congress as Overseer

OVERSIGHT of administration is one of the main functions of Congress, along with lawmaking and constituency service. It is sometimes referred to as Congress's neglected function, but it would be impossible to prove neglect from the two cases under study here. When things go wrong in ways that affect constituents, Congress is quick to come to attention. As two students of oversight have written, Congress as overseer responds to "fire alarms."[1] When supplemental security income and the disability review got under way, bells clanged all over the country.

The volume of congressional hearings and other inquiries, such as committee staff reports and General Accounting Office studies, was very large. Newly endowed with subcommittees in 1975 as a result of organizational reforms within Congress, the House Ways and Means Committee deployed two of them to investigate SSI. Its Subcommittee on Public Assistance held nine days of hearings in June 1975, which had no sooner concluded than the Subcommittee on Oversight opened a series of hearings that were to continue off and on for a year. Ten sessions were held. In the Senate, the Finance Committee instructed its staff to undertake a study of SSI in January 1975; the 270-page product, released more than two years later, was thorough and comprehensive. In the wake of the disability review, nine different committee and subcommittee units in the two houses held a combined total of twenty-seven days of hearings between March 1982 and May 1984. Nearly half the hearings were outside Washington.[2]

1. Mathew D. McCubbins and Thomas Schwartz, "Congressional Oversight Overlooked: Police Patrols versus Fire Alarms," *American Journal of Political Science*, vol. 28 (February 1984), pp. 165–79, is a much-cited theoretical essay.

2. Sometimes the committees collaborated, as when the Senate Special Committee on Aging and the Subcommittee on Social Security of the House Ways and Means

With all this calling to account, high-ranking officials of the Social Security Administration spent much of their time preparing and delivering testimony. Notably, among executive officials it is those at the agency level who must answer to oversight. Departmental executives—secretaries, under secretaries, assistant secretaries—who typically present an administration's proposals for legislation to Congress do not respond to inquiries about administration. They participate publicly only in takeoffs, not crash landings. The president and his immediate staff do not appear before Congress for either purpose, but are much more prominent in presenting proposals for action than in taking responsibility for administration.

Congressional oversight activity was of two broad kinds: remedy seeking and blame casting. The search for remedies yielded a flood of proposed bills in both cases. That very few actually passed can perhaps be taken as a sign, even if negative, of Congress's latent regard for administration. Designed to respond to constituents' grievances in highly specific and sometimes arbitrary ways, many of these bills would have compounded the SSA's administrative burdens. For example, thirty-eight senators joined with Claiborne Pell of Rhode Island to cosponsor the "Social Security Recipients Fairness Act," a piece of fantasy that provided, among other things, that in case of the theft of a check or a three-day delay in the receipt of a check, the SSA must issue a replacement within one day of notification by the client. In a similar resort to the device of arbitrary deadlines as a control on administrative performance, the bill also provided that any appeal not decided within ninety days would automatically result in a tentative decision in the appellant's favor, and that if this decision were later formally reversed, the amounts paid out by the government would be nonrecoverable. This bill did not pass, but it illustrates the spirit in which many members of Congress responded to the two sets of events. They were quick to align themselves with aggrieved constituents against the agency. Members of the committees having jurisdiction over legislation were more balanced. Particularly in the House, subcommittee leaders appeared cognizant of the need to weigh competing interests and claims and to devise legislative relief for the agency as well as its clients.

Committee held joint hearings in Chicago, Dallas, Boston, and Hot Springs, Arkansas. See the tabulation in Katharine P. Collins and Anne Erfle, "Social Security Disability Benefits Reform Act of 1984: Legislative History and Summary of Provisions," *Social Security Bulletin*, vol. 48 (April 1985), app. A, p. 30.

REMEDY SEEKING

One of the principal purposes of congressional oversight is to lay the basis for corrective legislation. In both of these cases, the Ways and Means Committee in particular sought to produce such legislation. The results were meager for SSI and hard-won for the disability review. In the disability case, Congress was not able to act until 1984, after much damage had been done to the agency and its clients, and policymaking had largely been taken over by the courts.

For SSI, new legislation could offer minor palliatives at best. The SSA's problems stemmed fundamentally from having been assigned a major new task that was profoundly different from—and incomparably more difficult than—what it had long been doing. For this task, the agency had moreover lacked both sufficient trained manpower and sufficiently developed data processing capacity. Short of reversing history by repealing the law, which was out of the question, there was no "cure."

As of 1975, the executive leadership of the SSA was wary of seeking cures by statutory means, perhaps fearing that matters would only be made worse. When pressed to propose remedies, Commissioner James B. Cardwell hesitated:

> I think it would be a mistake to go rushing off in every direction, reacting to every problem that we run into, and reacting to every expression of concern of special interest groups that will come to this committee and will come before the Congress generally. . . .
>
> I would say at the risk of being thought too philosophical, that we are all members of a government that has a long concern with accountability, and being very concerned with equity. As someone once said before I got here, those two things are often mortal enemies.
>
> SSI is replete with arrangements which achieve both and are sometimes in conflict with each other. Selling ourselves as well as the Congress on the kinds of modifications that may be in the offing is going to take a great deal of articulation and careful presentation.
>
> In sum, I would say don't look to us for too many reform proposals for this session. But that doesn't mean we are not sensitive and concerned.[3]

3. *Supplemental Security Income Program*, Hearings before the Subcommittee on Public

Acting on cues from various sources—Cardwell's testimony, members of Congress, state officials, public and private organizations purporting to speak for SSI recipients—the Ways and Means Committee in 1976 devised a set of amendments to the program and got it accepted by the House. The committee's report outlined seventeen new provisions.[4] Some of these were wholly client-serving, such as a requirement that the SSA conduct and report to Congress on a specific program of outreach. Members of the Public Assistance Subcommittee were convinced that the SSA had been insufficiently energetic in advertising the new program.[5] Others, though arguably client-serving, stemmed at least in part from the SSA's suggestions for facilitating administration. For example, the original law had required that SSI payments to alcoholics and drug addicts be made through a third party having an interest in the recipient's welfare, who was expected to oversee use of the money. Cardwell reported that the provision was not being carried out because the federal government could not find responsible payees.[6] The committee bill made a qualified response: if the chief medical officer of the institution or facility where such an individual was undergoing treatment (treatment was a prerequisite for qualifying for SSI) certified that payment of benefits directly "would be of significant therapeutic value and that there is substantial reason to believe that he would not misuse or improperly spend the funds," then direct payments were allowed.[7] Whether this provision would simplify administration or further complicate it was debatable.

Singly or in combination, the seventeen proposed changes did not significantly alter the dimensions of the SSA's task, and most failed of enactment anyway. The Senate never acted on the House bill as a whole. In the next several years Congress made occasional ad hoc,

Assistance of the House Committee on Ways and Means, 94 Cong. 1 sess. (Government Printing Office, 1975), vol. 1, pp. 40–41.

4. *Supplemental Security Income Amendments of 1976*, H. Rept. 94-1201, 94 Cong. 2 sess. (GPO, 1976). For the House's action, see *Congressional Record*, August 30, 1976, pp. 28277–88. Most of the debate was concerned with a floor amendment that required the states to refrain from reducing supplemental payments in response to the federal government's granting of automatic increases in benefits indexed to increases in the cost of living.

5. Robert Ball would later recall that HEW Secretary Caspar W. Weinberger had discouraged the SSA from conducting a large-scale mail campaign to locate people who might be eligible, on the grounds that the government should not go out of its way to encourage applications for welfare benefits. Communication to author, October 30, 1989.

6. *Supplemental Security Income Program*, Hearings, vol. 1, pp. 10–11.

7. *Supplemental Security Income Amendments of 1976*, H. Rept. 94-1201, p. 6.

relatively minor changes to the program when it became convinced of their urgency. As a brief official history observed on SSI's tenth anniversary, "The legislative results of the oversight process have been selective."[8] Selective and few.

The disability review presented a different situation, one more susceptible to a statutory fix. That there were problems in the administration of disability insurance was well recognized even before the review got under way. For some years Congress had been concerned about the rising volume of appeals filed by applicants who had initially been denied benefits and by the rising tendency of administrative law judges to overturn state agency decisions. In the spring of 1981, when the effects of the disability review had yet to be felt, Representative J. J. Pickle, chairman of the Subcommittee on Social Security of the Ways and Means Committee, attempted to get at this problem with a proposal that would have required the same disability determination guidelines to apply at all levels of the adjudicative process. Pickle first attached this and several other provisions on disability insurance to a bill designed primarily to address problems of social security finance. When that bill failed to go anywhere, he tried in November 1981 to attach his disability amendments to still another piece of social security legislation, but that effort failed in committee. Had Pickle succeeded, some of the worst effects of the review might have been mitigated.

Having failed to act in anticipation of those effects, Congress was forced to react to them. Starting in the spring of 1982, five different committee units were substantially involved—the Ways and Means and Finance committees, of course, as the committees with legislative jurisdiction, and also the Subcommittee on Oversight of Government Management of the Senate Governmental Affairs Committee, the Senate Special Committee on Aging, and the House Select Committee on Aging, which staked out a role in oversight with hearings, followed in some instances by legislative proposals. Some of these committees, including notably Ways and Means, operated through more than one subcommittee.[9]

It appeared for some time that differences over disability policy were too deep to be resolved. The House was under Democratic control. The Senate was controlled by Republicans, but closely divided on disability issues. It had trouble reconciling internal differences as

8. John Trout and David R. Mattson, "A 10-Year Review of the Supplemental Security Income Program," *Social Security Bulletin*, vol. 47 (January 1984), p. 8.

9. Congressional actions are summarized in Collins and Erfle, "Social Security Disability Benefits Reform Act of 1984."

well as those with the House. Late in 1983 the two houses managed to agree on a fragmentary, temporary measure that permitted persons dropped from the rolls before October 1, 1983, to continue collecting benefits while their appeals were pending (if the appeals were denied, benefits had to be repaid). This act also required that beginning on January 1, 1984, face-to-face hearings be held at the first stage of appeal, within the state agency. (Previously, appellants did not receive a face-to-face hearing until they reached an administrative law judge.) However, more fundamental issues—what the standards for disability determination and redetermination should be and where the burden of proof should lie in redeterminations, with the individual or the government—continued to elicit sharp, emotional, and paralyzing conflict.

While outrage mounted at the conduct of the review, Reagan administration officials and long-standing critics of the disability program in Congress, such as Senator Russell B. Long, remained determined to proceed, unshaken in the belief that many recipients were collecting benefits to which they were not entitled and the government should defend its financial integrity. During 1982 and 1983 the administration made a number of changes designed to alleviate the worst effects of the review—for example, it broadened the definition of exempt persons and stopped reviewing the mentally ill—but it resisted corrective legislation, a position dictated by the Office of Management and Budget over the objections of the secretary of Health and Human Services.[10] Representative Pickle at one point suggested that the administration's unilateral announcement of reforms was meant to undermine his effort to produce a bill.[11]

What forced opposing factions in the legislature and executive to compromise and at last collaborate on a bill was the prospect that they would be totally displaced as policymakers by the courts. Late in February 1984 the Court of Appeals for the Ninth Circuit ruled against the secretary of HHS in a major class action, finding that benefits could not be terminated without a demonstration of substantial improvement in the recipients' medical condition or clear error in the

10. David Whitman, "Television and the 1981–84 Review of the Disability Rolls," in Martin Linsky and others, *How the Press Affects Federal Policymaking: Six Case Studies* (Norton, 1986), pp. 342–43.

11. *Social Security Disability Insurance,* Hearing before the Subcommittee on Social Security of the House Committee on Ways and Means, 98 Cong. 1 sess. (GPO, 1983), pp. 40–42. For a summary of the administration's remedies, see ibid., pp. 39–40; and *Social Security Disability Reviews: A Federally Created State Problem,* Hearing before the House Select Committee on Aging, 98 Cong. 1 sess. (GPO, 1983), pp. 518–31.

original decision.[12] Similar decisions had already been rendered in class actions in five district courts around the nation. By spring, twenty-eight class actions dealing with medical improvement were pending, and the affected population ranged up to 230,000—potentially everyone removed from the rolls since March 1981 who had not yet been restored via individual appeals. The possibility loomed that the review could be *completely* reversed by the courts. Already nearly twenty states were operating under court-ordered eligibility criteria or were subject to moratoria pending implementation of court orders.[13] Under these circumstances, legislation was essential if the review were to be preserved at all. Accordingly, within a few weeks in the spring of 1984 the House passed a bill; opposing factions in the Senate broke a two-year deadlock, paving the way for a floor vote; and the secretary of HHS suspended reviews "until new legislation is enacted and can be effectively implemented" while pledging the department's "full cooperation" in working with Congress.[14]

The legislation that emerged in the fall of 1984 (the Social Security Disability Benefits Reform Act) followed the lead of the courts on the crucial issue. It provided that the secretary of HHS could terminate a beneficiary's entitlement to insurance or SSI for the disabled only if at least one of the following conditions were met: (1) the individual had medically improved; (2) new medical evidence and a new assessment of the individual's capacity demonstrated that he or she had benefited from advances in medical or vocational therapy or technology or had undergone vocational therapy and was now able to work; (3) on the basis of new or improved diagnostic techniques or evaluations, the individual's impairment was not as disabling as originally presumed; or (4) an earlier determination was found to be in error. There were numerous other provisions. This was a detailed and subtle law, with much of the hair splitting common to compromises that are worked

12. *Lopez* v. *Heckler*, 725 F.2d 1489 (1984).

13. Here and more generally in this account of legislation, I rely on Carolyn L. Weaver, "Social Security Disability Policy in the 1980s and Beyond," in Monroe Berkowitz and M. Anne Hill, eds., *Disability and the Labor Market: Economic Problems, Policies, and Programs* (Cornell University, New York State School of Industrial and Labor Relations: ILR Press, 1986), pp. 29–40. Weaver was on the staff of Senator Robert Dole, chairman of the Finance Committee, while the legislation was being considered. Also see Patricia Dilley, "Social Security: Political Philosophy and History," in Arthur T. Meyerson and Theodora Fine, eds., *Psychiatric Disability: Clinical, Legal and Administrative Dimensions* (Washington: American Psychiatric Press, 1987), pp. 373–409. Dilley worked for the majority staff of the Ways and Means Committee.

14. Linda E. Demkovich, "Administration About-Face on Disability Could Be a Political Blessing in Disguise," *National Journal*, April 28, 1984, p. 824.

out between sharply antagonistic, closely balanced forces in regard to complex subject matter. As the conference report noted, the agreement was an attempt

> to strike a balance between the concern that a medical improvement standard could be interpreted to grant claimants a presumption of eligibility, which might make it extremely difficult to remove ineligible individuals from the benefit rolls, and the concern that the absence of an explicit standard of review . . . could be interpreted to imply a presumption of ineligibility or to allow arbitrary termination decisions, which might lead to many individuals being improperly removed from the rolls.[15]

Also, Congress sought to reclaim control over the program from the courts by providing that no class actions relating to medical improvement could be certified after September 19, 1984, if they involved termination decisions previously made by the SSA.

In January 1986 the SSA resumed conduct of reviews, which thereafter proceeded with less controversy.[16] Legislative action, when it finally came, proved quite effective.

BLAME CASTING

Much of congressional oversight activity is not designed to culminate in remedial legislation. Rather, it is designed primarily to fix blame for government's poor performance on the executive branch or the other political party. Conceivably it contributes in the long run to the devising of remedies by adding to the stock of information about what went wrong, but any such result is tenuous. In the short run, it yields politically rewarding publicity for the congressional practitioners and public humiliation for the agency.[17]

Blame casting is far easier than remedy seeking because it can be accomplished rhetorically. Extensive knowledge, far from a requirement, may actually be a handicap. Blame casting requires very little

---

15. *Social Security Disability Benefits Reform Act of 1984*, H. Rept. 98-1039, 98 Cong. 2 sess. (GPO, 1984), p. 26.

16. Spencer Rich, "Government Resumes Effort to Verify Disability Claims," *Washington Post*, May 14, 1986, p. A24.

17. The pioneering analysis of policymakers' desire to avoid blame is R. Kent Weaver, "The Politics of Blame Avoidance," *Journal of Public Policy*, vol. 6 (October–December 1986), pp. 371–98.

concerting of activity within Congress; given a suitable committee position and staff support, one or two members can engage in it. Nor does it require cooperation from the executive except insofar as administration witnesses must attend hearings in order to be berated. In the U.S. system of government, it is their custom to appear. Moreover, for this activity Congress has a spontaneous and powerful ally in the press, which ordinarily finds the cause of bureaucratic failures in the bureaucracy itself, a proximate, vulnerable, and easily caricatured target.

The most aggressive and unabashed blame casters are committees that lack primary legislative jurisdiction and instead are oriented toward particular constituent groups—the select and special committees on aging, in these cases. These committees have become very active and also, in the case of the House committee, very large.[18] "Press releases are their reason for being," a former staff member of the Ways and Means Committee remarked contemptuously.[19] Legislative committees, exemplified here by Ways and Means in the House and Finance in the Senate, are inhibited by greater knowledge, by a palpable sharing of responsibility, and by a need to maintain amicable working relations with executive officials. Yet even these committees' working relations with the executive may be undermined by partisan differences. The SSA's misfortunes with SSI and the disability review occurred when Republicans controlled the executive and Democrats controlled at least one house of the Congress. As a result, the Democratic-controlled committees were more inclined toward blame casting than they would have been had their own party been the object. Also, the very engagement of these committees with the fortunes of their programs may give rise to a sharp, nearly personal sense of grievance if they feel that executive collaborators have misled them. The report of the Senate Finance Committee staff on SSI came close to charging that the executive had sold the legislature a false bill of goods.

Of the several techniques of blame casting, by far the most common is simple exposure and attack. Congressional committees indict an agency's performance by amassing evidence of its defects. They do this directly, by putting questions to executive witnesses and by reporting what they have heard from the members' own constituents. Just as often they amplify indictments prepared by others, by providing a platform for them. These others, in a politically active, highly

18. See Roger H. Davidson, "Congressional Committees as Moving Targets," *Legislative Studies Quarterly*, vol. 11 (February 1986), p. 23.

19. Interview, Patricia E. Dilley, August 30, 1988.

organized society, are numerous, articulate, and often quite well informed. Thus, for example, when the House Select Committee on Aging held a hearing on the disability review in June 1983, it amassed a record of fifteen statements from members of Congress and testimony from a twice-wounded Vietnam veteran and Medal of Honor winner who had lost his benefits; the organizer of the Alliance of Social Security Disability Recipients, a group spontaneously formed in North Carolina and claiming 2,700 members; the governor of Arkansas and four high-ranking legislative or executive officials from other states; and three officials from the SSA. Appendixes included a background paper prepared by the committee staff; case histories of denials submitted by a member of Congress; studies of the disability review by a special commission of the Massachusetts legislature and by an interagency task force in Michigan, each exhaustive and laden with its own appendixes; and prepared statements from the National Association of Counties and National Association of Disability Examiners.

This was an impressive and highly informative record, but hardly more so than that put together by the Subcommittee on Social Security of the Ways and Means Committees in a hearing only ten days later. That committee heard four officials from the SSA, one from the General Accounting Office, four members of Congress, and representatives of numerous state agencies and professional associations such as the American Association of Psychiatric Services for Children, the Commission on Legal Problems of the Elderly of the American Bar Association, the American Mental Health Counsellors Association, the American Psychiatric Association, the American Psychological Association, the Task Force on Social Security of the Consortium for Citizens with Developmental Disabilities, the National Multiple Sclerosis Society, the National Mental Health Association, the Mental Health Law Project, and the National Senior Citizens Law Center. It too reproduced the interagency task force report from Michigan, but while these numerous committee records contain some duplication, the general impression is of material more than sufficient to go around.

A second technique of blame casting is to charge the agency with failure to conform to legislative intent. Members of Congress often said that they never intended the disability review, and of course that was true in a qualified sense; no one intended a review of the kind that occurred. Disappointment and disillusionment were also themes of the congressional reaction to SSI, particularly as expressed in the Senate Finance Committee's staff study. SSI "was to provide income support in a manner which resembled as closely as possible the dignified and unobjectionable approach of the social security programs, and it was expected that [it] would be managed with the accuracy and efficiency which the Social Security Administration had traditionally brought" to them, the report said. However, SSI bore "too little resemblance" to the efficient program that Congress intended to establish. "The administering agency has repeatedly ignored the law in making policy decisions which run directly contrary to the statute and its legislative history; these policy decisions have distorted the nature of the program and have significantly increased the difficulty of administering it."[20]

At the time laws are enacted, congressional intentions are rarely stated with precision. Legislative histories embody generalized hopes for beneficial results, obscuring differences within the legislature and failing to anticipate anything like the full range of costs and consequences, let alone attempting to specify what costs and consequences Congress will tolerate.[21] To chastise agencies for failing to conform to legislative intentions therefore is ordinarily more than a little unfair. However, to the extent that purposes and assumptions are spelled out in legislative documents, they are likely to have been derived from executive sources. For legislative actions the executive itself has proposed, it supplies rationales in the normal course of advocacy, and for what anyone proposes, it will supply cost estimates. To the extent Congress adopts such material as its own, there is rough justice, after all, in complaining if things do not work out as the executive indicated. To a considerable extent, Congress's "intentions" are defined by the executive through calculated guesses or promises about the effects of proposed legislation.

Using estimates supplied by the SSA, a Ways and Means Committee report in 1979 had projected very modest savings from the disability review. In the short run, administrative costs were expected to exceed savings. Savings were projected to reach $123 million in 1984, a relatively trivial sum. If this could be taken as a fair guide to what Congress expected at the time it acted, then the magnitude of the actual event would surely have come as a surprise. Still, to speak of congressional *intentions*, as congressmen did during oversight, implied more precision of purpose than ever existed. The purpose, after all, was to remove ineligible persons from the rolls. How many there were,

20. *The Supplemental Security Income Program*, Committee Print, Senate Committee on Finance, 95 Cong. 1 sess. (GPO, 1977), p. 3.

21. See Robert A. Katzmann, *Institutional Disability: The Saga of Transportation Policy for the Disabled* (Brookings, 1986), chap. 2.

no one in 1980 knew (or pretended to know until the GAO report broadcast the SSA's tentative findings). What the review established, above all, was the great difficulty of ascertaining how many there were in a way that would generally be accepted as legitimate. In this situation, congressional oversight cast blame on the executive for failing to conform to an intention that was ill defined if only because the executive itself had been unable to assist reliably in defining it.[22]

By contrast, in the case of SSI the executive had been all too helpful. Armed for advocacy, it had taken the lead in asserting that SSI would set a new standard for dignity and efficiency. The Senate Finance Committee had been skeptical about federalizing administration. It had required much more persuading than the House Ways and Means Committee. Afterward it pretended to have believed what it was told in order to prove that its intentions had been betrayed.

There was more than casual, instinctive blame casting here. There was sharp disillusionment at having been misled about the SSA's capacities. "The Congress chose this agency because of its reputation for accurate, efficient, humane, and dignified administration," the staff report said. "It was expected [which is to say, "we were told"] that the Social Security Administration would be able to administer the SSI program within its existing administrative processes with relative ease. . . . In urging the federalization of income maintenance programs in the period from 1969 to 1972, executive branch officials had placed great emphasis on the improved quality of administration which could be expected from federally run programs as compared with existing State welfare programs."[23]

In charging specifically that the SSA had failed to conform to the law, the report sought to establish that the agency was to blame for

22. In an exchange with the acting commissioner of social security in 1985, one member of Congress acknowledged the great difficulty of ascertaining Congress's intentions in regard to the disability review. Representative Hal Daub said: "The way we have acted in Congress over the last 6 or 8 years would be enough headache for any well-intentioned bureaucrat. I know how difficult it has been for you and your staff to try to keep up with crystal balling what Congress meant. You are never going to get it perfect. We are always going to have a different view of what our intent was given pressures." Public statements of such candor are, of course, quite rare. *Implementation of the Social Security Disability Amendments of 1984*, Hearing before the Subcommittee on Social Security of the House Committee on Ways and Means, 99 Cong. 1 sess. (GPO, 1985), p. 27. However, it is not unusual for members of Congress to assure SSA officials privately that their criticisms are not really meant to be as severe as they sound. Without quite saying so, they convey that the severity is for public consumption. Interview, Elliot Kirschbaum, former SSA associate commissioner for policy, July 27, 1989.

23. *Supplemental Security Income Program*, Committee Print, pp. 5, 8.

the SSI's failing to become a uniform, relatively simple national program rather than a federally administered reincarnation of all the old state programs. This was a sensitive point. Because the Finance Committee in the summer of 1973 had devised the legislation that required states to hold individual recipients harmless by supplementing federal payments—and required the SSA to administer these mandatory supplements—it was vulnerable to the charge of having crucially subverted the executive's design. The Finance Committee deserved much of the blame for the program's having become so hard to administer; executive officials had occasionally hinted as much. The staff report replied, first, by complaining that the executive had declined to cooperate in securing relief for individuals whose benefits would have dropped under SSI, and, more to the point, by arguing that the executive created its own problems by agreeing to administer so many variations in state supplemental payments. "Departmental policy governing State supplementary benefits departs from clear legislative intent in a way that has distorted the basic purpose of the SSI program and has contributed heavily to the Department's inability to properly manage and control it," the report said.[24] Thus, far from shouldering blame, it contrived to turn the complex, variable, decentralized nature of the new program into one more instance of executive perversion of legislative instruction.

Two additional approaches to blame casting are detectable, both with marked signs of partisan motivation. One is to suggest that poor administrative performance results from a willful effort to discredit social programs. The other invites agency officials to put blame upon their executive supervisors at the departmental and presidential levels.

Officeholders in American government routinely impute political motives to other officeholders, especially ones who belong to the opposing political party or as administrators are currently accountable to it. Thus, for example, when SSA Commissioner Cardwell objected

---

24. *Supplemental Security Income Program*, Committee Print, p. 10. Intent in this instance was signified both by statutory language that required states electing federal administration of their supplemental payments to abide by federal rules and procedures and by a lengthy passage in a Ways and Means Committee report. The thrust of these statements, which originated with the executive, was to endorse the greatest possible degree of uniformity. "In general," the report said, "it is anticipated that the same rules and regulations would be applied to both Federal and State supplemental payments with the only difference being the level of such payments. However, the Secretary could agree to a variation affecting only the State supplemental *if he finds he can do so without materially increasing his costs of administration and if he finds the variation consistent with the objectives of the program and its efficient administration*" (p. 69).

in an executive session that raising SSI benefits literally on the eve of the program's start would make administration much more difficult, Representative James Burke, a liberal Democrat who headed the Social Security Subcommittee of the Ways and Means Committee, discounted his objections as Republican-inspired.[25] Burke sincerely disbelieved administrators' claims that they needed a substantial amount of time, on the order of weeks or months rather than days, in which to prepare computers for a change in benefits.[26] Administrative arguments are generally discounted as surrogates for political ones.

At the extreme, the view that politics motivates all administrative conduct leads to the charge that poor administrative performance is willful. In both of the cases here, Democrats would sometimes suggest that Republican administrations' lack of sympathy for social programs caused them to engage in administrative sabotage. In a hearing on SSI, for example, Representative Fortney H. (Pete) Stark remarked to Commissioner Cardwell that "it would seem to people far less paranoid than I that if one were trying to wreck a national health insurance program and prove that HEW was incompetent to supervise one, that the people who are running SSI would do just what you are doing— showing [that] you can really wreck programs by purposefully being incompetent."[27] The same partisan, paranoid theme crops up in the Democrats' reaction to the disability review. In a prepared statement, Claude Pepper, the chairman of the House Select Committee on Aging, observed that "as part of a plan to undermine confidence in the social security system and the invaluable protection it offers, the cruel and callous policies employed to strike terror into the hearts of crippled people all across America could not be more successful."[28]

A milder, far more credible variant of this theme was Chairman Pickle's charge, in response to HHS's hint in March 1984 that it was about to announce an eighteen-month moratorium on disability reviews, that the administration was trying to sabotage corrective legislation.

25. Interview, Sumner G. Whittier, former director, Bureau of Supplemental Security Income, December 5, 1986.

26. Interview, J. William Kelley, former staff member, House Ways and Means Committee, August 24, 1988.

27. *Administration of the Supplemental Security Income Program*, Hearings before the Subcommittee on Oversight of the House Committee on Ways and Means, 94 Cong. 2 sess. (GPO, 1976), vol. 3, p. 26. Cardwell fought back: "Mr. Stark, you wreck them by your accusations and by reaching the conclusions you keep articulating. You do as much as anybody by saying we don't know what we are doing."

28. *Social Security Disability Insurance Program: Cessations and Denials*, Hearing before the House Select Committee on Aging, 97 Cong. 2 sess. (GPO, 1982), p. 3.

News of the administration's plan immediately preceded a House vote on a bill. Pickle made a sharp reply:

This moratorium is a cruel hoax offering false promises of relief to the disabled while, in fact, helping to bring about the total and complete disruption of the disability insurance program. This proposal is a clear admission by this administration that their management of the disability program is a complete failure. . . .

In my opinion this is just one more example of a streak of meanness toward Human Services which runs throughout this administration. The bill that we are hoping can be passed immediately is desperately needed to restore order to a program which in the past few years has been reduced to chaos.[29]

In a rhetorical setting so sharply partisan, it becomes impossible to advance plausibly, let alone win support for, any proposal on the ground that administrative considerations require it. As a rule, the elected participants in American government do not believe that administrative considerations genuinely and independently exist.

Partisan motives also are often, though not necessarily, at the root of the wedge-driving tactic that congressional overseers like to use with agency witnesses. As one way of casting blame, they invite agency officials to blame executive overseers. "Did you get the personnel from the OMB that you wanted?" Senator Edward M. Kennedy disingenuously inquired of Commissioner Cardwell regarding SSI. "Over the period of the last 3 years, what is it that you have requested and what have you received?"[30] Thus Congress allies itself with the agency against the administrative presidency, not so much to support the former as to indict the latter. Agency officials, constrained by loyalty to the president, discreetly decline to contribute to the indictment. Cardwell replied to Kennedy that the SSA had requested more manpower than it got, but that "everyone" in the executive branch and in Congress had accepted the erroneous assumption that federal manpower requirements would be much lower than those of the states. Republican members of Congress were in general less sharply critical

29. *Social Security Disability Reviews: The Human Costs*, Joint Hearing between the Subcommittee on Social Security of the House Committee on Ways and Means and the Senate Special Committee on Aging, 98 Cong. 2 sess. (GPO, 1984), pt. 3, pp. 2–3.

30. *Future Directions in Social Security*, Hearing before the Senate Special Committee on Aging, 94 Cong. 1 sess. (GPO, 1975), pt. 12, pp. 990–91.

of the administration than Democrats, but did not go so far as to come
to the administration's defense.

WITH THE AID OF THE PRESS

Media coverage of both events was heavy. Cast often as exposés of
the SSA, these stories complemented congressional exposure and attack,
sometimes contributing directly to it.

For SSI, the most important coverage was a series of front-page
stories that ran in the *Washington Star* for six weeks beginning in mid-
August 1975. Under the running headline of "Social Security Scandal,"
the series featured such individual headlines as: "$403,798,830.74 in
Overpayments"; "Welfare Payments Wrong 23% of the Time"; "States
Fight Back"; "$179 Million Overpayment for Year Irks California";
"Fixing Welfare Errors Costly in Overtime"; "Other Programs Infected"; "Judge Acts to Protect U.S. Welfare Clients"; "Computers
Go Haywire to Tune of Millions." The series concluded with several
pieces that purported to explain what went wrong. These did not
focus exclusively on the agency. On the contrary, the first of them
dealt with Senator Russell B. Long's insistence on changing the law
in the summer of 1973 to assure that no recipient would have benefits
reduced: "A Senator's Clout Sparked the Mess in Overpayments."
The second concentrated on the agency, but not in a way that suggested
misfeasance. Its theme was that established SSA bureau chiefs, "the
barons," out of pride and a will to dominate, had failed to support the
"outsider" who had been made the first chief of the Bureau of
Supplemental Security Income. Still, the overall impression was of
blundering and, worse, "scandal," at the agency.[31]

Officials of the SSA replied as best they could. First the new
commissioner, James B. Cardwell, wrote to protest that "there is no
scandal," that the series lacked "objective context," and that "erroneous
payments . . . are a fundamental characteristic of each and every
benefit payment system operated at any level of government."[32] Later
the outgoing acting commissioner, Arthur E. Hess, wrote a long piece
for the *Star* that patiently and carefully explained the complexities of

31. The first "news" story ran on August 15 and the last on September 28. The
more analytical pieces appeared on October 6, 7, and 8.

32. *Washington Star*, August 16, 1975, p. A5.

the situation and defended the legitimacy of many so-called overpayments.[33] Both pleaded for simplification of the program.

In the case of the disability review, coverage was divided between print and visual media. The "horror stories"—cases of obviously disabled persons who had lost their benefits—were well suited to portrayal on television. Typical segments of TV coverage began with interviews of pathetic victims of the review, proceeded to scenes in which disaffected examiners, administrative law judges, and doctors criticized it, and concluded with defensive comments from SSA officials.[34]

Print coverage was heavy nationwide. Between 1981 and 1984 hundreds of stories appeared in newspapers around the country recounting the suffering of thousands of individuals who had been cut off. Coverage was especially heavy and prominent in the *New York Times* and was complemented there by numerous pieces of editorial opinion specifically aimed at the agency. A *Times* editorial said that the agency had taken Congress's command to review disability cases "as a license for bureaucratic mayhem."[35] *Times* Columnist Anthony Lewis cited the SSA's nonacquiescence in court decisions as one example of a profound and growing contempt of the Reagan administration for the rule of law.[36]

On TV, coverage was concentrated on the CBS network, which ran four "horror story" segments, two each on the morning and evening news, and several updates on the progress of reform legislation. NBC ran one report on the nightly news, and PBS did one documentary show. There was also a great deal of local coverage. SSA officials

33. Arthur E. Hess, "Reply to Our SSI Stories: Problems Being Tackled, Goals Being Met," *Washington Star*, September 7, 1975. Overpayments, Hess explained, often were not simply errors, but resulted from: "the deliberate judgment to give the benefit of the doubt to thousands of blind, aged or disabled persons to pay the higher of two possible amounts when it was clear that a payment was due at once"; deciding "to activate payment systems even though not all the accounting facets were in place, because to hesitate any longer would have put in mortal jeopardy payments to three million people"; paying in advance, as required by law, to meet a recipient's expected needs, only to find later that changes in circumstance caused the payment to be greater than necessary; the SSA's being placed under court restraining orders to continue payments that it knew should have been stopped; and differences of judgment between state and federal authorities, auditors and quality assurance reviewers, and administrators and judges.

34. Whitman, "Television and the 1981–84 Review," pp. 313–14.

35. "Why Drive Troubled People Crazy?" April 20, 1983, p. A26.

36. "A Profound Contempt," May 21, 1984, p. A17.

appeared in a number of these to make defensive answers to accusatory questions. "We're not playing God," Associate Commissioner Sandy Crank said on CBS. "We are not out to kill people," Deputy Commissioner Paul Simmons said.[37]

Because a theme of this coverage was that the Reagan administration was abusing vulnerable members of society, the White House became involved. It had not otherwise taken much notice of the disability review. The president himself saw and reacted to a local news story on WRC-TV in Washington. "What are we doing?" the president asked, after seeing this portrayal of a family in which a disabled father had lost his benefits.[38]

Wishing to avoid blame, the Reagan White House reacted in two ways. First, it counterattacked the media with charges of inaccuracy. Concentrating on the poignancy of individual cases, reporters almost never pointed out, for example, that the review had originated in a congressional enactment in 1980 or that the statutory standards for receipt of disability benefits were quite strict. Second, members of the White House staff urged SSA officials to seek ways of moderating the review generally and of assuring a politically acceptable outcome in at least one highly publicized and acutely embarrassing case—that of Master Sergeant Roy Benavidez, a Mexican-American who had received the Congressional Medal of Honor from President Reagan for his bravery in the Vietnam War.[39]

The heavy volume of media coverage caused the White House to view the disability review as above all a problem of presidential public relations, while congressional Democrats were encouraged to see it as an opportunity to secure TV exposure. In preparation for a Senate Budget Committee hearing at which HHS Secretary Richard Schweiker was to testify, an aide to Senator Jim Sasser of Tennessee wrote him in March 1982:

A television crew from *Sixty Minutes* is supposed to cover this hearing. . . . There is a good chance if you ask Mr. Schweiker about the problems of the new accelerated disability review procedures you may get some good press. Especially since I have been talking with someone from CBS in New York on this matter who is doing a documentary in April for Bill Moyers' *Journal*.

37. Whitman, "Television and the 1981–84 Review," pp. 310–12, quote at p. 312.
38. Whitman, "Television and the 1981–84 Review," pp. 316–17.
39. Whitman, "Television and the 1981–84 Review," pp. 328–42.

There have been numerous reports outlining problems with removing eligible people from the Disability rolls according to a quota system. CBS was interested in a letter that our office received which was unsigned but went to the very heart of the callous indifference and cruelty of the system of disability reviews. You could read this letter to the Secretary as it would be an interesting human interest piece.

Sasser did read the letter to Schweiker and ask whether the SSA was using a quota system. Schweiker replied that it was not. The exchange failed to get on TV.[40]

IT IS AT THE oversight stage that an agency feels the full impact of the separation of powers. Under the system of separated powers, although the agency has several sources of command, it has no reliable source of protection when things go wrong, as they did in the two instances under study here. Because no single institution is preeminently in charge of agency conduct, none must accept responsibility when it falters. In distress, it is isolated, a naked object of blame.

Oversight is marked by particularly sharp conflict between the executive and the legislature. The structural and (sometimes) partisan differences between the executive and the legislature that are inherent in a system of separated powers, when combined with electoral dynamics, give Congress a powerful incentive to use oversight in an intensely critical way, casting executive agencies in the worst possible light. Members of Congress seek to demonstrate to constituents that they are not at fault for misfortune at the hands of government and that they are eager to listen to and redress grievances.

Congress's oversight of both SSI and the disability review was abundant and to a considerable extent self-serving. Partisan conflict, reinforcing interbranch conflict, was especially sharp in the disability review. Although congressional committees that are specialized by function, and thus have responsibility for legislation, are somewhat inhibited from casting blame on the executive and exploiting public grievances for political ends, committees that are specialized by constituency are under no such constraint. Thus special committees on aging in both cases functioned as especially critical overseers.

The administrative agency bears the brunt of this scrutiny of "the executive." The scrutiny certainly is not borne primarily by the

40. Whitman, "Television and the 1981–84 Review," p. 313.

president and his immediate staff, nor even by his appointees at the level of the executive departments. They do not appear before Congress to account for administrative actions; agency officials do.

Agency leaders shoulder blame before Congress or construct discreet evasions rather than plead that the president was at fault. The administrative presidency's claim on the loyalty of agency leaders is strong enough that they do not take refuge in the excuse that the OMB has cut their budgets, even if it is true. The president has enough control over the agencies, principally through the power of appointment, to assure that the public statements of agency heads do not implicate *him* when blame is being apportioned.

Part IV
Conclusion

CHAPTER 9

An Administrative Perspective

THE PICTURE that emerges from the preceding six chapters is of an agency badly buffeted by external forces, its ability to do what is asked of it largely taken for granted. It is not viewed as a valuable public resource to be husbanded, nor as a tool that needs care and maintenance and can be used effectively only by those who comprehend how it functions. Persons who presumably would give painstaking attention to instructions on how to use a pasta machine or a piece of video equipment make major policy decisions with virtually no thought to whether a complex organization of human beings can reasonably be expected to execute their commands. The difference lies in the fact that organizations of human beings, unlike mechanical or electrical devices, are thought to be infinitely pliable. It is of course true that people are more pliable than mechanical or electrical devices—but they are also less predictable and therefore require a greater effort to understand.

In this chapter I summarize and elaborate upon three themes: institutional features of American government inescapably impose handicaps on administrative performance; policymakers in general lack concern for administration; and even when they try to anticipate the administrative consequences of their policy choices, they are liable to err.

STRUCTURAL HANDICAPS

The institutional context in which the Social Security Administration operates—what I will call its policy-producing environment—puts many obstacles in the way of its performing well.

First, the environment is unpredictable. Whereas the chief executives of private, profit-making organizations can within limits define their own agendas, executives of public agencies have theirs thrust upon them. Nor do agenda items emerge in a measured, steady, predictable way. Proposals for action are likely to be fraught with a false urgency, dictated by the results of elections just past or the hoped-for results of elections soon to be held. Electoral dynamics, in combination with the fixed, four-year presidential term, encourage newly elected chief executives to sponsor bold departures in policy that inevitably entail administrative risks. Supplemental security income originated and the disability review was accelerated in this way.

The results of legislative deliberation, and their timing, are uncertain until an enactment actually occurs. It is therefore hard for executive agencies to plan. They do not know what they will be commanded to do or when they will be commanded to do it until legislative action has been concluded. For a long time, it appeared that the Senate would not approve SSI. While the SSA had a planning effort formally in place, it lacked both urgency and realism. Then, in the late summer of 1972, the Senate acted quite suddenly, and the agency was galvanized into action, with a little over a year to prepare for a major new responsibility.

The chances are that whatever an agency is commanded to do, it will be expected to do quickly. Congress does not act unless convinced of the popularity of its actions; once it decides to act, it becomes impatient to realize, and receive credit for, the benefits. Besides, a general and no doubt well-founded belief that bureaucracies are normally sluggish makes politicians seek ways to force deadlines on them.

Second, the policy-producing environment is unstable. Laws change constantly, not necessarily in gross terms, but at least in operational detail—and operational detail is what administration consists of. What happened to SSI between its enactment in the fall of 1972 and its inauguration in January 1974 is a vivid, extreme example. Congress kept fine-tuning the law to deal with new or newly discovered problems, while the SSA struggled to prepare to administer a law that would not hold still. It would have been different, of course, if the changes had been designed to facilitate administration, but that was not the case. Although the SSI example is extreme, it is not anomalous. Congress is never idle. Its temper, as Woodrow Wilson observed more than a century ago, "is strenuously legislative."[1] A strenuous legislature,

1. *Congressional Government* (Johns Hopkins University Press, 1981), p. 193.

because it is prolific, requires a strenuous administration. Moreover, the spirit of the law is as susceptible to revision by Congress as the letter. In disability insurance, the revision of spirit that occurred in the late 1970s was at least as important as the revision of the letter that occurred in 1980.

A third feature of the policy-producing environment, richly illustrated by these cases, is conflicting cues. The separated institutions of American government give separate guidance. In the absence of a coordinating force, their instructions often conflict, for the institutions are constituted on different principles and tend to have different policy biases. The president and Congress are separately accountable in their own ways to their particular electorates, and the courts are as nearly autonomous as any institution in a democratic society can be. At any particular time, the primary institutions also embody partisan or ideological preferences peculiar to that time (even if they do not do so in equal measure). Each has its own conception of what an important agency, deeply engaged in direct relations with the public, ought to be doing. Each has a constitutional right to seek to influence the agency's conduct. Each has a particular set of institutional weapons it uses to that end.

To say that an agency must often operate without clear guidance is an understatement. Rather, it becomes the object of an institutional struggle, waged more or less intensively depending on the issues and stakes associated with its functions at any given time. Sometimes it must operate under conditions of intense institutional conflict.

In SSI, the presidency conceived of a simple, uniform, rights-oriented, thoroughly rationalized national program, consistent with its preference for rationalizing measures. Congress, which is notably more heedful of variety, special cases, and vested interests, enacted an extremely complex, contingent, qualified, and variable one—and then the courts finished the job by insisting on administrative adjudication tailored carefully to the individual case. In the disability review, Congress and the presidency ordered a review of the rolls, the SSA responded in a way that was faithful to its published regulations and established routines, and the courts pronounced the response illegitimate. As the review unfolded, conflict among the guiding institutions intensified. The Reagan presidency was telling the agency to proceed under existing rules; the courts were saying it could not do so, but must adopt a medical improvement standard; and Congress was torn between the two positions, unable to act.

Nor are interbranch conflicts the only ones an agency must cope with. Even considered individually, the branches do not display a high degree of consistency. They have more than one role, and different roles yield different policy biases.

The policymaking presidency tends to sponsor bold innovation. It favors acts that depend for their success on concentration of central authority. The administrative presidency, by contrast, is fiscally oriented. Like Congress, it is reluctant to pay the costs of truly national programs. Thus, in the case of SSI the policymaking presidency insisted on imposing a major new administrative burden on the SSA while the administrative presidency resisted giving it the support to do the job. In the disability review, the policymaking and administrative presidencies were essentially allied in support of cost-saving innovation, but not to the degree that the Reagan administration would have been willing to contemplate a federal takeover of state disability agencies.

Congress likewise changes as it shifts from policymaker to overseer and provider of constituency service. As a policymaker, Congress has enacted strict standards of eligibility for disability insurance, but its individual members complain when standards are applied with strictness to their own constituents. As a policymaker, Congress objected in the late 1970s that the program was being run too loosely and it compelled fresh constraint; but when constraint bore heavily on constituents, Congress as overseer quickly drew back and assailed the agency.

There is some distortion, of course, in generalizing about the inconsistent roles of Congress, as if Congress were a monolith. Different committees have different roles; for example, the committees having legislative jurisdiction over the SSA's programs—the House Committee on Ways and Means and the Senate Committee on Finance—were less zealous overseers in the disability case than the committees on aging, which were specialized by constituency. This observation only reinforces the general point: all of the institutions to which the SSA is accountable have divisions of internal structure. Congress is fragmented by house, party, committee and subcommittee, and district constituencies. The presidency is divided between the Executive Office of the President and the departments, and each of those is divided and subdivided. The courts are divided along territorial and hierarchical lines. The presidency and the courts possess some hierarchy, in contrast to Congress, which has virtually none, but in none of the three branches is internal coordination effective enough to assure clear and consistent guidance to an administrative agency. The SSA's intensely controversial practice of nonacquiescence, for example, originated in response to the inconsistencies of judicial action.

To some extent, the conflicts among and within an agency's supervisory institutions get worked out. Very intense conflicts, such as that of the early 1980s in the disability review, necessitate resolution. In SSI, the highly complex law produced by Congress survived— Congress "won"—and the SSA had to learn to live with it. In the disability review, Congress eventually did act, settling some of the most important issues. Things settle down. Yet some of the conflicts an agency faces are truly unresolvable. There is no way, for example, of settling for all time whether the disability program should be strict or lenient. The contending social forces cannot be put to rest by the stroke of a statutory pen. Many of the conflicts the agency faces are not at bottom artifacts of institutional properties, but reflect fundamental conflicts of value and opinion within the society. Governing institutions are "merely" the medium through which they find expression. Furthermore, to the extent the conflicts are shaped by the different biases of these mediating institutions, the differences largely inhere in the constitutional design. Constituted on different principles to perform more or less distinct governing functions, the branches were designed to be in tension with one another. Thus the fact that they are in tension is unremarkable, but it is necessary to remark on because of its adverse implications for administration. Uncertainty and confusion, which are endemic to the policy-producing environment in the United States, are dysfunctional for administration.

In addition to coping with an unpredictable, unstable environment that produces conflicting cues, an administrative agency must also depend on leadership that routinely changes with presidential elections, if not more often. SSA commissioners came and went very rapidly in the years under study here. An agency is most likely to be devoid of leadership at the moment most likely to be critical for policymaking, namely, the transition between presidencies. The SSA had no head at the outset of the Reagan administration when the disability review was infused with additional momentum.

Furthermore, the agency is likely to depend critically on state-level administrative collaborators. A constitutional legacy of decentralization, combined with the unwillingness of both Congress and the administrative presidency to pay the costs of truly national programs, means that federal agencies are forced to enter into cooperative arrangements with state governments, which retain residual policymaking and administrative roles. The SSA's dependence on state agencies for initial determinations of disability is an example. Under the stress of the disability review, this relation undermined the SSA's ability to act. State governments ceased cooperating with it. In SSI, by contrast, the SSA was obliged to carry out a function on the states' behalf—the tables of interdependence were turned—in a highly exceptional arrangement that proved a plague on the federal agency.

The institutional setting, then, is not merely a source of cues. It does more than send messages. It also shapes the agency's capacity for response by constraining its leadership and compromising the autonomy of even its administrative operations.

There are plenty of opportunities in such an institutional setting for things to go wrong with administration. Whatever emerges as policy in the form of statutory instruction has an ambiguity usually born of elaborate bargaining and compromise. At most, the statute defines an enterprise—it points the agency in a direction—but the agency must then set out at its peril. As the enterprise develops and a course of action is pursued, unanticipated costs and consequences will become apparent. Bearing a heavy burden of uncertainty, the agency also risks bearing a heavy burden of blame if things go badly. Numerous congressional committees are quick to expose error and place all blame on the executive branch.

The president, however, does not ordinarily accept blame. He can decline to take responsibility on behalf of the agencies because he does not head the government—not even, unambiguously, the executive portion of it. Separation of powers has plainly deprived him of authority over the government as a whole, and only a little less plainly deprived him of authority over the executive part. Were his authority to command executive agencies unambiguous rather than being shared with Congress and the courts, his responsibility would be unambiguous too. Because he is, like Congress, responsible to an electorate, he has a powerful political incentive to distance himself from agencies that are in trouble. Though he is not, like Congress, their public critic, neither is he their visible and vocal defender. He does not ordinarily choose to draw on his stock of power and prestige to save their reputations. Presidents were not very visible as SSI and the disability review deteriorated into administrative debacles. Especially in the disability review, the overriding concern of the White House was to combat adverse publicity in order to protect the president's public relations.

Nor do department officials step into the breach. The Constitution positively forbids the simultaneous holding of executive and legislative offices, so that the president's cabinet members do not sit in Congress and answer to it directly and daily, as do ministers in a parliamentary system. Departmental officials do not normally testify in oversight hearings; it was social security commissioners and their staffs who appeared in the dozens of days of hearings that were held on SSI and the disability review. Only technically does a department secretary answer in court. Although Health and Human Services secretaries nominally were the defendants in the SSA's cases and although the Department of Justice did the litigating, as it generally does for executive agencies, the costly defeats in court during the disability review were indubitably defeats for the SSA. It suffered the loss of esteem.

The default of the president, who is the agencies' putative leader, combines with the assertiveness of Congress and the courts to make administrative agencies the fall guys of American government. As every institution's subordinate, they are obliged to answer to each and are permitted to talk back to none.

LACK OF CONCERN FOR ADMINISTRATION

In policymaking by elected officials and their staffs, politics overrides administration, as one would expect. They are concerned above all with how attentive constituencies will react to their choices and with the distribution of costs and benefits among their constituencies. How policy is to be implemented is a concern of a much lower order. What the effects of implementation will be on federal administrative agencies is hardly a concern at all.

Not being much interested in administration, elected officials prefer to entrust it to the administrators, who are presumed to know about it if anyone does. However, legislative and executive policymakers often distrust administrators. Just what form the distrust takes is likely to depend on whether the agency head is a career specialist or a political generalist. Distrust may develop because administrators are thought to protect their own programs excessively or because they fail to display sufficiently impressive levels of managerial competence, policy and program expertise, or articulateness. Often they are judged wanting in deference to policy and political guidance or excessively deferential to such guidance from the "wrong" source.

Also, trust in administrators falls when programs are faring badly. Then presidential and congressional policymakers do not hesitate to assert control over administration. This was the case with the disability review. The seemingly uncontrolled growth of the caseload in the mid-1970s positively invited intrusion. SSI presented a very different case. Confidence in the SSA and its incumbent head, Robert M. Ball, was extremely high. His constant presence in the virtually endless legislative sessions on welfare reform was testimony to the policymakers' respect for his expertise, which in their eyes covered a wide range of policy and administrative matters. They wanted and needed him to be on hand. Among other things, his presence seemed to assure that administration was being attended to.

Yet agency heads, even very expert and experienced ones, know less about what their organizations can do than policymakers would like to believe, and certainly less than would justify political officials' abdication of independent judgment. There are many reasons for this, including the amount of time that leaders of major agencies must devote to participating in policymaking. Interactions with political supervisors in the capital become quite consuming. Agency heads who spend their time negotiating with or advising congressional committees, department secretaries and under secretaries, Office of Management and Budget officials, and other members of the policy-producing environment in Washington cannot also stay personally abreast of the condition of field operations, the effects of new technologies, and the many other variables that may affect administrative performance. They are heavily dependent on subordinates to keep them informed and deprived of time to listen to them.[2]

Agency leaders may also have less incentive to make reasoned, well-informed estimates of organizational capacities than one might suppose.

---

2. My analysis is heavily influenced by descriptions of Robert Ball's activity during the early years of the Nixon administration, when welfare reform was constantly under negotiation. Ball's engagement in external relations at that time was extreme. An agency leader's use of time may vary with the incumbent and with political circumstances. For a journalistic portrayal of the social security commissioner's job, see "A Day in the Life of a Government Executive," in Charles Peters and Michael Nelson, eds., *The Culture of Bureaucracy* (Holt, Rinehart and Winston, 1979), pp. 79–87. This description of the schedule of James B. Cardwell, Ball's successor, describes an extremely full and fragmented day, divided physically between Washington and Baltimore and divided cognitively among a wide range of issues and demands. One event is the commissioner's weekly staff meeting with all bureau directors and assistant commissioners. It is perfunctory. "Within 10 minutes, everyone present has either spoken or declined to speak" (p. 85). Herbert Kaufman included the commissioner of social security in his systematic observations of six federal bureau chiefs over the course of a year in the late 1970s. He concluded that the chiefs as a group spent about 25–30 percent of their time on external relations. The bulk of their time (55–60 percent) was devoted to receiving and reviewing information for all purposes. *The Administrative Behavior of Federal Bureau Chiefs* (Brookings, 1981).

Organizational leaders in any milieu, public or private, tend to emphasize the strengths and obfuscate the weaknesses of their organizations in order to sustain morale internally and elicit confidence externally. Candor is not intrinsic to the role; a certain amount of calculated delusion is. In a political setting, which is to say in a public agency, incentives to present the *appearance* of success are especially powerful, because such organizations are so heavily dependent on others' confidence. Agency leaders therefore do not ordinarily testify to Congress or to presidential officials that things are going badly in their agencies unless events have given them no choice.

In persuading others of how good their organizations are, they are also likely to succeed in persuading themselves. The most successful of them may have become successful precisely by not knowing the limits of organizational capacities, even by acting as if limits did not exist and thus daring to risk innovation. One of the ways in which leaders motivate staffs is by articulating high expectations, which with luck are then fulfilled. By setting impossible goals, they seek to stimulate and inspire—and in the end to discover that the goals were not impossible after all. Also, pride and a sense of proprietorship inhibit the identification of organizational incapacities. Psychologically, it is not easy for successful leaders to acknowledge what cannot be done.

Even if agency leaders were fully able to define organizational capacities and detect their limits, however, it would still be unrealistic to expect them to insist on those limits contrary to the well-advertised preferences of political superiors engaged in presidential and congressional policymaking. Cooperation with political superiors is a constitutional obligation, a condition of their retaining office, and a condition of their being able to achieve whatever policy or administrative goals they may be pursuing independently. Ordinarily they have agendas of their own, which they cannot hope to realize without the support of elected officeholders. Under such influences, they will cope with the policy preferences of political superiors rather than insist, to the contrary, on administrative considerations, which have a somewhat speculative quality in any case because of the difficulty of knowing organizational capacities with certainty in advance.

Furthermore, the fact that they operate under political constraints becomes one more obstacle to their being fully informed about conditions within their organizations. To the extent that external constraints dictate choices, there is no point in inviting potentially conflicting advice or information from organizational subordinates, who would only have to be rebuffed in the end. And to the extent that the potential givers of contrary advice or information themselves sense the political constraint—and in the politically supercharged environment of Washington they are likely to sense it very keenly—they will be deterred from speaking out. Thus external pressures tend to inhibit internal conversation. The absence of internal conversation in the SSA on the subject of accepting responsibility for means-tested assistance, after several decades in which agency leaders had emphasized that this was not their mission, is quite striking.

Finally, it is hard for organization leaders to estimate administrative capacities because in a governmental setting so much depends on the support and cooperation of other actors. Governmental agencies are far from autonomous. In SSI, the SSA depended on the presidency and Congress to authorize adequate staffing promptly, and in the disability review it depended on the performance of state agencies, to cite only two obvious examples.

The assumption that pervades policymaking is that the agency will be able to do what is asked of it because by law and constitutional tradition it *must*. It does not occur to presidential and congressional participants that the law should be tailored to the limits of organizational capacity. Nor do they seriously inquire what the limits of that capacity may be. There is a pervasive overestimate of the efficacy of law as a determinant of administrative behavior.

MISCALCULATION

In addition to lack of concern with administration, and perhaps more fundamentally, the failure to tailor tasks to organizational capacities appears to stem from the fact that policymakers have no way of judging capacity except through trial and error. The great difficulty of estimating administrative feasibility defeats consideration of it. The resort to trial and error occurs to some extent by default, in the absence of any better technique. The evidence of this is that when calculations of organizational capacity and administrative feasibility are attempted, they are quite likely to be mistaken. Several kinds of errors were evident in these cases.

—An overestimate of the capacity of data processing to simplify and facilitate administration. SSI rested explicitly on an assumption that the superior data processing capabilities of the federal executive branch would make the program relatively easy to administer. The SSA had been an early and successful user of automated data processing techniques, a fact that it had advertised perhaps too well for its own good. Policymaking officials credited its capacity to perform extraordinary feats.

The SSA did perform an extraordinary feat by getting checks out in January 1974. An independent study group created by the Department of Health, Education, and Welfare later pronounced this a "remarkable" achievement.[3] Yet the new computer system would not attain a satisfactory standard of performance for several more years. The Senate Finance Committee staff concluded that the difficulties experienced with SSI's computer systems "reflect[ed] an erroneous overconfidence in the ability of the Social Security Administration to develop a sophisticated system which would work under circumstances which virtually guaranteed that it could not work."[4] Official postmortems on SSI invariably cited the failure to allow sufficient time for computer development as a crucial cause of the ensuing failures of administrative performance.

The problem of course did not lie in the limitations of technology per se. In principle, computers could do what Nixon administration officials and the SSA leadership had promised. The problem lay rather in the mismatch of human expectations, developmental skills, and policy processes with the technology. It was not possible to develop the software needed to serve a new, very complicated, and constantly changing program in the time available. Afterward, it was judged that two or three years would have been required.[5] In view of the changeability of the law, any estimate of the time required to prepare for implementation is not very meaningful. Policy patchwork, which is standard practice, leads to software patchwork, which is technically hazardous. An independent, university-based computer expert told Congress that because the initial deadline was unrealistic, many computer versions of SSI had to be developed. The overlapping of different versions then exacted costs in performance.[6]

Ironically, it proved particularly difficult in SSI to achieve interfaces

3. SSI Study Group, "Report to the Commissioner of Social Security and the Secretary of Health, Education, and Welfare, on the Supplemental Security Income Program," January 1976, p. 201. Chaps. 4–7 of this document are reproduced in *Oversight of the Supplemental Security Income Program*, Hearings before the Subcommittee on Oversight of the House Committee on Ways and Means, 94 Cong. 2 sess. (Government Printing Office, 1976), pp. 114–254.

4. *The Supplemental Security Income Program*, Committee Print, Senate Committee on Finance, 95 Cong. 1 sess. (GPO, 1977), p. 3.

5. *Oversight of the Supplemental Security Income Program*, Hearings, pp. 9–10.

6. *Oversight of the Supplemental Security Income Program*, Hearings, pp. 258–59.

with other federal benefit programs, including above all those of the SSA itself and of the Veterans Administration—a task at which the SSA naturally was expected to excel. The failure to offset social security benefits was the principal source of error in SSI payments.[7]

In the wake of SSI, various outside analysts concluded that the SSA's reputation for mastery of computer technologies had been exaggerated, such that policymakers misjudged its capacities. As of the early 1970s the SSA was not in fact on the frontiers of data processing. A report of the congressional Office of Technology Assessment concluded in 1986 that at the time SSI was enacted, the SSA's work load had become "too large, too complex, and too dependent on automated processing to be handled by SSA's existing work force with existing technology."[8] Had policymakers perceived this, they might have been more hesitant to proceed with SSI.

—An exaggerated perception of the extent to which the culture and ideology of the organization shape the task, rather than vice versa. Policymakers persuaded themselves that SSI would be different from state-run welfare programs because the SSA was different from state welfare agencies. Imbued with the concept that beneficiaries had a right to their benefits, the SSA preserved their dignity and self-respect while helping them to obtain what they were entitled to. Policymakers assumed that the SSA staff would bring the same attitudes to the new program, contributing to its transformation. They did not inquire whether the more potent causal forces might run in the opposite direction, with the organization being shaped by its function.

When SSI was instituted, it became apparent that tensions between administrators and clients were endemic to a means-tested program. The very fact of the means test tended to put them in a mutually antagonistic position, and for the SSA's staff the antagonism was heightened by the perception that the agency's traditional clients were being made to suffer poorer service for the sake of the new, more difficult ones. Commissioner James B. Cardwell described his observations for a congressional committee in 1975:

> I visited offices in New York City and Harlem and Manhattan . . . and the first thing I encountered there was a group of young social security employees who were upset. They didn't like this

7. *Oversight of the Supplemental Security Income Program*, Hearings, p. 29.
8. Office of Technology Assessment, *The Social Security Administration and Information Technology*, OTA-CIT-311 (October 1986), p. 14.

program, they did not like what they had to do, they did not like the attitude of the beneficiaries, they didn't like the way they were being treated by the local public assistance office with whom they had to deal, and they were up in arms.

One of the first things I tried to do in that visit was to calm down that group of people. It was a shocking experience to me. These were the young employees, not the traditionalists. They were the people you would have expected to be the most socially minded of our workers. But they had people spit in their eye and people threaten them with bodily harm, and they were upset.

I deliberately went back a year later to look at the same offices where we had had extreme problems . . . and I found in the year that a lot of that had smoothed out. Yet we are constantly encountering among our own employees, among the unions that speak for them, expressions of concern that social security isn't what it used to be. It isn't what it used to be because of SSI partly, perhaps fundamentally, but also because they have had to lower the quality of services as they see it for their traditional clients.[9]

—A tendency to judge the capacities of an organization by the reputation of its chief executive. In the milieu of policymaking, agencies are conflated with their leaders. This may happen because policymaking communities tend to be small—at its end stages, policymaking is dominated by a few persons even in a pluralistic and democratic system—and small policymaking communities become self-absorbed, their members preoccupied with the particular motives and reputations of fellow members. It may also happen because one of the few practical ways policymakers have of judging an organization's ability is to infer it from that of the organization's most visible member. The implicit premise is that the quality of organizational leadership *determines* organizational capacities or, alternatively, that organizational leaders, especially those who are careerists and have risen through the ranks, *represent* the quality of the organization.

Neither premise is foolish. Both have a good deal of plausibility. Yet the personalizing of agencies can be misleading, especially as their size and the complexity of their tasks increase. It seems likely that

9. *Supplemental Security Income Program*, Hearings before the Subcommittee on Public Assistance of the House Committee on Ways and Means, 94 Cong. 1 sess. (GPO, 1975), vol. 1, p. 37. See also *Administration of the Supplemental Security Income Program*, Hearings before the Subcommittee on Oversight of the House Committee on Ways and Means, 94 Cong. 1 sess. (GPO, 1975), vol. 1, pp. 25, 32–33.

Robert Ball's widely celebrated ability contributed in 1969–72 to policymakers' overestimating the capacities of the organization he led.

—An assumption that the performance of federal agencies is invariably superior to that of state agencies. In 1972, the year in which SSI was enacted, the Advisory Commission on Intergovernmental Relations initiated a survey of public attitudes toward the three levels of government in the American federal system, asking respondents from which level they felt they got the most for their money. If this may be interpreted as a contest for esteem, the federal government came out comfortably on top, favored by 39 percent of the respondents, with the states on the bottom, favored by only 18 percent.[10]

Among political elites, the prevailing view of state governments was unflattering in the extreme. They were charged with being "indecisive," "antiquated," "timid and ineffective," "not willing to face their problems," "not responsive," and "not interested in cities," according to a former governor of North Carolina who wrote a book in their defense.[11] A study for the Citizens Conference on State Legislatures, a reform group, observed that "they have generally been regarded, at least in recent memory, as among the last bastions of political reaction and regression."[12]

Officially, the Nixon administration did not share any such view. The doctrine of federalism that it propounded in 1969–72 called, not for centralization of functions at the national level, but for a "sorting out" that would make the federal government responsible for income maintenance while the states would be in charge of providing social services.[13] Nevertheless, in practice executive planning for SSI was subtly affected by an assumption that the national government was the federal system's *best* government—the most competent, efficient, and technologically sophisticated. Given the prevailing stereotype of state governments, it became easy to adopt and hard to question the view that supplanting state welfare agencies with the SSA would be

10. Advisory Commission on Intergovernmental Relations, *Changing Public Attitudes on Governments and Taxes, 1984*, ACIR pub. S-13 (Washington, 1984), p. 1. Localities were in the middle, favored by 26 percent of the respondents; 17 percent responded "don't know."

11. Terry Sanford, *Storm over the States* (McGraw-Hill, 1967), p. 1.

12. Citizens Conference on State Legislatures, *The Sometime Governments: A Critical Study of the 50 American Legislatures* (Bantam, 1971), p. 14.

13. On sorting out, see Johannes Althusius [Richard P. Nathan], "New Federalist No. 3," *Publius*, vol. 2 (Spring 1972), pp. 132–37. This essay argues that the income transfer function should ultimately be performed entirely and exclusively by the federal government. It cites support for this choice in the experience of federal systems generally.

an improvement per se. And, even if state governments were not perceived individually to be of inferior competence, a *system* of state administration was assumed by central planners to be crucially defective because it lacked uniformity. The planners were unwilling to rely on the various techniques that American federalism offers for combining national standard setting with state administrative performance.

After SSI was enacted and the SSA's urgent need for more staff became plain, the plainer also became the naiveté of the original assumption that the federal agency could run SSI with half the work force that the states needed. Also in retrospect, analysts discovered some virtues of state administration. The independent study group reported hearing

> repeated testimony to the effect that SSI clients are served less effectively under the new program than they were under the State-run program. One reason for the poorer quality of service stood out from the rest—the fact that each client is no longer handled by a particular case worker responsible for his claim. The decreased personalization . . . fails to meet the SSI clientele's special needs and results in errors and consequent delays.[14]

The competence of administrative organizations is not determined by their location in the federal system. The perception that it is was one of the leading misperceptions of 1969–72.

—An underestimate of the susceptibility of administrative organizations to political direction. In anticipating the effects of the disability review, officials in the Executive Office of the President also employed a stereotype. They assumed that administrative agencies would not be disposed to reverse their own earlier decisions and were quite astonished when so many recipients began to be terminated.

The stereotype may have been correct but misapplied under the circumstances. Decisions are made at so many levels in disability determinations that state agencies making initial redeterminations of eligibility were not necessarily reversing themselves, but rather were challenging the decisions of various appeals officers. The review invited them to second-guess those who had second-guessed them, and they responded by faithfully following their own routines. On this interpretation, presidential officials were right in thinking them devoted to

14. SSI Study Group, "Report," in *Oversight of the Supplemental Security Income Program*, Hearings, pp. 229–30.

routines, and wrong only in inferring the actual consequences in the particular case.

But presidential officials were probably influenced as well by another stereotype, that agencies are impervious to political direction, especially when it instructs them to curb benefits. In the years immediately preceding the review, policymakers had developed an unusually strong consensus that the disability program was out of control and something must be done about it. They conveyed this view to administrators with unusual clarity and urgency, whereupon field employees—acting under pressure, in a hurry, often with imperfect information in individual cases, and with the high degree of discretion inescapably present in disability determinations—gave them what they had signaled they wanted. They were astonished by that, too. When policy direction develops consistency and momentum, administrators may become quite responsive to it, despite the policymakers' view that bureaucratic roles will inhibit a response.[15]

This list is not exhaustive. An examination of other cases, or a more penetrating look at these, would reveal miscalculations of other kinds. Some of these particular miscalculations are probably less likely to occur today than they were ten or twenty years ago. Experience with computer technologies has accumulated sufficiently to encourage awareness that technological success depends on development and application. Public and elite attitudes toward state governments have become more favorable while confidence in the competence of the federal government has declined, so that there is less disposition to assume automatically that the states are of inferior competence.[16] There may be a greater willingness to weigh the pros and cons of centralized versus decentralized administrative arrangements.

The experience of SSI may itself have contributed importantly to these changed perceptions. When it was enacted, its sponsors had

15. Compare the analysis of why independent regulatory commissions cooperated with deregulation in Martha Derthick and Paul J. Quirk, *The Politics of Deregulation* (Brookings, 1985), chap. 3, esp. pp. 93–94.

16. In 1984, 24 percent of the respondents to a poll of the Advisory Commission on Intergovernmental Relations said that they got the most for their money from the federal government; 35 percent said from local government; and 27 percent said from state government. Thus in twelve years the federal and state governments had traded places in this poll. ACIR, *Changing Public Attitudes on Governments and Taxes, 1984*, p. 1. Between 1972 and 1978 the federal government was consistently rated ahead of state and local governments. Since then the results of this poll have been erratic. As of 1988 federal, state, and local governments were about equally rated. Debra L. Dean, "Closing the Gap: State and Local Governments Fare Well in ACIR Poll," *Intergovernmental Perspective* (Fall 1988), pp. 23–24.

begun to think of it as a trial run for a more encompassing federalization of income support programs. Robert Ball wrote in 1972 that "any failures in administration will give a black eye to proposals for welfare reform in general. . . . Both the opportunity for a demonstration of Federal efficiency and the potential for failure are very large."[17] In the event, the experience was not encouraging, and when a major piece of legislation addressing the defects of aid to families with dependent children finally passed in 1988, it depended heavily on federal-state collaboration.[18]

Although the propensity to make any particular kind of miscalculation will change with experience and new perceptions, it is unlikely that knowledge about organizational performance—and the ability to apply such knowledge in the course of policymaking—is ever equal to the need.

17. "Assignment of the Commissioner of Social Security," December 14, 1972, copy in author's files, pp. 53–55.

18. Julie Rovner, "Welfare Reform: The Issue That Bubbled Up from the States to Capitol Hill," *Governing*, vol. 2 (December 1988), pp. 17–21.

CHAPTER 10

The Changes Brought
by Big Government

THE MORE ONE contemplates American government as a setting
for administration, the more one wonders how administrative agencies
are able to function at all. Yet some of them have apparently managed,
historically, to perform very well. For the first several decades of its
existence, the Social Security Administration enjoyed an excellent
reputation. It was often cited as a model of competence. It delivered
checks reliably, in the right amounts, at a very low cost, using the
latest in office technologies. The salient features of the governmental
setting were the same then as now. The dynamics of electoral
competition in a democracy, the separation of powers, and federalism
are constitutional properties of the American government. If they
handicap administrative performance, there is no reason, on the face
of it, to suppose that they only recently began to do so. Nor is it likely
that officeholding policymakers of the past were more concerned with
administration or more insightful about it than the incumbents of
today.

In this chapter I ask what, if anything, has changed over time in
the relations between the SSA and its institutional supervisors. I argue
that the early SSA was in many ways insulated from supervision, but
that as government has grown—and specifically as the SSA and its
programs have grown—its early autonomy has steadily eroded. Institutional surveillance has much increased, and with it the associated
obstacles to administrative performance.

THE ERA OF INSULATION

Through much of its history, which began with enactment of the
Social Security Act in 1935, the SSA had limited relations with the

192

presidency; a close, highly cooperative relation with Congress, dependent mainly on the leadership of the House Ways and Means Committee; and relatively mild scrutiny from the courts.

The presidency had little independent capacity for policy planning and initiation and supervised the SSA very lightly.[1] The fact that social security programs had their own revenue source, an earmarked tax, contributed to this insulation. Until adoption in 1969 of the unified budget, which consolidated all trust funds with traditional items, the financial transactions of social security were recorded separately from those of the rest of the government and were consequently spared close inspection from the president's Bureau of the Budget.[2] Commissioners of social security enjoyed long tenure—sixteen years in the case of Arthur J. Altmeyer (1937–53), eleven years in the case of Robert M. Ball (1962–73). The president was sufficiently uninterested in asserting command over the agency that commissioners did not always change even when party control of the presidency changed.[3]

The Ways and Means Committee, under the prolonged and very effective leadership of Wilbur Mills (a member from 1942–76, chairman from 1958–74), developed a deep interest in social security policy, mastery of the subject matter, virtually exclusive jurisdiction over it within the House, a high degree of success in winning support on the House floor (where the committee's bills were usually considered under a closed rule), and a superior bargaining position in conference vis-à-vis the Senate Finance Committee. Ways and Means did not use subcommittees, rarely engaged in oversight, and had little staff of its own, necessitating heavy reliance on the SSA. Its relation with the agency was collaborative, not critical. The two shared expertise and an attitude of proprietorship toward social security programs.[4] Spared dependence on general revenues, social security programs were also spared scrutiny from congressional appropriations committees.

The courts decided very few social security cases; in calendar year 1960 there were only 337 filings.[5] When they shaped social security

---

1. Martha Derthick, *Policymaking for Social Security* (Brookings, 1979), chap. 3, esp. pp. 69–76, 80–85.

2. Derthick, *Policymaking for Social Security*, p. 36.

3. Derthick, *Policymaking for Social Security*, pp. 18–19, 178–81.

4. Derthick, *Policymaking for Social Security*, chap. 2.

5. *Committee Staff Report on the Disability Insurance Program*, House Committee on Ways and Means (Government Printing Office, 1974), p. 76. Susan Gluck Mezey reports that in the fifteen years from 1955–70, a total of slightly under 10,000 disability claims were filed in federal district courts, whereas 10,000 claims were filed in 1982 alone. *No Longer Disabled: The Federal Courts and the Politics of Social Security Disability* (Greenwood

policies through statutory interpretation—as in *Kerner* v. *Flemming*, which in 1960 advanced a liberalizing interpretation of disability law— Congress reacted critically. It was inclined to resist judicial intrusion.[6]

Because one party (the Democrats) controlled the political branches most of the time, the agency was spared the tension that comes with changes in party. The SSA was more than a decade old and quite well established before the Republican party was able to win either house of the Congress, and it was nearly two decades old before the Republicans won the White House. Policymaking proceeded in an evolutionary, if halting, fashion. The agency dominated executive planning of policy initiatives. It proposed steady increments to the basic program of old age and survivors' insurance, broadening the types of coverage offered and the classes of population covered. Always the changes were within the framework of the "insurance" program, financed with a payroll tax and creating benefits by right, independent of need.[7]

Not until the disability program was enacted in 1956 did the administration of social insurance have to depend significantly on state governments. Then state administration of disability determinations was provided for as one of numerous concessions to conservative opponents of disability insurance. Specifically, the American Medical Association did not want the medical profession to have to do business directly with the federal government.[8] Until then the Bureau of Old Age and Survivors Insurance was not engaged in intergovernmental relations, in contrast with its companion agency, the Bureau of Public Assistance, which administered grants to the states for aid to the aged, blind, dependent children, and disabled. In all, the SSA as administrator of social insurance enjoyed a high degree of insulation from the features of the institutional environment described in this book.

The SSA's freedom, moreover, extended to the implementation of

---

Press, 1988), p. 122. Of course, the fact that the number of cases was small for many years does not necessarily mean that the decisions were insignificant.

6. Patricia Dilley, "Social Security Disability: Political Philosophy and History," in Arthur T. Meyerson and Theodora Fine, eds., *Psychiatric Disability: Clinical, Legal, and Administrative Dimensions* (Washington: American Psychiatric Press, 1987), pp. 373–409. Congress only modified *Kerner* v. *Flemming*, however, rather than reverse it. See Jerry L. Mashaw and others, *Social Security Hearings and Appeals: A Study of the Social Security Administration Hearing System* (Lexington Books, 1978), p. 75. For an account of Congress's response to judicial rulings adverse to the agency, see Frederick B. Arner, *A Model Disability Structure for the Social Security Administration*, Report to the Alfred P. Sloan Foundation, Grant B 1988-38 (September 1989), pp. 76–78.

7. Derthick, *Policymaking for Social Security*, chap. 11.

8. Derthick, *Policymaking for Social Security*, p. 302.

new programs. The enactment of disability insurance in 1956 and medicare in 1965 presented the agency with major administrative challenges. Medicare was especially daunting. It involved policy development in areas of great controversy, in which health care providers, organized labor, and consumers generally had a deep interest. Thousands of new employees had to be hired, hundreds of new district offices had to be established, contracts had to be negotiated with Blue Cross and other private insurance companies, and agreements with the states had to be worked out to provide for quality reviews of provider institutions. All of the elderly people in the country had to be asked to decide whether they wanted to participate in part B, the voluntary portion of medicare that covers doctors' fees and requires participants to pay premiums.

The attitude of the Johnson administration through all of this, Robert Ball would later recall, was "that we were in charge and handling the thing well." The administrative presidency both permitted implementation "without a lot of second guessing and clearances" and encouraged other agencies to cooperate with the SSA. Similarly, Congress refrained from making legislative changes during the initial stages of implementation. At one point, the Senate Finance Committee appeared about to intervene in regulations governing reimbursement of health care providers, but Ball as commissioner was able to fend it off with help from the General Accounting Office and the Health Benefits Advisory Council, a group of expert advisers.[9] However, the SSA's insulation came to an end in the late 1960s and early 1970s.

THE LOSS OF AUTONOMY

Changes gradually occurred in the agency's setting independently of developments in the social security program. Presidential politics became competitive; Republicans began to win the office frequently, although Democrats continued to predominate in Congress. The Executive Office of the President expanded and heightened its effort at supervision of executive agencies.[10] Policy planning shifted to the

9. Memorandum from Ball to author, October 30, 1989. On the early administration of medicare, see Herman Miles Somers and Anne Ramsay Somers, *Medicare and the Hospitals: Issues and Prospects* (Brookings, 1967), chap 2.

10. There are many accounts of the growth of the presidential office. Among them are: Thomas E. Cronin, *The State of the Presidency* (Little, Brown, 1980), pp. 243–47; Fred I. Greenstein, "Change and Continuity in the Modern Presidency," in Anthony King, ed., *The New American Political System* (Washington: American Enterprise Institute

White House and departmental staffs, especially in regard to income support, which was established as a presidential issue with Lyndon Johnson's declaration of war on poverty. For some years thereafter, welfare reform remained on the agenda of presidents and their domestic policy planners. The SSA felt the effect of these developments without being their cause or even their particular target. Other agencies were also affected. Likewise, in the 1960s and 1970s the courts began to apply heightened scrutiny to federal agencies. The "new administrative law" showed less deference than formerly to agency judgments and a greater willingness to engage in policymaking. The judiciary became active across a broad front. If anything, the SSA felt the effects of the judicial revolution later than most agencies.[11]

Even when changes occurred specifically in the SSA's relations with its institutional supervisors, the causes were not necessarily to be found in social security affairs, or at least not exclusively so. The Ways and Means Committee lost much of its preeminence in the House and underwent internal changes—it was enlarged, subcommittees were created, staff members were added, the use of the closed rule and of executive sessions was curbed—as part of a more encompassing reform of legislative organization and procedures in the mid-1970s.[12] This disrupted the SSA's intimate collaboration with the committee and opened up social security policymaking to a wider range of influences, but the changes had not been designed with that specific end in view.

---

for Public Policy Research, 1978), pp. 45–85; and Terry M. Moe, "The Politicized Presidency," in John E. Chubb and Paul E. Peterson, eds., *The New Direction in American Politics* (Brookings, 1985), pp. 235–71.

11. Broad treatments of the expanded role of the courts include: Donald L. Horowitz, *The Courts and Social Policy* (Brookings, 1977); Richard B. Stewart, "The Reformation of American Administrative Law," *Harvard Law Review*, vol. 88 (June 1975), pp. 1669–87; R. Shep Melnick, *Regulation and the Courts: The Case of the Clean Air Act* (Brookings, 1983); and Jerry L. Mashaw, *Due Process in the Administrative State* (Yale University Press, 1985). On the prolonged success of the SSA in court, see, for example, Lance Liebman and Richard B. Stewart, "Bureaucratic Vision," *Harvard Law Review*, vol. 96 (June 1983), pp. 1959–60. This essay is a review of Jerry L. Mashaw, *Bureaucratic Justice: Managing Social Security Disability Claims* (Yale University Press, 1983).

12. For accounts of the reform of the Ways and Means Committee, see Catherine E. Rudder, "Tax Policy: Structure and Choice," in Allen Schick, ed., *Making Economic Policy in Congress* (Washington: American Enterprise Institute for Public Policy Research, 1983), pp. 196–220; and Randall Strahan, *New Ways and Means: Reform and Change in a Congressional Committee* (University of North Carolina Press, 1990). For a fascinating, spontaneous description of the changes by a leading member of the committee, see Barber B. Conable, Jr., "Changing Tax Policy in a Changing Congress," *Tax Foundation's Tax Review*, vol. 41 (February 1980), pp. 7–10.

Along with these general institutional changes, and to some extent following from them, certain events in social security also drew attention specifically to the SSA and its programs. First was the deeply troubled beginning of SSI, which marked the agency's fall from grace. Then there was a sharp, unanticipated rise in the cost of the disability insurance program, which by the mid-1970s was suffering from chronic actuarial deficiencies and overwhelming work loads at each of the several levels of the determination and appeals process.[13] Partly because of this experience with disability insurance, the program as a whole then fell victim to fiscal crisis. Revenues from the payroll tax recurrently fell short of expenditures beginning in 1975. Restoring the balance between social security spending and revenue became an urgent objective of the Ford, Carter, and Reagan administrations. Congress in 1977 and again in 1983 had to enact extraordinary measures to close the gap.[14]

In addition to its heavily publicized fiscal problems, which became a cause for public alarm, the SSA began to experience difficulties with data processing that threatened its core functions—maintaining the records and distributing the benefits for old age and survivors' insurance. As of the early 1980s, the agency had limited access to its most important data sets, which were stored on over 500,000 reels of magnetic tape. Over 30,000 production operations each month required 150,000 tapes to be handled several times, introducing human errors that were estimated to consume about a quarter of available computer hours.[15] Errors were increasingly creeping into the agency's routine operations.[16] There were hints that possibly one day the checks would not go out on time. Whereas the SSA in the past had been described as any administration's "fair-haired boy" because it dispensed millions of checks efficiently and uneventfully, by the mid-1970s the glow was gone.[17] A series of articles in the *Washington Post* in 1977 described the

13. *Committee Staff Report on the Disability Insurance Program*, Committee Print, House Committee on Ways and Means, 93 Cong. 2 sess. (GPO, 1974).

14. For an account of the 1977 legislation, see Derthick, *Policymaking for Social Security*, chap. 19; for the sequel in the early 1980s, see Paul Light, *Artful Work: The Politics of Social Security Reform* (Random House, 1985).

15. Office of Technology Assessment, *The Social Security Administration and Information Technology*, OTA-CIT-311 (October 1986), p. 41.

16. *Social Security: How Well Is It Serving the Public?*, Hearing before the Senate Special Committee on Aging, 98 Cong. 1 sess. (GPO, 1984), pp. 35ff.

17. On the SSA as "fair-haired boy," see Derthick, *Policymaking for Social Security*, pp. 80–81, quoting Charles I. Schottland, commissioner of social security in the Eisenhower administration.

agency as a case of "government gone awry."[18] In trouble, it invited attention.

Both because the institutional milieu changed and because its programs were under stress, the SSA lost control of its agenda and became highly vulnerable to supervision. Whereas for the first four decades of its existence changes in the agency's programs stemmed fundamentally from its own policy planning, initiatives now came from other sources. Whereas nominal supervisors had for decades performed very little oversight of any kind, now they performed oversight of every conceivable kind as aggressively as they could. Social security commissioners changed often, and presidents and secretaries of Health, Education, and Welfare sought out candidates who would take a detached, critical approach to the agency and its programs. The commissioners initiated reorganizations and assessments of performance. The Office of Management and Budget scrutinized the agency's budget, and the HEW secretary's office scrutinized its regulations. Various well-staffed congressional committees, the General Accounting Office, and special study groups produced hearings, reports, and analyses in profusion; courts reversed disability determinations by the thousands and then, as the review took effect, tens of thousands. The loss of autonomy was comprehensive; it occurred on every institutional front.

In volume and share of expenditures, the agency's basic program of retirement and survivors' insurance did not suffer, for it was protected by partisan political processes and pressure group support more than by any power lodged in the agency itself. The fiscal crises of social security ended with fresh infusions of revenue in 1977 and 1983 that left the core program in strengthened condition. In the battle for public funds, it beat out every domestic competitor. After President Reagan suffered politically from trying to cut it, he ceased trying, and it became untouchable.[19] But presidential efforts to control the agency did not diminish; they may even have intensified.

The SSA's losses in autonomy were cumulative and interacting. As one institutional supervisor intervened, opportunities were created for

18. March 29, 1977, p. 1. The story was one in a three-part series by Haynes Johnson that portrayed the SSA, not altogther unsympathetically, as a locus of bureaucratic pathology.

19. Joseph A. Pechman, ed., *Setting National Priorities: The 1983 Budget* (Brookings, 1982), pp. 116–18; and David A. Stockman, *The Triumph of Politics: How the Reagan Revolution Failed* (Harper and Row, 1986), pp. 181–93, 401–04.

others. SSI epitomized this effect. It began as a presidential intervention in the SSA's programs that the SSA leadership acquiesced in. That Commissioner Ball *did* acquiesce in it, that he had a genuine enthusiasm for the policy change, should not obscure the fact that the change did not originate with the SSA. Unlike the addition of survivors' insurance in 1939, the major expansion of old age insurance coverage in 1950, and the addition of disability insurance in 1956 and health insurance (medicare) in 1965, SSI was not the agency leadership's idea. Able though the leadership was to suppress doubts about mixing need-tested assistance with social insurance, it would not have independently conceived of this very dubious departure from established practice. From this presidential intervention flowed the administrative trauma described in preceding chapters, and both the fact of trauma itself and the particular properties of SSI attracted a host of critical overseers. SSI contributed to, if it did not straightforwardly cause, numerous erosions of the SSA's independence. Because SSI was financed with general revenues, it opened the agency to greater scrutiny from appropriations committees. Because the SSA replaced the states as administrators of need-tested assistance, it fell heir to the judicial and administrative controls that had been imposed on them. With SSI came *Goldberg* standards (although *Mathews* v. *Eldridge* briefly stayed the spread of such thoroughgoing judicial supervision to the SSA's insurance programs). With SSI came quality control procedures and the publication of error rates, which led straight to the further trauma of the disability review. With SSI came devastating publicity and equally devastating congressional investigations. The agency suddenly became fair game.

The disability review likewise illustrates the SSA's new vulnerability, and how, as autonomy is breached, further breaches follow, compounding one another. In 1980 Congress ordered periodic review of the disability insurance rolls—a measure of modest significance, it seemed. Then data on rates of ineligibility were broadcast by Congress's arm of oversight, the GAO, drawing on findings that had been produced by the SSA itself in the wake of presidentially sponsored efforts to improve control of the agency. These data were seized on by a newly installed, zealous presidency as a potential source of billions of dollars in budget savings. The combined influences of Congress and the presidency then led the SSA into the conduct of an administrative operation that proved utterly vulnerable to judicial reproof. Judicial reproof then deprived it of the cooperation of its field agents, the state governments.[20] In this whole affair, the SSA was from beginning to end acted upon by others rather than being an independent actor. Its role stands in the starkest possible contrast to that which the agency played almost thirty years earlier, when its leaders, with organized labor's help, planned and promoted passage of disability insurance. The agency's leaders were then prime movers in the maelstrom of American government; their successors now were passive victims.

In sum, while the U.S. Constitution has not changed, certain features of institutional structure and functioning have changed in ways that very much affect relations between the SSA and its institutional superiors. Courts and the presidency have become much more vigilant and intrusive. Congress has become more critical. And the SSA has become a more vulnerable and inviting subject of scrutiny as its programs have run into financial and administrative trouble.

THE EFFECTS OF GROWTH

One reason that the SSA now invites scrutiny is that its role in government has changed in a fundamental way. The early SSA combined program building or policy initiation with administration. As the program building progressively succeeded, the administrative function grew, both absolutely and relatively. Of itself, this very change in roles contributed to the change in the relation between the agency and its environment.

Institutional features that today are inimical to administration positively assisted the agency's program building. Federalism, which hampers administration by dispersing authority, obscured the costs of program growth by spreading them. The propensity of the president to sponsor policy initiatives gave program enlargement much of its legitimacy and political impetus (while the lack of any independent planning capacity at the presidential level meant that the president relied very heavily on the agency to define initiatives). If the president was unreceptive to agency proposals, as was true with some qualifi-

20. The state agencies with which the SSA cooperates, like the SSA itself, became vulnerable to political supervision over time. An SSA source observed that the state disability determination agencies "were largely invisible to state government, especially at the political level, and were consummately loyal to SSA" before the disability review began. "It was when the political levels within the states realized the economic impact on their states of what was happening that they became aware of the existence of the state agencies." Memo to author from Jean H. Hinckley, former deputy director of SSA Office of Disability Programs, December 7, 1989.

cations during Republican presidencies, then the separation of powers, combined with weak parties, meant that agency leaders, with the help of organized labor, could take the proposals directly to Congress, which as a general rule was Democratic and much more receptive. In regard to program formation, interbranch and interparty differences could enhance agency autonomy and create room for maneuver, but when administrative concerns have been paramount and blame has been apportioned for error, the same institutional features have contributed to the agency's exposure and isolation.[21]

As program building succeeded and as programs matured, the SSA's administrative tasks became more varied, larger in sheer volume, and more complex. Title II of the Social Security Act, the foundation of the social insurance program, consisted of a mere 4 pages when enacted in 1935, but had grown to 50 pages by the early 1950s and to nearly 200 by the early 1970s when SSI was enacted. This did not include medicare, which was enacted as a separate title. Types of benefits had proliferated and calculations of benefits had grown complex.[22] The number of beneficiaries, which had grown from 222,500 at the end of 1940 to 3,477,200 by the end of 1950, was a staggering 26,228,600—13 percent of the population—at the end of 1970. Disability insurance and medicare were both much harder to administer than the basic program and entailed dependence on contractors—state agencies in the former case, private insurance carriers in the latter. The SSA's adjudicative system, devoted almost wholly to deciding disability cases, grew in crude numbers to exceed the federal judicial system. In fiscal year 1976, the SSA'S 625 administrative law judges disposed of 180,000 cases, whereas the judicial system of the United States, including district, circuit, and supreme courts, consisted of 505 judges who disposed of 129,683 civil and criminal cases.[23] The SSA staff rose from 11,169 in 1950 to 50,395 in 1970 and would have had to rise much more but for the use of contractors. Furthermore, in 1969 Congress gratuitously gave the SSA responsibility for administering a special program of benefits for coal miners disabled by black lung disease, an unrelated activity that was not even included in the Social Security Act.

Reviewing the administrative condition of the program in 1972,

21. On how institutional features affected program building, see Derthick, *Policymaking for Social Security*, chaps. 1–9.

22. Changes in the statute over time are conveniently summarized in tabular form in *Social Security Bulletin*, Annual Statistical Supplement, 1984–85, pp. 1–38.

23. Mashaw and others, *Social Security Hearings and Appeals*, p. xi.

shortly before the enactment of SSI, the SSA's assistant commissioner for administration, Jack S. Futterman, noted that the growth of program responsibility had caused the SSA's measured work load (a composite figure representing such elements as the volume of claims taken, benefits computed, and earnings records updated) to more than double in the preceding six years. Futterman characterized growth in the fifteen-year period from 1950 to 1965, during which the work load had risen at an average annual rate of 10 percent, as "steady and evolutionary." The expansion of 1965, which broadened cash benefit programs besides adding medicare, was by implication revolutionary. It had "temporarily swamped" the agency, whose operating system had been "severely strained" in 1966 and 1967. Furthermore, since then the agency had been under severe pressure to economize. The number of full-time employees had declined by more than 2,000 between June 1968 and June 1970 even as work loads were rising. Futterman went on to describe the ways in which the agency had coped, of which the most important was advances in the use of automatic data processing. But while Futterman's assessment was on balance optimistic, promising SSA employees that they could face further increases in responsibility "with a substantial measure of reassurance," an astute reader might have discerned here a warning that if the agency had ever had slack resources, they had certainly been used up. (Futterman himself was astute enough to warn in advance that SSI would probably be more difficult to assimilate than medicare because it was not a new program but one that would be converted from those of more than fifty other governments.)[24]

By the early 1970s, then, it might have been difficult for the SSA to absorb additional administrative burdens even if they had been thoroughly consistent with its experience, traditions, and ethos. Instead, the assignments that now came to it from above were alien and pitted it for the first time against its clients—SSI because it required application of a means test whereas the insurance programs had granted benefits by right, the disability review because it entailed a large-scale withdrawal of government benefits from long-time beneficiaries. No such thing had ever been attempted before by the SSA, whose historic experience was with adding new classes of benefits and beneficiaries. No such thing, it is probably safe to say, had been attempted before in the history of the U.S. government.

24. Jack S. Futterman, "Administrative Developments in the Social Security Program since 1965," *Social Security Bulletin*, vol. 35 (April 1972), pp. 3–9.

Because the SSA was now pitted against its clients, it was also pitted against the judiciary, the institutional refuge of the aggrieved individual. Responsible for a caseload of millions, and under pressure steadily from the presidency and intermittently from Congress to bring the disability portion of that caseload under control, the SSA applied management techniques that were routinized and impersonal in the extreme. For that very reason, these techniques tended to jeopardize the agency in the courts, with their expectation of individualized and rationalized justice.

Virtually all of the changes described thus far—in the SSA, in the primary governing institutions, and in the relations between the two—may be ascribed directly or indirectly to the growth of government. In time, as government in general and social security in particular became very large, social security proved to be underfinanced and its administering agency to be overburdened. Meanwhile, the supervisory institutions grew more complex organizationally and became more vigilant and demanding in an effort to respond to the problems that came with government growth. Then they too began to fall victim to the effects of growth.

This last point is worth exploring briefly because it bears on the critique of institutional performance that has been the main theme of this book. Quite possibly the performance has in some respects deteriorated with time and the growth of government. It is plausible to suppose, for example, that the tensions between the policymaking presidency and the administrative presidency have increased over time as the former has come to bear an ever greater burden of public expectation and the latter has had to cope with large chronic budget deficits. Contemporary analysts of the courts have frequently observed that as caseloads have grown inconsistencies among the circuits have multiplied.[25] It seems likely that the modern Congress, in session constantly with a large agenda of long, complex bills, is less able to deliberate over them at length—and thereby to gain confidence in its decisions—than its more leisurely predecessors of several decades ago.

It is hard to imagine, for example, that a contemporary committee of Congress could apply to any piece of legislation the care that the House Ways and Means Committee brought to considering the Social

---

25. Stephen L. Wasby, "Inconsistency in the United States Courts of Appeals: Dimensions and Mechanisms for Resolution," *Vanderbilt Law Review*, vol. 32 (1979), pp. 1343–73. More generally on the effects of expanded work loads on the courts, see Richard A. Posner, *The Federal Courts: Crisis and Reform* (Harvard University Press, 1985).

Security Act Amendments of 1950. In near-daily executive sessions from April to August 1949, the staff twice presented every section of the bill and a companion bill for public assistance, first for a tentative vote and discussion, later for the final vote.[26] This more leisurely, deliberative Congress of a generation ago did not necessarily pay a great deal of attention to administrative considerations; still less did it refrain from making decisions that in the eyes of an administrative agency were irrational and inconvenient, such as its choice in 1956 of state administration of disability determinations in order to placate the American Medical Association. In search of compromise and to serve partisan and constituency-serving ends, or merely to satisfy the idiosyncratic preferences of particular members, it has always wrought havoc on the executive's most cherished designs. Yet greater leisure and deliberation presumably protected Congress at least from making outright mistakes, that is, decisions that it never intended to make because they were inconsistent with its own preferences. Thirty years ago Congress had time to read what it was enacting. Thus, one supposes that the Senate Finance Committee would have been less likely then to make the kind of mistake it made in passing SSI, when its chairman failed to realize that individual recipients had not been held harmless. The legislative consequences of this mistake proved very harmful to administration.

None of this is to suggest that enactments a generation ago were any less likely than modern ones to have unanticipated consequences. Yet the older Congress had greater room for error. When government was smaller, simpler, and in its program-building phase, new laws had fewer consequences. As government programs grew in number, an action in any one was increasingly likely to have unanticipated effects on others. As more and more citizens became clients and beneficiaries of more and more programs, changes in programs had wider and deeper effects on their lives. Not very many years ago, no one would have credited the notion that people would have committed suicide (as disability recipients were alleged to have done during the review) because of decisions made by the federal government.[27] Lawmaking has become unstable largely because it has come to have such a wide range of impacts. The machinery that has been created and is now deeply embedded in the society demands constant tinkering as its

26. Derthick, *Policymaking for Social Security*, pp. 43–44.

27. For example, see *Oversight of Social Security Disability Benefits Terminations*, Hearing before the Subcommittee on Oversight of Government Management of the Senate Committee on Governmental Affairs, 97 Cong. 2 sess. (GPO, 1982), pp. 494–98.

interactions with the society become manifest; a change in one place necessitates another somewhere else, in an endless process. Congress, like the SSA but perhaps more so, is confounded by complexity. It finds it harder to manage mature programs today than it did to create new ones a generation ago.[28] Acts of creation, especially in social security, tended to have gradual effects.[29] Actions taken to manage mature programs have immediate and potentially profound consequences for hundreds of thousands or millions of people.

If the SSA's problems are indeed traceable in significant measure to the nature of the policy-producing environment, in combination with the growth of government, it should not be alone in experiencing such problems. Other federal agencies should be similarly afflicted. How typical the recent experience of the SSA is can be established only by prolonged and close study of a variety of agencies. I will briefly examine the Internal Revenue Service (IRS), the agency most nearly comparable to the SSA in size and scope of interaction with the citizenry.

ANOTHER AGENCY UNDER STRESS

Like the SSA, the IRS is charged with administering a complex law that is subject to constant change. An opponent of tax reform in 1986, arguing for a moratorium on changes in the tax code, reported to readers of the *Washington Post* that the IRS was already unable to write regulations fast enough to keep up.[30] He calculated that nearly 6,000 subsections of the Internal Revenue Code had been changed in six separate pieces of legislation enacted between 1976 and 1984.

The extreme instability of tax law is probably attributable to the numerous and conflicting objectives embedded in it, according to another analyst. "If, in former eras, politicians liked to throw money at problems, more recently they like to throw tax laws at problems." Policymakers pursue various goals through the tax code: equity, promotion of desired activities through incentives, and macroeconomic

28. Generally on the effects of government's growth on political institutions, see Lawrence D. Brown, *New Policies, New Politics: Government's Response to Government's Growth* (Brookings, 1983).

29. On the incremental nature of the program, see Derthick, *Policymaking for Social Security*, pp. 288–89.

30. Harold I. Apolinsky, "The Changes Just Cost Money," *Washington Post*, April 6, 1986, p. C8. See also Hilary Stout, "Tax Law Is Growing Ever More Complex, Outcry Ever Louder," *Wall Street Journal*, April 12, 1990, p. 1.

objectives, including economic efficiency. The pendulum of policy choice swings back and forth as one objective—and then, in reaction, its alternative—is preferred. More fundamentally, though,

> the basic reason the pendulum swings back and forth relates to politics and the short-term nature of the focus of our political system. Congressmen are elected every two years. Chairmen of major committees such as House Ways and Means and Senate Finance generally want to respond to the pressures of their committee members to produce something notable in each Congress. Presidents want to leave their mark on the system. Secretaries of the Treasury and assistant secretaries for tax policy who seek to make a difference come and go. Everyone who comes into power feels he or she should improve things.[31]

These descriptions of tax policy make it sound very much like social security policy—only more so.

For the IRS as for the SSA, obligations have exceeded organizational capacity. The filing year of 1985 produced a much-publicized crisis, characterized by computer breakdowns, overloaded telephone lines, record backlogs of unprocessed returns, hundreds of millions of dollars of erroneous or delayed refunds, incorrect dunning notices, and unjustified threats to seize property. There were also cases in which IRS employees hid or destroyed documents in order to meet production quotas. The next tax year went more smoothly, but evidence of declining organizational performance persisted. Whereas the IRS had audited over 2 percent of returns in 1980, by 1986 the proportion had fallen by half.[32] A prominent theme in analyses of these events is the

---

31. Stanford G. Ross, "Federal Tax Policy," in *Business, Work, and Benefits: Adjusting to Change* (Washington: Employee Benefit Research Institute, 1989), pp. 135–59. I have simplified Ross's analysis somewhat. He identifies five leading "tendencies" of tax policy under the headings of equity, incentives, efficiency, fairness, and fiscal circumstances. Ross served briefly as social security commissioner during the Carter administration.

32. Leading journalistic accounts of the IRS's troubles include: "Auditing the IRS," *Business Week*, April 16, 1984, pp. 84–92; Kathy Sawyer, "The Breakdown of America's 'Tax Factories,' " *Washington Post*, October 22, 1985, p. A1; Sawyer, "The Mess at the IRS," *Washington Post National Weekly Edition*, November 11, 1985, p. 6; Gary Klott, "The I.R.S. Loses Its Muscle," *New York Times*, April 6, 1986, sec. 3, p. 1; and Hilary Stout, "Deep Problems at IRS Cause the U.S. to Miss Billions in Revenue," *Wall Street Journal*, January 2, 1990, p. 1. For congressional sources, see *IRS Tax Payment Posting Problems in Philadelphia Service Center*, Hearing before the Subcommittee on Oversight

great difficulty of achieving computer modernization and of realistically anticipating the benefits to be achieved from it. Another theme is the inability of overworked and undertrained staffs to give correct, consistent answers to taxpayers.

Like the SSA, the IRS must cope with two Congresses—one a high-minded maker of policy for the country as a whole, the other a determined protector of individual constituents who are aggrieved by the agency's application of the law. As a maker of policy, Congress favors vigorous collection of revenue in order to keep the government solvent. As a provider of constituency service, it complains that the IRS is abusive and overly zealous.[33]

Also like the SSA, the IRS suffers from institutional guidance that is unclear and conflicting. The more conceptually and politically difficult the subject matter, the more vague and elliptical the guidance tends to be. At about the time the SSA was struggling with the disability review, the IRS was caught up in a hotly contested interbranch conflict over whether it had authority to grant tax-exempt status to educational institutions that practice racial discrimination. In the fall of 1982 the case of *Bob Jones University* v. *U.S.* was argued before the Supreme Court. At issue was interpretation of a law that provides tax exemptions for "corporations (or other organizations) organized and operated exclusively for religious, charitable, scientific . . . or educational . . . purposes." Dating from the 1930s, this law said nothing about racial discrimination.

The reaction of the IRS in 1967, when it first confronted the question of whether it could deny tax-exempt status to schools that discriminated, was that it lacked such authority, but it changed its position three years later, in response to a ruling by a three-judge panel of the U.S. District Court of the District of Columbia. The

---

of the House Committee on Ways and Means, 99 Cong. 1 sess. (GPO, 1985); *IRS Philadelphia Service Center Problems*, Hearings before the Subcommittee on Administrative Practice and Procedure of the Senate Committee on the Judiciary, 99 Cong. 1 sess. (GPO, 1986); *IRS Plans for Service Center Operations in 1986*, Hearing before the Subcommittee on Oversight of the House Committee on Ways and Means, 99 Cong. 1 sess. (GPO, 1986); and *1986 Tax Filing Season*, Hearing before the Subcommittee on Oversight of the House Committee on Ways and Means, 99 Cong. 2 sess. (GPO, 1986).

33. Rose Gutfeld, "IRS Faces Pressure to Raise Collections—But Not Get Tough," *Wall Street Journal*, December 24, 1987, p. 1; and *Taxpayers' Bill of Rights*, Hearings before the Subcommittee on Private Retirement Plans and Oversight of the Internal Revenue Service of the Senate Committee on Finance, 100 Cong. 1 sess. (GPO, 1987).

court held that an organization whose activities are illegal or contrary to public policy is not entitled to privileges and immunities ordinarily afforded to charities.[34] The district court ruling was not definitive, however, and litigation proceeded in the case of Bob Jones University, which had lost its tax-exempt status in the mid-1970s.

Early in January 1982, the Treasury Department, speaking for the Reagan administration, announced that in the absence of further guidance from Congress the IRS would revert to its pre-1970 position that it lacked authority to deny tax-exempt status to institutions that discriminated. It seemed possible that this decision would render the *Bob Jones* case moot.

The administration's position originated with officials in the Justice Department who thought they saw an opportunity to force Congress to do its duty and clarify the law. The question would then be removed from the courts, whose discretion the Reagan Justice Department was committed to curbing. The administration submitted clarifying legislation to Congress and elicited a vituperative response. Congress did not like being told by the executive what it was supposed to do. Democrats enjoyed the administration's embarrassment, for there had been a massive outcry in response to the Treasury announcement, and not even Republicans wished to vote on clarifying legislation if they did not have to. The issue came to an end in the spring of 1983, when the Supreme Court ruled against Bob Jones, holding that the IRS did not exceed its authority by interpreting the law to require denial of tax-exempt status to schools that discriminated.[35]

IRS officials were pawns in this affair, not prime movers. The agency's commissioner and counsel had dissented from the Reagan administration's decision and insisted that the under secretary of the Treasury give them an order in writing to change the IRS position.[36]

What happened to the IRS in the *Bob Jones* case was less prolonged and damaging than what happened to the SSA in the contemporaneous case of the disability review. The IRS was not publicly blamed for the Reagan administration's decision. But the case nonetheless illustrates

34. *Green* v. *Connally*, 320 F. Supp. 1150 (1971).
35. *Bob Jones University* v. *U.S.*, 461 U.S. 574 (1983).
36. This account is based on "The Case of the Segregated Schools," C94-83-531, PLP-83-011, Harvard University, Kennedy School of Government and Harvard Law School, 1983. On the role of the Justice Department, see also David Whitman, "Ronald Reagan and Tax Exemption for Discriminatory Schools," in Martin Linsky and others, *How the Press Affects Federal Policymaking: Six Case Studies* (Norton, 1986), pp. 259–60.

vividly the kinds of interbranch conflicts that American government generates, with their attendant pulling and hauling upon the agencies.

This quick look at the IRS suggests that the situation of the SSA is not unique. Other agencies labor under comparable handicaps. The closing chapter will consider corrective measures.

CHAPTER 11

Where to Look
for Improvement

AS OF 1990 the turmoil that supplemental security income and the disability review caused has subsided.[1] The Social Security Administration is administering SSI benefits for 4.5 million persons, and on behalf of the states that have chosen federal administration of their supplemental payments (about half the states numerically, accounting for the great bulk of the cases), it is administering 1.9 million such payments. SSI remains a much harder program to administer than retirement and survivors' insurance, but major problems with systems have been resolved, and field staffs have grown accustomed to the inherent difficulties of means-tested income payments. Disability reviews, which were halted in 1984, were resumed in January 1986. Initially they proceeded at a low level, but the volume has since increased; in fiscal year 1988, 317,900 cases were reviewed out of a caseload of 2.8 million. Under the revisions of law and procedure made in reaction to the events of 1981–83, the reviews have ceased to be controversial.

Conceivably, the turmoil described in this book should be dismissed

---

1. This is not to imply that the Social Security Administration is in a stable state. It has been further roiled by reductions in staff. President Reagan's fiscal 1986 budget announced plans to reduce agency employment, which then was approximately 80,000, by 17,000 over a five-year period. As the cuts took effect, morale fell. In a survey by the General Accounting Office in 1988, 44 percent of field office managers and 64 percent of field office employees reported that morale in their units was low or very low. *Delivery and Quality of Public Services Furnished by the Social Security Administration,* Hearings before the Subcommittee on Social Security of the House Committee on Ways and Means, 99 Cong. 1 sess. (Government Printing Office, 1985), p. 3; and General Accounting Office, *Social Security: Staff Reductions and Service Quality,* HRD-89-106BR (June 1989). This report compares data for 1988 with earlier surveys of agency morale, showing a significant short-run decline.

as merely the inescapable cost of policy innovation. Major policy change can never be expected to work smoothly from the start. Implementation must be to a considerable extent incremental, experimental, and adaptive. Statutory provisions, regulations, administrative procedures, and computer programs all will need "debugging" in the ordinary course of events. Public agencies adapt to policy changes because they have no other choice. They develop new routines to meet the new demands, as happened in SSI. Seeing havoc, policymakers devise remedies, as Congress eventually did in the disability review. Public agencies are rarely abolished, and they are not swallowed up by the competition.[2]

It is partly for this reason that those who issue commands to public agencies rarely pause to ask how effective those commands are likely to be, whether the agencies can be expected to fulfill them, or how they will be affected by the attempt. They justifiably come to take the existence of the agencies for granted. Less justifiably, they also take for granted the agencies' resilience. They assume that the necessary adaptations will occur.

Nevertheless, even from the perspective of 1990, with the administration of SSI and periodic disability reviews functioning routinely, it seems unwarranted to dismiss the initial problems as merely those that could be expected to occur with any innovation in policy and organizational tasks. Under Secretary John G. Veneman's assurance to Congress that SSA could take on responsibility for SSI "with no disruption to its current functions" embodied a truly monumental miscalculation. The suggestions of 1981 that more than 500,000 cases could be removed from the rolls can now be juxtaposed with the fact that, after much trauma for both the SSA and its clients, the actual number removed was 83,360.[3] It is appropriate to pose now the question that policymakers failed to contemplate sufficiently in advance: did the policy gains outweigh the administrative costs?

2. Herbert Kaufman, *Are Government Organizations Immortal?* (Brookings, 1976).

3. Late in 1989 the General Accounting Office published a statistical summary of the review. It concluded that the number of terminations by SSA and the state agencies had reached 315,910. The figure of 495,000 that the SSA had been reporting had been inflated by duplicate counting and inclusion of cases that were not part of the review process. Of the 315,910, 63 percent had been reinstated through appeals. Seven percent had died, and 4 percent had qualified for retirement insurance. Only 26 percent—a total of 83,360—were alive and no longer receiving insurance payments. *Social Security Disability: Denied Applicants' Health and Financial Status Compared with Beneficiaries',* HRD-90-2 (November 1989), pp. 43–46.

It is possible that today's recipients of SSI feel themselves to be less stigmatized than did yesterday's recipients of welfare payments from state and local agencies. It is likely that net welfare entitlements for the aged, blind, and disabled are greater than they would have been had SSI never been enacted.[4] In 1990 the maximum federal monthly payment for an individual is $386 and for a couple, $579. Payments are adjusted automatically to reflect increases in the cost of living. All but two states are supplementing the federal payment. As of June 1989, in states using federal administration the average monthly payment to SSI recipients (federal payment and state supplemental combined) ranged from $196.76 in Arkansas to $403.47 in California. The same or similar results could have been achieved, though, by incremental elaboration of grant-in-aid conditions, the conventional method of extending national controls over the states. The grant-in-aid strategy would have yielded a complicated mix of uniformity and diversity, but so, as it happened, did SSI—with the difference that the SSA is the administrator.

In regard to disability reviews, the crucial question is whether it is again true that a person once on the rolls has a virtual guarantee of staying on. Has the program simply returned to the *status quo ante*, or will the statutory requirement of 1980 that cases be regularly reviewed for continuing eligibility be carried out? And if carried out, will it result in terminations, or has it been nullified by the amendments of 1984, which require a showing of medical improvement before termination can occur?

Statistics that contain an answer to such questions are only beginning to become available. They show that a higher percentage of the caseload is being reviewed now than in the late 1970s, before the requirement of periodic review was imposed (8.3 percent in 1988, compared with 2.4 percent in 1978). The proportion of initial cessations upon review has, however, dropped sharply (from 46.4 percent in 1978 to 11.5 percent in 1988), presumably as a result of the 1984 amendments. Furthermore, a substantial fraction of those who are initially terminated

4. For a set of appraisals on the tenth anniversary of SSI, see *A 10th Anniversary Review of the SSI Program*, Hearing before the Senate Special Committee on Aging, 98 Cong. 2 sess. (GPO, 1984); and *The Supplemental Security Income Program: A 10-Year Overview*, Committee Print, Senate Special Committee on Aging, 98 Cong. 2 sess. (GPO, 1984). Analyses of SSI in operation have consistently estimated the rate of participation among the elderly at 50–60 percent of those who are eligible. It seems possible that many of the aged, at least, continue to be deterred by the stigma attached to means-tested assistance. Whether it is administered by a federal "insurance" agency or a state "welfare" agency may not matter much to them.

succeed in having that decision reversed on appeal. After appeals are completed, the proportion of cessations drops below 10 percent.[5]

It seems likely that as the events of 1980–84 recede in time, they will come to be seen as just two more swings of the policy pendulum in disability insurance—the swing of 1980–81 toward stringency, followed by a reaction against it in 1984. The price that was paid—in hardship to beneficiaries and opprobrium cast upon the SSA from judicial, legislative, and journalistic sources—will be seen not as the inevitable price of desirable policy change, but rather as the price of policymaking by pendulum swings.

WHY FUNDAMENTAL CORRECTIVES ARE UNATTAINABLE

In this book I have sought to portray a number of handicaps to administration that arise out of its setting in American government. The handicaps identified have been of three kinds. Some have been inherent in the structural features of American government. Others arise out of policymakers' lack of concern for administration, and others out of their inability to perceive the administrative consequences of policy choice. These handicaps have been both heightened and laid bare by the growth of government. As chapter 10 showed, the Social Security Administration's exposure to environmental influences has increased as its programs have multiplied, matured, and grown more complex. It also showed that the SSA is not alone in being an agency under stress.

Partisans of the SSA have reacted to its recent problems by trying to restore its old autonomy through executive reorganization. They propose to make the SSA independent of the Department of Health and Human Services and place it under the direction of a three-member, bipartisan board with six-year, overlapping terms. It is unlikely, however, that mere measures of executive organization can significantly reverse a development that stems fundamentally from the great growth of agency programs and affects the agency's relations with every part of the government. At most, the proposed reorganization would insulate the agency to some extent from presidential supervision

---

5. *Background Material and Data on Programs within the Jurisdiction of the Committee on Ways and Means*, 1989 ed., Committee Print, House Ways and Means Committee, 101 Cong. 1 sess. (GPO, 1989), pp. 50–54.

and the effects of presidential transitions—at the cost, however, of subjecting it to management by a committee.[6]

Realistically, remedies to such problems can be sought only within very narrow limits. To the extent that the problems lie in fundamental features of American government, not much can be done—or ought to be done.[7] Unpredictability and instability in statutory guidance for administration are a price of democracy, which guarantees that governments will change regularly, following election contests between the candidates of rival parties. They are also the price for the benefits of a system that is responsive to a pluralistic society. Much of the mutation in law, after all, comes from Congress's need to constantly seek reconciliations of incompatible goals and conflicting interests. The reconciliations it arrives at in any given law often last only a very short time. Congress wants to satisfy everyone, and since it cannot satisfy everyone at once, it tries to satisfy every interested party—and to honor every competing policy objective—in rapid turn.

Conflicting cues to administrators are one price to be paid for the United States' own particular version of democracy, which values diffusion of governmental power while lodging an unusually large share of power in courts as the bulwark of constitutional rights. Correspondingly, although having to share administrative power with state governments may reduce the effectiveness of federal agencies, such

6. The proposal for reorganization owes something to the experience of SSI. High-ranking agency executives believed then that the need to clear all their actions with HEW officials seriously hampered implementation of the program. Similarly, the effort to recreate a multimember board, the original form of the agency, derives some of its current impetus from the experience of the disability review. Agency partisans have tended to place all the blame for what happened on the Reagan administration and to infer that the agency should be protected from the sudden changes in presidential policy that can occur during transitions. A proposal to make the SSA independent of HHS was approved by both the Senate Finance Committee and House Ways and Means Committee in 1989. However, it failed of enactment when it was dropped from the Senate version of the reconciliation bill. The House version provided that the agency would be headed by a three-member bipartisan board, whereas the Senate version called for a unitary agency head.

7. Not everyone would concur that nothing can or need be done. Not everyone takes the separation of powers for granted. Modern arguments calling for revision of the constitutional system appear, for example, in James L. Sundquist, *Constitutional Reform and Effective Government* (Brookings, 1986); and Donald L. Robinson, "The Renewal of American Constitutionalism," in Robert A. Goldwin and Art Kaufman, eds., *Separation of Powers—Does It Still Work?* (Washington: American Enterprise Institute for Public Policy Research, 1986), pp. 38–64. The difficulties posed for administration, however, have not usually been prominent among indictments of the separation of powers.

arrangements also have the virtues of federalism. One is to adapt governmental action to particular local circumstances; the continuing diversity and decentralization in the supplemental security income program may be generally beneficial, even if inconvenient for the SSA. Another virtue is, once again, the diffusion of governmental power. The decision of numerous state governments to cease cooperating in the disability review may be interpreted as a sign of the structurally compromised authority that handicaps the SSA, but it may also be viewed as one way in which an ill-conceived, unjust exercise of federal government power could be brought to heel. Diffusion of power, so deeply and pervasively characteristic of American government, is both bad and good. It undermines the effectiveness of administration, but it also thwarts abuses of power from any governmental source.

Similarly, to the extent that problems arise out of the size of government, not much is to be done. They are the price that must be paid for Americans' collective desire to have the benefits of big government, income security foremost among them. Inevitably if illogically, Americans also resent the costs and inconveniences of big government. Big bureaucracies tend to be blamed for those costs and of course to be seen as a cost and inconvenience themselves. Hence, as bureaucracies' responsibilities increase, they are subject to stricter critical scrutiny and are given only grudging, minimal support. A gap opens between what they are asked to do and the resources they are given. This gap, while not precisely measurable, appears to be growing generally.[8] Administrative dysfunction is becoming widespread, even endemic.

SOME MODEST PRESCRIPTIONS

In an arresting book, John A. Rohr has argued that administrative agencies have an obligation to act as a balance wheel in the constitutional system "by choosing which of [their] constitutional masters [they] will favor at a given time on a given issue."[9] However, rather than impose

8. In addition to evidence already presented on agency distress, see, for example, Milton D. Morris, *Immigration: The Beleaguered Bureaucracy* (Brookings, 1985), on the Immigration and Naturalization Service; and "The First Federal Agency," *Washington Post*, August 24, 25, and 26, 1986, on the Customs Service. For a general scholarly account of American government's abuse of bureaucracy, see William T. Gormley, *Taming the Bureaucracy: Muscles, Prayers, and Other Strategies* (Princeton University Press, 1989).

9. *To Run a Constitution: The Legitimacy of the Administrative State* (University Press of Kansas, 1986), p. 182.

this awesome additional charge on already stressed agency leaders, I would prefer to cultivate the precept that each of the branches has responsibility for the agencies' performance and well-being. In my view, agencies have enough trouble meeting operational goals without also bearing the imponderable duty of maintaining balance among the constitutional branches.

It needs to be recognized that administrative considerations represent a legitimate, even central and urgent, claim upon the attention of all policymakers; that organizational capacities are a necessary and proper topic of reasoned inquiry, integral to policymaking; and that responsibility for nurturing those capacities—and using them intelligently—is borne generally by all the constitutional branches, not just by agency heads.

To improve administrative performance and forestall the kind of trauma analyzed here requires both learning from the past and anticipating the future. Neither is easy to do in any large-scale human enterprise. In regard to public administration, the government's effort to learn and anticipate has been conspicuously less than commensurate with the stakes. It has been inhibited by the priority that elected officeholders give to political and policy goals; by a constitutional tradition that casts doubt on the legitimacy of administrative power, making agencies an object of suspicion; and by a deeply ingrained pragmatism in policymaking. American lawmakers tend to believe, or act as if they believe, that there is no way of knowing what the effects of a law will be until it is tested. Then whatever turns out to need fixing can be fixed. There is a good deal to be said in defense of this attitude. Realistically, implementation has to respond to experience. Adjustments will be made successively as experience accumulates. However, extreme pragmatism increasingly becomes a luxury as government becomes more centralized, with power concentrated at the national level, and more active, with a widening range of responsibility. Under such conditions, the ramifications of error are so great that it becomes increasingly important to avert it or limit the risks if possible. Too many people are harmed when something is "broken," and the constant fixing takes a heavy toll in administrative turbulence.

Policymakers need a dispassionate and regular source of information and advice about the capacities of federal administrative agencies. There is need for a concentrated, self-conscious effort at organizational learning. The most promising place in which to develop such a function is, I believe, the generalist staff agencies of Congress.

In constitutional theory, the executive branch might seem the more logical place to turn to. As chief administrator, the president would seem to have a greater incentive and responsibility than Congress to know how well the organizations in his branch are faring. Yet the agencies are not really "his" any more than they are the legislature's in the U.S. system, and the legislature is not likely to place credence in the executive's appraisals of itself. Despite occasional efforts to lodge responsibility for management in the Office of Management and Budget, budget savings are historically its overriding priority. That priority has only been confirmed in recent years as budget deficits have grown. In the cases here, the OMB appears strictly as watchdog, critic, and economizer. Its role in SSI was confined to unrealistically limiting the SSA's requests for personnel. Its role in the disability review was to seize on it in 1981 as a source of very large budget savings, and thereby to increase the pressure on the SSA and its state agents to perform. In doing this, it displayed ignorance of the consequences for recipients.

Congress is the more promising place in which to locate responsibility for appraising agency capabilities. Not that its agents are dispassionate: committee staffs usually have very pronounced partisan and programmatic biases, and the generalist units (the Congressional Research Service, Congressional Budget Office, General Accounting Office, and Office of Technology Assessment), even though nonpartisan and disinterested by comparison with committee staffs, share the institutional biases of the legislative branch. Created to help Congress, they do so largely by finding the flaws in executive performance. The GAO, which urged the SSA to accelerate the conduct of disability reviews in the spring of 1981, for that reason bears a share of responsibility for the consequences of acceleration. Yet it received none of the blame because legislative agents virtually monopolized the function of assigning blame. Soon after the review got under way, the GAO set to work criticizing the SSA's conduct of it.[10]

Nonetheless, the generalist staff agencies of Congress have potential for useful service as appraisers of the administrative capacities of executive agencies. Some of that potential is detectable in this book. Ironically, these congressional agents are shown here to display more sensitivity to administrative issues than does the president's staff. While the GAO appears mainly as a critic of the SSA's performance, it also provided testimony to Congress sympathetically describing the mag-

10. See statement of Gregory J. Ahart, director of GAO's Human Resources Division, in *Oversight of Social Security Disability Benefits Terminations*, Hearing before the Subcommittee on Oversight of Government Management, Senate Committee on Governmental Affairs, 97 Cong. 2 sess. (GPO, 1982), pp. 233–52.

nitude and complexity of the statutory burdens on the SSA.[11] Similarly, Congress's Office of Technology Assessment appears in this book, not as an actor in either key event, but as the producer of a report that is the principal source of information on the evolution of the SSA's data processing capacities.[12]

Were this kind of congressional staff product to be produced more comprehensively and systematically, it would help to reduce the deficits of concern and perception that have been identified in this analysis. Congressional staff sources might, for example, regularly produce state-of-the-agency reports on the major federal agencies, describing their activities and assessing their capacity to meet their responsibilities. Such reports would describe their major statutory assignments, the personnel and technologies with which the assignments are performed, trends in performance measures, leading problems, and signs of organizational health or pathology. Such reports would not need to appear annually; were they to do so, they would quickly degenerate into boilerplate. Once or twice a decade would be more feasible.

The GAO has already taken steps toward general evaluations. Coinciding with the 1988 election, it produced a series of twenty-four "transition reports," identifying in general terms leading issues that incoming officeholders would face. Some of these focused on major issues of policy, such as the budget deficit, revenue options, and international trade, but most focused on issues associated with the functions of executive departments or independent agencies, for example, Health and Human Services, the IRS, and NASA. These agency-focused reports laid out very broad agendas for improving administrative performance.

The GAO's transition reports were very brief and general. Closer to the state-of-the-agency report being recommended here—indeed, an apt model for it—is a study of the SSA that the GAO released in the spring of 1987.[13] Subtitled *Stable Leadership and Better Management Needed to Improve Effectiveness*, this 246-page document was much fuller and more analytical than its trite title would suggest. It opened with a

11. Statement of Joseph F. Delfico, associate director of GAO's Human Resources Division, in *Social Security: How Well Is It Serving the Public?* Hearing before the Senate Special Committee on Aging, 98 Cong. 1 sess. (GPO, 1983), pp. 35–46.

12. Office of Technology Assessment, *The Social Security Administration and Information Technology*, OTA-CIT-311 (October 1986).

13. General Accounting Office, *Social Security Administration: Stable Leadership and Better Management Needed to Improve Effectiveness*, HRD-87-39 (March 1987).

portrait of the SSA's structure and functions. Chapter 2 described the SSA's programs and institutional environment, in phrases suggestive of the analysis set forth in this book ("social security programs are complex," "short legislative lead times can adversely affect implementation," "dilemmas resulting from trying to serve conflicting interests," "SSA is highly dependent upon others to accomplish its mission"). Fourteen subsequent chapters covered such subjects as the organization's leadership, internal structure, financial management, internal decision processes, budgeting, policy formulation and implementation, automatic data processing, operational efficiency, performance measurement, and personnel management. If one were to design a format for state-of-the-agency reports, it would be hard to improve on the example set by this publication. Any policymaker wishing to assign new tasks to the agency or to elicit improved performance of established tasks would find it immensely informative.

It may be objected that general evaluative portraits would have limited applicability to any particular policy issue. Information and advice on administrative questions might be futile if they were not well integrated with, and responsive to, actual policy deliberations. Yet general reports at least provide background and context for policy deliberation, potentially elevate the level of concern by their mere existence, and presuppose the development of staffs specializing in consideration of administrative questions. The staffs themselves then could be drawn upon for advice on particular issues if members of Congress wanted to do so.

State-of-the-agency reports, if confined to the major executive bureaus and prepared only once or twice a decade, would not necessarily add very much to the work load of congressional agencies. They could draw heavily on source material already developed by Congress in committee hearings and GAO reports, the reports of the inspectors general of the departments, annual reports and other documents produced by the agencies themselves, and publications of the Administrative Conference of the United States. They could be contracted out. A great deal of information exists that is not now synthesized in a comprehensive, generally accessible form.

The GAO, which produced its report largely with its own resources, has a staff of forty persons assigned full time to reviewing the SSA. For the report it synthesized some of its own previous work and reviewed studies done by the HHS inspector general, the SSA, and contractors. It examined the SSA's operating data, including budget and financial reports, quality assurance reports, work measurements, Senior Executive Service contracts and merit pay plans, automatic data processing contracts, training course descriptions, staff allocation procedures, and debt collection activity. It interviewed between 300 and 400 SSA employees who were divided between headquarters and the field and among a variety of functions and organizational units. It also interviewed outside experts and former HHS and SSA officials, including five former SSA commissioners or acting commissioners. Finally, it generated important new data, with questionnaires administered to nearly 2,000 lower-level and mid-level SSA employees designed to elicit their perceptions of organizational problems. While this kind of effort could not be made for every agency or even for important agencies every year, the GAO's performance in this case demonstrates the capacity of a concerned official evaluator to analyze a federal agency in depth.

With or without general state-of-the-agency reports, a more systematic effort should be made to analyze the administrative consequences of major legislation that is impending. For years, the legislative reference staff of the OMB has reviewed bills to assure that they are consistent with presidential policies. Also, the OMB and the Congressional Budget Office estimate financial costs of legislation. What is needed is a comparable effort to estimate administrative costs and consequences. Assuming the addition of staff competent in institutional analysis, this effort might be lodged in the OMB and CBO, although it would likely be subordinated there to the budgeting function. On the congressional side, the GAO might be the more logical site, given its current evolution as an evaluator of administrative capacity.

A proposal for administrative analysis of impending legislation was advanced several years ago by an experienced public servant, Rufus Miles, as one conclusion to a study of several cases of policymaking that suffered from insufficient attention to administrative effects. Miles recommended that proposed legislation should be analyzed carefully to determine "just how the bill would be administered, how many people would be required to administer it, what its impact would be on state and local institutions and private businesses in terms of administrative burden, the advantages and disadvantages of contracting out significant portions of the administrative processes . . . , how the necessary coordination with other programs would be achieved, and . . . what the incentives and disincentives are that would affect the way in which the program would influence the institutional and individual behavior of those who would be the beneficiaries of the legislation."[14] He added that the analysis should also show what options were considered to achieve the purposes of the legislation and the reasons for choosing the preferred option over those rejected.

To Miles's list of criteria I would add an appraisal of the administrative burden specifically on federal agencies and an analysis of the technologies, incentives, and disincentives that would be brought to bear on the activity of federal agency employees. Such analyses should specifically include an estimate of the lead time required for an agency to prepare for new tasks. Where relevant, these estimates also should cover the development of computer technologies. Such estimates would of course be rough guesses, but probably not more rough than the estimates of financial costs that government agencies regularly produce.

THE IMPLICATIONS OF SCALE

Different kinds of policy change require different prescriptions for implementation. Ideally, administrative analysts would develop an ability to identify the crucial variables. Lead times, for example, are often but not always crucial. They were crucial in the case of SSI, which involved a fundamental revision of the SSA's central tasks; a major expansion in the size, and change in the socioeconomic composition, of its clientele; and development of computer technologies that were new to the agency. In retrospect, it seems impossible that all this could have been accomplished in the time allotted even if Congress could have somehow been compelled to leave the law alone after enacting it.

As a problem of administration, the disability review contrasted in most important respects with SSI. Rather than an expansion of benefits, it entailed a contraction, which greatly increased the political hazards. Rather than involving fundamentally new tasks and technologies, it involved expanding the scale and increasing the pace of well-established routines. Having more time in which to recruit and train state personnel might have helped, but lack of time for preparation was probably not crucial in this case. In the disability review, central planners suffered a failure of foresight. No one anticipated what would happen when impersonal reviews of records were conducted on a massive scale to meet a policy objective on which there was only superficial, unstable

14. Rufus E. Miles, Jr., "A Costly Deficiency in Public Policy Formulation," in Theodore W. Taylor, ed., *Federal Public Policy: Personal Accounts of Ten Senior Civil Service Executives* (Mt. Airy, Md.: Lomond Publications, 1984), pp. 81–114, quote at p. 112.

agreement and then were in turn scrutinized by courts, individual congressmen, and the media.

Different as the two cases were, they had at least one trait in common: large scale. These were not incremental efforts; they were massive and encompassing. In SSI, the agency took on responsibility for all recipients in all categories (aged, blind, disabled) all at once. The disability review was to cover, in the span of three years, all the disabled who were not classified as permanently so—and the agency started off by defining the group subject to review expansively and then concentrating first on those classes of cases judged most likely to include ineligible persons. Proceeding comprehensively ordinarily increases administrative risks; proceeding partially and incrementally reduces them, if only by revealing piecemeal where they lie.

When the federal system is conceived of as an aid to experiment and a means of adjusting policy to particular circumstances, it offers opportunities for proceeding incrementally and partially. In these cases, however, it was perceived instead as an anomaly and inconvenience. Underlying both of the efforts described in this study was a strong centralizing, standardizing impulse. That impulse was at the core of the creation of SSI and was an important feature as well of the Disability Amendments of 1980, one purpose of which was to effectuate improved control over the state agencies. The law redefined the SSA's relation with the states in regulatory, as opposed to contractual, terms. However, as these cases suggest, the pursuit of nationalization can have perverse results. It was an irony of SSI that it resulted in a more decentralized SSA: the agency acquired responsibility for administering variations among and within the states, and newly increased discretion was lodged in the field-level claims representatives as performers of the federal agency's core tasks. It was an irony of the disability review that the newly regulated states, treated in the law as mere subordinates of the federal government, proceeded to assert governmental prerogatives by ceasing to cooperate in carrying out the review. And it was a further and deeper irony that an effort to rationalize and centralize the disability program culminated in a transfer of power from the SSA to a more decentralized institution, the federal courts.

When programs involving a large volume of cases and many discretionary decisions at dispersed locations are being administered in a vast and socially heterogeneous country, centralization has limits. The limits inhere in the administrative enterprise. The center tends to lose control as volume and complexity increase in programs that necessarily lodge a great deal of discretion at the field level (as is true in both means-tested income support and the disability insurance program). It is tempting, and perhaps logical, for those who want to rationalize programs and maximize central control over them to fight the institutions of federalism, which they take to be the root cause of diversity. But those institutions are not the sole source of fragmentation, and in some circumstances they may not be the most fundamental one. Federalism is an institutional accommodation to, as well as a cause of, diversity. The designers of policy change and the analysts of administrative technique at the national level, when confronting the institutions of federalism, need to weigh the case for accommodation against that for centralized (or centralizing) alternatives. Accommodation may have costs, but so, ordinarily, does centralization. A more careful weighing in both of these cases, especially that of SSI, might have led to a less radical attempt at centralization, one less costly to the SSA. As learning accumulates, one lesson may well be that decentralized organizational structures (like incremental processes) have the advantage of limiting the risk of large-scale error.

POLICYMAKERS AS CONSUMERS OF ANALYSIS

In the Ways and Means Committee postmortems on SSI, when academic sources produced recommendations for more administrative analysis, Robert Ball reacted skeptically. Speaking specifically of medicare but obviously with general implications, he observed that "administrative ease and feasibility is a relative thing compared to social advance sometimes. If we had really been required to explain— first of all, we did not know—but if we had been required to explain the [administrative] intricacies of Part B before the Congress adopted it . . . , I don't think we would have it yet."[15] Administrative analysis is the enemy of policy innovation, as well as politics.

Administrative analysis will not be consumed if the president and Congress have no interest in consuming it. On the evidence I have presented in this book, there is not much reason to suppose that they are interested unless there are political incentives to be interested. Therefore one important task of analysts, both public and private, is to demonstrate that present policymaking practices have administrative costs of a kind that politicians would care about were those costs to

---

15. *Administration of the Supplemental Security Income Program*, Hearing before the Subcommittee on Oversight of the House Committee on Ways and Means, 94 Cong. 2 sess. (GPO, 1976), vol. 5, p. 42.

be specified. These are costs not just in inconvenience, disruption, and damaged morale in administrative agencies, but also in wasted money in the federal government's budget and in hardships to citizens. The haste with which SSI was initiated demonstrably increased its financial cost. When faced with uncertainty, the SSA chose as a general rule to err on the side of beneficiaries, thus making millions of dollars in overpayments. Its being overburdened had ramifications for all of its activities, including disability determinations and reviews. SSI was one, though by no means the only, contributor to the explosion of the disability rolls in the mid-1970s.

Whether the disability review saved or cost the government money on balance would probably be hard to calculate, particularly if one chose to include the costs of the policy changes that followed in its wake, embodied in the Disability Benefits Reform Act of 1984. However, it would not be hard to make the case that over time, fluctuations and inconsistencies in policy guidance have contributed to gross inefficiencies in administration, or that in the particular case of the review, speed, scale, and lack of foresight unnecessarily inflicted severe hardship on vulnerable persons.

For legislative policymaking to pay greater attention to administration does not necessarily require a high degree of interest or initiative on the part of members of Congress. It requires of them enough tolerance of administrative analysis to permit small staffs for that purpose to develop and to engage in dialogue with committee staffs specialized by subject matter. All else being equal—that is, assuming the absence of political costs—they can be expected to tolerate staff attention to administrative practicalities. In general, they prefer avoiding trouble to creating it. Only the most cynical students of American politics, dedicated to the proposition that congressmen are relentlessly self-serving, would suppose that congressmen *want* bureaucracy to perform poorly so that they can come to the rescue of aggrieved individuals, or that they don't mind if it performs wastefully as long as the waste helps them to win reelection.[16]

Presidents, who run a greater risk than Congress of being held

16. For the cynical view, see Morris P. Fiorina, *Congress: Keystone of the Washington Establishment* (Yale University Press, 1977); and Kenneth A. Shepsle and Barry R. Weingast, "Legislative Politics and Budget Outcomes," in Gregory B. Mills and John L. Palmer, eds., *Federal Budget Policy in the 1980s* (Washington: Urban Institute Press, 1984), pp. 343–67. This paragraph benefited from the author's conversations with James M. Verdier and Stephen J. Verdier and an interview with Michael Stern (all former congressional staff).

responsible for administrative performance and who have a strong institutionalized interest in efficiency, therefore presumably have at least some incentive to be receptive to administrative concerns if the basis for concern can be demonstrated. Of the main institutional sources of administrative supervision, it is the judiciary that is least likely to develop sensitivity to considerations of administrative cost and capacity. Unlike the president or Congress, the courts bear no political costs from poor administrative performance and have no responsibility for supplying administrative means. At the same time, the history recounted here suggests that judicial intrusion is not necessarily gratuitous. It responds very much to the quality of administrative performance, which in turn depends heavily on the quality of policymaking by the political branches. If the legislature and executive performed better—that is, if they exerted a steadier, more effective, more collaborative control over policy and the ensuing administrative action—the scope for judicial action would be correspondingly narrowed.

IT IS AN IRONY of the constitutional scheme that it has led in modern times to so much mutability in the law. There was nothing that James Madison, the principal architect of the constitutional structure, hated more. "To trace the mischievous effects of a mutable government would fill a volume," he wrote in *Federalist* number 62— and then proceeded to fill the rest of that essay with impassioned statements on the subject. Domestically, mutable policy "poisons the blessing of liberty itself":

> It will be of little avail to the people, that the laws are made by men of their own choice, if the laws be so voluminous that they cannot be read, or so incoherent that they cannot be understood; if they be repealed or revised before they are promulgated, or undergo such incessant changes that no man, who knows what the law is today, can guess what it will be to-morrow. Law is defined to be a rule of action; but how can that be a rule, which is little known, and less fixed?[17]

Today's laws are so voluminous and change so often that they are not understood by the people who administer them, let alone the mass of citizenry to whom they apply. As of the mid-1980s, the SSA was issuing program instructions—that is, interpretations of laws, with

17. Edward Mead Earle, ed., *The Federalist* (Modern Library, n.d.), pp. 405–06.

guidance for implementing them—to field staff at the rate of thousands of pages per month.[18]

It is history's cruel insult to a great man that much of the mutability stems from the most fundamental features of the American governmental regime. Republicanism gives elected officials incentives to legislate frequently. The embrace of a vast and heterogeneous society— what Madison, in the context of 1787, called "enlarging the sphere," with consequences that today are called "pluralism"—requires that many different interests and objectives be honored. Separation of powers means that there are several competing policymakers, each authoritative in its own right. Alone, these structural features might not make for mutability, but in combination as the institutional context of today's hugely expanded obligations and expectations of government, they certainly do. This is the setting in which public agencies must do their work, and it is not auspicious for them.

18. GAO, *Stable Leadership and Better Management Needed*, p. 123. These pages were for the program operations manual system (POMS), which was created as a unified system in 1978 in order to consolidate instructions previously contained in 230 different instruction manuals. POMS contains about 38,000 pages. By no means all of the changes that headquarters makes are attributable to changes in the law. Many are attempts to make the manual itself clearer or to adapt it to the introduction of new technologies.

Index